Amarillo

Amarillo

The Story of a Western Town

PAUL H. CARLSON

Texas Tech University Press

This book is typeset in Garamond, Birch, and Brush Script. The paper used in this book meets the minimum requirements of ANSI/NISO Z39.48-1992 (R1997). ∞

Designed by David Timmons

Library of Congress Cataloging-in-Publication Data
Carlson, Paul Howard.
Amarillo : the story of a western town / Paul H. Carlson.
p. cm.
Summary: "History of the founding of Amarillo and its progress from a small cowtown to the second largest city on the Texas High Plains. Includes social, cultural, economic, and political aspects of the city's development through its 118 years"—Provided by publisher.
Includes bibliographical references and index.
ISBN: 978-0-89672-587-4 (cloth)
ISBN: 978-1-68283-311-1 (paper) 1. Amarillo (Tex.)—History. 2. Amarillo (Tex.)—Civilization. I. Title.
F394.A4C37 2006
976.4'825—dc22

200605719

First paperback printing 2026

Texas Tech University Press
Box 41037
Lubbock, Texas 79409-1037 USA
800.832.4042
ttup@ttu.edu
ttupress.org

For my grandchildren
Tim, Ashley, and Kelli McLaurin
Kyle and Jennifer Carlson
Dylan Carlson

Contents

Illustrations

Maps

Preface

Some twenty years ago two friends and professional colleagues, B. Byron Price and Frederick W. Rathjen, produced *The Golden Spread*, a brief, illustrated history of Amarillo and the wider Texas Panhandle. It is an exceptional example of its genre, but it is no longer in print, and, while it covered Amarillo, it did not concentrate on the city. Moreover, the authors tilted their attention toward the Panhandle region's colorful pioneer past. Thus, some need existed for a new history of Amarillo, one that placed the modern city at the core of the study.

This book represents an effort to produce such a history. Amarillo, through its economic and political strength and its deep cultural influences, dominates much of the Texas Panhandle. The city is the marketing and commercial hub of a broad region, one that laps over into Oklahoma, Kansas, Colorado, and New Mexico. It is also a regional center for health care and for social and cultural activities of all kinds. This book, then, is an attempt to provide a broad, chronological sweep of the social, cultural, political, and economic history of Amarillo and to show how Amarillo has developed as the major urban center for the larger Texas Panhandle.

Amarillo is unique. Perhaps every city is. Yet there are few places of comparable size that have been the subject of as many country songs and western ballads. Indeed, Alan Jackson, Emmylou Harris, Neil Sedaka, and James Durst each recorded a different song titled "Amarillo." Other popular recordings using the city's name include Bob Wills's "When You Leave Amarillo," George Strait's "Amarillo by Morning," Carol Hall's "The Bus from Amarillo," and Terry Allen's "Amarillo Highway." Yet the country ballads hardly capture the essence of the city as it exists today. Contemporary Amarillo is a community whose citizens overwhelmingly support its cultural and intellectual life, such as live drama and fine arts generally and its superb symphony orchestra particularly. That does not mean it has outgrown country and western music—far from it. Clearly, Amarillo is a community whose city and citizens proudly embrace a western past that includes frontier images of long-booted cowboys, heady cattle drives, rowdy saloons, and busy railheads. The unusual dynamic keeps present-day Amarillo firmly rooted in its western past, or, as a recent postcard suggests, Amarillo is a bit western frontier and a bit space age—a contemporary city in which the Old West, both the real and the imagined, remains hearty. This book's subtitle, "The Story of a Western Town," embraces the city's country and western music connections, its rural, western traditions, and its strong but modern cowboy-rancher customs.

But, in most ways, Amarillo is no longer a "western" town. Indeed, with a population of some 176,000 people in 2006, it is one of the two largest urban communities on America's western High Plains. It is a thoroughly modern city, urbane in temperament and cosmopolitan in outlook. Still, large numbers of its citizens embrace informality of dress and speech, rural ideals, pickup trucks, country and western music and western dance halls, "cowboy" steak houses, and similar manifestations of the mythic Old West and so keep Amarillo solidly anchored to its deep agrarian roots, pastoral traditions, and rural heritage. This strong dichotomy of outlook helps explain the grand attractiveness of Amarillo, a marvelously uncommon city with an extraordinary history.

For help on this book I owe thanks to many. Stanley Marsh 3 suggested that it be written, provided research support, and then got out of the way. Byron Price and Fred Rathjen provided a framework. David

Weir of Amarillo handled some research chores. Patt Perry in the Southwest Collection at Texas Tech University and her assistants Ben Vasquez, Christopher Taylor, Katie Vardeman, and Robbie Eck were especially supportive. They retrieved materials, assisted with computer searches, photocopied documents, and made researching a pleasant task. Their thoughtful help speeded the research and writing process, and for their assistance I am highly grateful.

Many other people provided help, including Freedonia Paschall, Bruce Cammack, Tai Kreidler, Randy Vance, Lynn Whitfield, Monte Monroe, Peggy Ariaz, Debbie Shelfer, and Alwyn Barr. Rob Weiner, a music historian at the Mahon Library in Lubbock, and Curtis Peoples of the Southwest Collection at Texas Tech provided information on country ballads. The staff at the interlibrary loan office at the Texas Tech University Library was courteous and efficient. Librarians at the Amarillo Public Library, including Gail Brown and Judith Sample, aided my research from the outset, and Rob Groman of the library's Special Collections Department helped beyond measure, especially with photographs. Mylynda Bettis at the Amarillo Independent School District offices provided historical information, and Betty Bustos at the Panhandle-Plains Historical Museum found pictures and other images for the book.

Garry Nall, Fred Rathjen, Leland Turner, Leroy Matthiesen, A. G. Mojtabai, Lamar Lively, Jean Stuntz, and Kevin Sweeney read early drafts of separate chapters, or parts of them, and Ty Cashion of Sam Houston State University read major portions of the manuscript, suggesting changes, offering ideas, and providing information. I am grateful for their advice, but I alone accept responsibility for whatever faults and weaknesses remain. Finally, I owe a deep debt of gratitude to my wife, Ellen, who, as always in the past, was once again patient and understanding through the long process of research and writing.

Amarillo

1

The Golden Spread

Amarillo, the Queen City of the Texas Panhandle, dominates what agriculture reporter Garland "Cotton John" Smith called "the Golden Spread"—that expansive range country spreading across the wide Canadian and upper Red River valleys and stretching into the bordering states of New Mexico, Colorado, Kansas, and Oklahoma. It is a beautiful land. And Amarillo, with a population of 176,000, extends its political, economic, and cultural reach beyond its immediate vicinity to the very limits of the Panhandle, some twenty-six or more counties in far northwest Texas, and the larger Golden Spread.

Amarillo is a western city. But in substantial ways its image and character are midwestern. The winters in the Texas Panhandle, for example, are mildly severe, and summer winds, like those in South Dakota and Nebraska, are hot and dry. The number of African Americans and Hispanic Americans in Amarillo has been, until very recently, proportionately small. Some of the area's first railroads, such as the Atchison, Topeka, and Santa Fe, connected Amarillo and the Texas Panhandle with the Midwest, especially Chicago. Likewise, Route 66, the famous highway that ran through the very heart of Amarillo and the Texas Panhandle, connected the city with the Midwest.

In some ways, Amarillo's background and outlook are also midwestern. Many of the region's early settlers, for example, came from midwestern states such as Iowa and Illinois, bringing with them social, cultural, and intellectual norms different from those in Texas. Many of the first people to raise livestock in the Panhandle marketed their animals in Kansas City, Omaha, and Chicago, causing them to look to the Midwest for economic support, guidance, and leadership. In recent years, livestock feeding, rather than grazing, has become an important part of the Panhandle economy, as in the Midwest.[1]

Yet the Amarillo country has not always been oriented toward the Midwest. For almost a thousand years Indian people of the Texas Panhandle looked westward, toward the Rio Grande and what is modern New Mexico for economic support from other western tribes. Trade and commerce were common between the Mogollons and the Anasazis of the Southwest and people in the Panhandle. They grew such southwestern-derived crops as corn, beans, and squash. In return, Panhandle inhabitants provided people in the Southwest with animal hides, dried meat, flint for weapons and tools, and other items. By the time Europeans arrived in the area, the trade had enjoyed a long history.

The western orientation of Panhandle inhabitants continued after Spaniards entered the upper Rio Grande country in the sixteenth century. Indeed, it may have increased, for the Europeans brought with them horses. And, once mounted, Indian people, particularly the Apaches, Kiowas, and Comanches, expanded their range of territory, increased the interaction between people of the Texas Panhandle and the people of the upper Rio Grande, and encouraged Spaniards to ply their trade among the people of the southern Great Plains.

Focus on eastern trade sputtered as Spaniards settled at San Antonio, La Bahia, and Nacogdoches. When Americans from the United States entered Texas, the eastern orientation increased, and after the war with Mexico, when Texas had become part of the United States, it solidified—for a time. American explorers in the 1850s and soldiers and traders later were largely responsible for strengthening that relationship.

The Golden Spread

Amarillo's economic, cultural, and social influence extends into five states.

But it did not last. The arrival of farmer-stockmen and townspeople from midwestern states in 1890 and afterward once again changed the region's orientation. Marketing and commercial needs, transportation networks, and family and personal interests all turned people of the Texas Panhandle toward the Midwest. Amarillo is part of Texas, granted, and it has important political ties to the capital in Austin, but in many ways the city is as much midwestern as it is southern or Texan.

Amarillo sits in the heart of the Texas Panhandle. Although it is the seat of Potter County, the city in recent years has expanded south into northern Randall County. About thirty-six hundred feet above sea level, it enjoys an invigorating climate. The weather, compared to the Midwest, is dry; the nights are cool, the mornings brisk. The average low temperature in January is 21 degrees; the average high temperature in July is 92 degrees. The city receives an annual rainfall of about 19.6 inches. A bit of snow falls during the winter months.[2]

Amarillo and much of the Panhandle below the Canadian River lie on a high tableland called the Llano Estacado, which stretches southward from the Canadian River Valley to the Edwards Plateau and eastward from the Pecos River Valley in New Mexico to the Caprock escarpment, a sharp natural uplift that fronts the Rolling Plains. Wide, treeless, and semiarid, the Llano is an immense area, mostly level with some gently rolling features. The soils are sandy, sandy loam, chocolate loam, and clay. Grass dominates the vegetation.

In the Amarillo area, at the northern edge of the Llano Estacado, there is little surface water, but the head streams of East and West Amarillo creeks begin in the city itself. When water is present, the creeks flow north to empty into the Canadian River, the major watercourse of the Panhandle.

The general area surrounding Amarillo has long been something of a crossroads. Water in the Amarillo creeks, in Wild Horse Lake within the limits of modern Amarillo, and at Tecovas Spring a few miles to the west, along with easy access to water in the Canadian and upper Red rivers, encouraged overland travelers to encamp in the area. Wild game in the form of bison, deer, pronghorns, and such smaller animals as rabbits add to the attractiveness of the region.

Undoubtedly, because of these same attributes, Clovis and Folsom peoples, among the first humans in North America, visited what is modern Amarillo. Clovis people were hunters and foragers whose culture in the Panhandle region lasted from roughly 11,400 years ago to about 10,800 years ago. They sought a wide range of animals and collected wild plant foods. On the Llano Estacado and in the Texas Panhandle country, they often hunted smooth-skinned, or Columbian, mammoths and short-faced bears, but deer, ancient horses and camels, giant ground sloths, pronghorns, small rabbits, and other animals also formed part of their diet. When available, now-extinct straight-horned bison represented the mainstay of their economy, providing food, clothing, and a source of tools.

The people probably lived in scattered bands. Perhaps thirty to fifty persons from several interrelated families comprised each band. They maintained small, informal sociopolitical organizations, for larger ones were not needed. They moved often, following the highly mobile big game animals along their familiar haunts. Other than their tools and weapons, they carried few possessions.

Over time Clovis people adapted to new conditions. As they did so, their lifeways evolved and their societies changed. Eventually, the people and features that identify their culture either disappeared from the scene or, perhaps more likely, faded into a variety of local traditions.

On the Llano Estacado, the Folsom culture became dominant. It extended from 10,800 years ago to about 10,200 years ago. Folsom people possessed much in common with their Clovis predecessors. They were foragers and big game hunters who concentrated on ancient straight-horned bison rather than mammoths, for the elephantlike animals had all but disappeared. They hunted elk, deer, and pronghorns. Like other big game hunters, they also pursued many smaller animals, such as rabbits, raccoons, ducks, geese, squirrels, and turtles.

As with their Clovis forbearers, Folsom people moved about in scattered bands linked by kinship networks of perhaps thirty to fifty people. They followed the large straight-horned bison across the Plains and doubtless came together in larger units in the summer for social and political reasons. They migrated in cyclical patterns, returning to favorite camping spots and hunting places along marshy lakes, in swampy meadows, and at permanent springs.

The Folsom culture, like that of the Clovis, did not last. By 10,200 years ago it had begun to fade, and ultimately it disappeared. In addition, mammoths, ancient horses and camels, giant armadillos, short-faced bears, and some other Pleistocene-age animals had become extinct. And the environment was changing. Modern weather patterns began to emerge. Temperatures warmed. Streams, lakes, swamps, and marshy lowlands dried up. The Panhandle grasslands underwent a transformation, shifting to a mixed-prairie cover of short grasses such as grama and buffalo grasses.

As the Folsom tradition declined across the larger Great Plains, several regional traditions emerged. On the Llano Estacado their names are generalized as "Plainview," "Firstview," and "Late Paleoindian." Evidence of such cultures often exists at archaeological sites that Folsom people had occupied.

Plainview people were hunter-gatherers, much like their Clovis and Folsom ancestors. Although, as with their predecessors, they hunted deer, elk, and smaller animals such as rabbits, raccoons, turtles, and birds, their characteristic prey remained the straight-horned bison. They depended more than their forbearers did on seed collecting and root digging, suggesting the development of a varied diet on the Great Plains. The Plainview culture, it seems, employed more complex sociopolitical organizations than did other early groups. Their interrelated family bands were larger, and they held more frequent interband meetings. Their hunting techniques were more sophisticated, their trade contacts more frequent, and their nonmaterial culture more intricate.[3]

Some eighty-five hundred years ago the various Plainview cultures, in response to the shifting weather patterns and a changing environment that included a hotter, drier Great Plains, began to give way to new traditions. People began to cultivate some of the plants they had been gathering and to stay longer in one place. Over time such events ushered in what archaeologists and anthropologists call the Archaic period, a long, dry era with cultures distinct from earlier ones.

The Archaic period across what is today Amarillo lasted from about eighty-five hundred years ago to two thousand years ago. The period included a very long stretch of extensive drought, called the Altithermal. Weather patterns during the Altithermal continued to warm, vegetation cover continued to transform, and subsistence modes continued to alter.

People of the long Archaic period maintained hunting and gathering traditions that had existed for generations, but subsistence techniques, tools, and utensils focused more on food collecting than on food production through hunting. Their characteristic prey became modern bison, which had evolved from the older species and had by then adapted to grazing on the shorter, less coarse grasses that, as the warmer, drier climate emerged, were spreading through the Plains. Game was always important, but vegetable foods became the basis of the Archaic peoples' diet. They sought fruits, berries, nuts, tubers, and seeds on a seasonal round of collecting.

On the Llano Estacado and in the Texas Panhandle area, the Archaic period represented a time of change—slow change. A succession of richer, more versatile, and technologically more advanced cultures than the big-game hunting groups appeared. People adopted a wider range of tools and implements and used them for a greater variety of purposes than had earlier peoples. The development of pemmican is a good example of the changes. Developed, apparently, by Archaic people, pemmican is a form of preserved meat prepared mainly by women. The women would dry meat in thin strips, then, by pounding it, they would crush the dried meat and add bone marrow, crushed nuts or berries, and some animal fat. They would then stir the product together, pack it in a skin bag, and seal the bag with additional fat. Pemmican might keep for years. Hunters carried it with them, and the useful product spread widely across North America.

As time passed, Archaic life patterns tended to give way to more sophisticated practices. Social organizations became more complex. Nonmaterial culture traits grew in importance: for example, people took to using tobacco and spent more time on handicrafts. Although many features of the Archaic tradition persisted for several more centuries, life in the Panhandle country and on the Llano Estacado underwent a gradual adaptation to other subsistence modes.

Also, Amarillo continued to serve as a crossroads. The availability of water was one reason. Another was the Alibates flint quarries, located northwest of modern Amarillo. An agatized dolomite rich in magnesium carbonate, Alibates flint for centuries had been a popular stone for use in the manufacture of weapons and tools, such as spear and arrow points and knife blades.

Alibates flint quarries exist in few places. But along the Canadian River is a whole series of quarries, a few of them about three or more feet deep and ten feet in diameter. The outcrops cover an area of about ten square miles, and many of them are located along canyon rims. Some of the quarries today are part of the Alibates Flint Quarries National Monument, some 1,079 acres containing hundreds of small quarries and several sites that were Indian villages.

From the time that humans first occupied the Southern Great Plains Indian people visited the Alibates quarries. They dug out the colorful flint or gathered it from gravel in the Canadian River Valley downstream from the outcrops. Clovis and Folsom groups, people of the Archaic period, and other Native Americans through modern times all sought Alibates flint. They used the stone themselves or traded it to neighbors, who in turn traded some of it to more distant people. Sometimes people set up villages at the quarry sites. The villages, the quarry visitors, and the trade all contributed to the sense of a crossroads in the area.

The quarries encouraged the development of new groups in the Panhandle country. But the process was a slow one, and years—hundreds of years—passed. Hunters, visitors, and traders came and went. As people began to cultivate the foods they had been gathering, a gradual shift from food collecting to food producing occurred. Over time other new influences, such as a Plains Woodland tradition, emerged to change Southern Plains lifeways. The presence of an Eastern Woodland style of pottery in the Panhandle region suggests both the eastern influences and a more settled lifeway.

The Lake Creek site is a good example of the shift to a more settled lifestyle. Located in modern Hutchinson County, the site contains evidence of Eastern Woodland traditions as well as traditional southwestern, or Puebloan, influences. People first occupied the Lake Creek site sometime around A.D. 1000, abandoned it for a time, and then reoccupied it, but they did not stay there beyond about 1250. Lake Creek people probably cultivated a few crops of corn and maybe some beans and squash. They quarried and probably traded Alibates flint, made pottery that represented both Puebloan and Eastern Woodland traditions, hunted, and exchanged goods and ideas from both the Pecos and Mississippi valleys.[4]

Lake Creek also suggests the development of a Plains Village tradition, indicating an increased use of horticulture, technology that allowed for permanent homes and a more settled life, including more sophisticated ceramic work than what had been used earlier. It "is a culture," writes Frederick W. Rathjen, that exhibits Eastern Woodland "characteristics, including agriculture, which were refashioned and adapted to a Plains environment and fused with earlier Plains cultural traditions." The Plains Village tradition existed in western Kansas and Nebraska, in north-central Texas, and in central Oklahoma.[5]

In the Texas Panhandle, the Panhandle Aspect culture represents an important Plains Village tradition. It is characterized in part by the ruins of Antelope Creek, an archaeological site along the Canadian River Valley that dates from about 1200 or shortly afterward to about 1400. Antelope Creek people, like their Lake Creek predecessors, traded with, and borrowed ideas from, eastern and Puebloan groups. But, Antelope Creek also has important relationships with a group in the Upper Republican River area of western Nebraska, and, in fact, it may have developed from people who left Nebraska and moved south to the Canadian River.

Antelope Creek people cultivated corn and perhaps some beans and squash, hunted game animals and birds, and collected wild plant foods. They lived in substantial housing whose designs may have been Puebloan-derived: multi-roomed homes with stone-slab foundations that supported adobe and masonry walls reminiscent of southwestern Pueblo architectural styles. They used implements and weapons of bone, horn, wood, and stone. Their principal weapon was the bow and arrow, but evidence of the atlatl, a spear-throwing device, suggests other weapons were common. Everyday working tools included chipped knives, scrapers, serrated mussel shells, and others. Pottery was plentiful.

The people of Antelope Creek used Alibates flint; indeed, they controlled the most important sources of the stone. They used it to make some projectile points and traded both finished products and quarry blanks to distant places. Their trade contacts reached west to the Rio Grande pueblos and east to Caddoan communities in Louisiana and eastern Texas. They conducted sporadic trade with other Plains groups.

The Antelope Creek culture was sophisticated. Its population increased over the years, but then rather suddenly the culture disappeared. Drought, changing socio-economic conditions, and perhaps the appearance of Athapaskan-speaking groups, such as the Apaches, caused its decline. Whatever the cause, Antelope Creek people dispersed, perhaps moving northward to join people living along the upper Republican and Arkansas rivers. Perhaps some joined other groups to the east and southeast. By 1450 or so, their villages in the Canadian River Valley along the upper edge of the Llano Estacado had emptied.[6]

A half-century later, about 1500, various Apache groups dominated the Llano Estacado and the region around present-day Amarillo. Aggressive warriors and skilled hunters, the Apaches and their linguistic relatives had been moving south through the Great Plains for generations. Some moved into the Rio Grande and Pecos River country. Others challenged the Plains Villagers, took over some of the village sites, and expanded their hunting ranges.

On the Southern Plains, the Apaches were nomadic hunters. They moved around in small bands, or hunting groups, and came together in larger numbers during summer months. The men pursued bison, mainly, but took deer and smaller game as well. The women collected wild plant foods, including fruits, nuts, and berries. The Apaches lived in tentlike structures—tipis—skillfully constructed from poles and bison hides. They used bows and arrows, spears, and other weapons and tools made from bone, horn, stone, and wood. Apache families kept dogs, which women used as beasts of burden to haul household items, drag the tipis, or carry wood or other supplies.

In 1541 the famous Spanish conquistador Francisco Vasquez de Coronado and his eighteen hundred companions met at least one of the early Apache groups on the Llano Estacado. Coronado and his chroniclers described not only the Indian people they met but also the level plains, the dogs, the tipis, and the Indians' lifeways in general.

By 1600 Apache people occupied an enormous area of the Southern Plains east of the Rio Grande. They dominated the country from north of the Arkansas River to at least as far south as the upper Red River in the Texas Panhandle. They may have served as commercial hunters and middlemen in trade relationships between pueblo dwellers of the Rio Grande in New Mexico and the settled farming villagers, probably ancestral or Plains Wichitas, of the Central and Southern Great Plains.[7]

Once the Indian warriors acquired Spanish horses, sometime in the seventeenth century, Apache power and influence increased. Apache bands overran and absorbed some groups of Plains Wichitas, Coahuiltecans, and others. They came to dominate the Texas Panhandle and used the water sources in the Amarillo area as camping, hunting, and trading sites. Apache people traded dried meat, bison hides and robes, Alibates flint, and horses to Pueblo people in New Mexico and to Plains Villagers to the east for vegetable foods and other products they needed for their roving, hunting life on the Southern Plains.

Amid all this activity Europeans arrived, and the Indian world of North America would never be the same. Coronado and his men brought horses, cattle, sheep, goats, hogs, wool cloth, implements of iron, guns, and other items of European origin and manufacture. They also brought wheat and peaches, both of which became very important in the Southwest.

Other Europeans followed Coronado. On the eve of the seventeenth century, the land west of the Texas Panhandle became New Spain's far northern frontier. From the east came the French. The intrusive cultures' material goods quickly expanded ancient Indian trading networks. The Europeans also carried along various Old World diseases to which Indian people, lacking immunity to them, succumbed in large numbers. Small pox, rubella, and measles took the largest number of lives.

Meanwhile, Apaches, Utes, and other Indian groups who for generations had traded with the Pueblos came in contact with European goods. Through trade and theft they acquired iron weapons and implements, wool cloth and clothes, European foods, and horses—especially horses.

Apaches particularly took to horses. After the great Pueblo Revolt in 1680, an Indian uprising that caused Spaniards to abandon New Mexico for a decade, such eastern Apache groups as the Jicarillas, Mescaleros, and Lipans quickly became expert equestrians. Mounted on horseback, these Apaches spread their influence, increased their power, and extended their range of territory. As indicated above, they dominated the Southern Plains, including the Llano Estacado.

But, Apache hegemony did not last. Just as the Apache people's great strength was peaking in the early eighteenth century, others challenged them for the Southern Plains. Various Comanche groups led the assault.

Comanche people divided into a number of autonomous, independent groups. Related to Shoshones and Utes and other groups of the Great Basin country, the various Comanche divisions pushed south and east into the Southern Plains, pushed the Apaches aside, and attacked other Indian groups who stood in their way. In the early eighteenth century the Comanches acquired horses and adopted a horse-mounted, bison-hunting way of life. They became superb equestrians, skilled hunters, and aggressive warriors. Eventually, as some have written, they became "Lords of the South Plains."[8]

In most ways, Comanches became typical Plains Indians. They moved about in small hunting bands, came together in larger groups in summer, and centered much of their seasonal activities around communal bison hunts. They did not engage in horticulture. They lived in tipis that women built and owned, used dogs and horses to transport their possessions, and gathered wild foods of several kinds. But, unlike many Plains Indian tribal groups, the Comanches did not practice the Sun Dance, an important religious ceremony. Instead, Comanche religion remained an individual experience with each person seeking his or her own guiding spirits.

For the Comanches, as with most societies, a gender division of labor existed. Men hunted, defended the camp, and sought honor, prestige, and position through success in combat, acquisition of horses, hunting, and wise counseling. Women maintained the household, cooked the meals, made the clothing, and often dominated daily decision-making. They sought honor and prestige through skilled beadwork, proficient hide tanning, and successful child rearing. But, fathers and mothers, grandparents, and aunts and uncles all looked after the needs of children.

Coinciding with the Comanche rise to power was an increased Spanish presence in Texas and the Southwest. The avowed purpose was to extend the "rim of Christendom" for the Spanish king, but the realm was already in decline. Although Spanish activity in frontier areas actually increased, the overall power and influence of the Spanish slipped. As the empire waned, Spain's results on the far northern frontier were mixed at best. In 1800 the non-Indian population of Texas numbered only four thousand.[9]

Meanwhile, across the Texas Panhandle Comanche people had come to dominate human activity. Their new homeland, called Comancheria, extended over a huge territory that stretched from the Arkansas River south to the Edwards Plateau of Texas and from the Pecos River eastward to the Texas and Oklahoma Cross Timbers near the ninety-eighth meridian. Politically, the several independent divisions, or bands, exercised a power equal to their ability to make war. In 1800 the Comanche population reached perhaps eight thousand people.[10]

Changes came. Revolution through much of the Spanish world brought an independent Mexico into existence in 1821, and fifteen years later a revolution in Mexico's northeastern states created an independent Texas. Americans, who rushed by the thousands into Texas, had encouraged the split from Mexico, and in 1845 they led efforts that joined Texas to the United States.

Likewise, changes came to the Comanche world. Near constant warfare, such European-borne diseases as small pox and measles, and declining food sources negatively affected Comanche life. Social and cultural institutions changed, and populations declined. Under pressure from Americans, Texans, and other Indian groups, Comancheria shrank. White explorers and traders, soldiers and scientists, adventurers and settlers all moved into or through Comanche country.

Among those who ventured into Comanche country were Maj. Stephan H. Long and Josiah Gregg. As early as 1820, Major Long, who had been seeking the Red River, followed by mistake the Canadian River eastward across the Panhandle. Gregg, a Santa Fe trader, in March 1840 opened a road from New Mexico across the Panhandle. He traveled through present-day Oldham and Potter counties, camping at Tecovas Spring on March 13 and at Wild Horse Lake, within modern Amarillo, on March 14. A few days later, he moved into current Carson County and stopped about noon at a watering hole along Antelope Creek. He then followed the Canadian River eastward.

About 1843 William Bent, a trader from Missouri, and his partners set up a trading post, called Adobe Walls, near the Canadian River in modern Hutchinson County. They used it for trade with Comanches, Kiowas, Arapahoes, Cheyennes, and others, but, in part because Comanches alternately traded at and attacked the site, it was not successful. Six years later Bent and his partners blew up the post and abandoned the place entirely. Afterward the adobe ruins remained a conspicuous landmark.[11]

That same year, 1849, marked something of a turning point for Anglo-related traffic in the Panhandle region. The end of the war with Mexico, argonauts headed for the gold fields of California, and military expeditions in the area all meant an increase in activity among travelers, traders, and army personnel. Capt. Randolph B. Marcy, for example, in 1849 mapped the Fort Smith–Santa Fe Trail as a travel route through the Panhandle.[12] Three years later, leading a party of some sixty soldiers and civilians, he explored the North Fork of the Red River upstream to the divide between the North Fork and the Canadian, and he followed the Prairie Dog Town Fork of the Red to what he thought were its headwaters. Later in the decade, government-sponsored surveying crews, searching for a Canadian River–thirty-fifth parallel railway route to the Pacific Ocean, entered the Amarillo region.[13]

By the end of the 1850s the Canadian River Valley, in the heart of Comancheria, had become well known to Americans. U.S. Army explorers, scouts, and soldiers had traveled up and down the valley. Santa Fe traders seeking different routes to and from New Mexico and fur trappers searching for fresh trapping grounds had followed the Canadian River. Comancheros from Santa Fe and Taos used the river valley to reach their Indian trade partners beyond the Llano Estacado.

The Civil War slowed activity somewhat, but in the 1870s bison hunters arrived. Their actions in the Texas Panhandle angered Southern Plains Indians enough that Comanches, Kiowas, Cheyennes, and their allies in June 1874 attacked some bison hunters and bison-hide buyers at a tiny trade station, also called Adobe Walls, about a mile east from Bent's ruins. The white hunters and traders held off the Indian warriors, but the Comanches and Cheyennes widened their attacks across the Panhandle and extended them to settled regions to the east.

In response, the army sent in troops. Quickly, about three thousand soldiers from five different directions converged on the Panhandle. The campaign, which became known as the Red River War, lasted from

August to November. Col. Ranald Mackenzie and the Fourth Cavalry delivered a crushing blow when in the fall they destroyed five Indian villages in Palo Duro Canyon. Afterward, during the winter of 1874–75 most Indian groups who had been in the Panhandle returned to reservations in Indian Territory (Oklahoma). By June 1875 the "war" had ended.

In the aftermath of the Red River War, the federal government cleared Indian title to the Panhandle. Treaties, such as the Little Arkansas (1865) with the Cheyennes and Arapahoes and Medicine Lodge (1867) with Comanches and Kiowas, had established reservations in Indian Territory, but in addition the treaties had allowed the Southern Plains tribes hunting rights in the Panhandle. After the Red River War, the hunting rights were slowly terminated, and in 1878 and 1879 Indian people of the Southern Plains conducted their last tribal hunts in the region.

Also in the aftermath of the Red River War, sheepherders—"pastores" they were called—entered the Texas Panhandle. Many of the pastores, such as Casimero Romero, were former Comancheros. Familiar with the region, its lush grasslands, and its fresh water sources (springs along the escarpments and sweet-water tributaries of the Canadian River, which in those days, were abundant), the New Mexico wool growers in 1875 and afterward moved their families and their flocks down the Canadian River. They established herding camps and at least in one case—Tascosa—a small village along the river or its tributaries. From the river breaks, they grazed their sheep on the Llano Estacado's high tablelands, including around present-day Amarillo and its Wild Horse Lake. They marketed the annual wool clip and surplus lamb crop in Las Vegas, Taos, and Santa Fe.

Sheepherders did not stay long in the Panhandle. As early as 1876 cattlemen, led by Charles Goodnight, entered the Canadian River Valley. While Goodnight, after wintering his herds among the pastores, pushed into Palo Duro Canyon, others challenged the wool growers for the land. By 1882 most of the sheep men had returned to New Mexico.

Cattlemen, who like the pastores planned to use the lush grasslands of the Texas Panhandle to support their livestock, entered the region at a time when the American cattle industry was attracting eastern and foreign investment. Goodnight, for example, received financial support from John Adair, an Irish investment banker, to establish the JA Ranch. The Prairie Cattle Company, with headquarters in Edinburgh, Scotland, and its LIT brand, in 1880 moved thousands of cattle from Colorado and New Mexico into the Panhandle's northwestern fringe. The legendary XIT Ranch, owned by a Chicago syndicate, in 1885 took control of three million acres provided by the State of Texas in return for financing a new capitol building in Austin.

At or near the site of present-day Amarillo, cattlemen established several ranches. On the western edge of the future city, Joseph F. Glidden and Henry B. Sanborn in 1881 established their Frying Pan Ranch. On the Canadian River, north of modern Amarillo, the LX Ranch, a London-based company, in 1884 took over some two hundred thousand acres of rangeland that others, including early investors W. H. Bates and David T. Beals, had occupied. About the same time the huge T-Anchor Ranch, in present-day Randall County, purchased land and cattle along the southern edge. As early as 1883 large ranches, often known by their livestock brands—such as LS, LX, LIT, LE, Frying Pan, and T-Anchor—dominated Panhandle ranching.[14]

Cattlemen marketed their animals in the north. They sold some to the government for use on Indian reservations in the Dakotas, Wyoming, and Montana. Some cattle went to ranchers in Colorado, Nebraska, Wyoming, and elsewhere. They trailed other cattle to the Kansas railroad centers of Wichita, Ellsworth, and Dodge City, and from there the animals moved to slaughtering houses in Kansas City, St. Louis, Chicago, and Cincinnati.

In effect, the early 1880s represented a boom period in the western cattle industry. Cattle prices soared, and foreign and eastern capitalists poured money into land and cattle syndicates, including those in the Texas Panhandle. Ranchers put up barbed wire fences to enclose their ranges, moved to improve their longhorn stock by adding Shorthorns and Herefords, and expanded their herds. In the mid- to late 1880s disaster came as overstocked ranges led to declining prices, extended drought ruined the grass, and terribly cold winters destroyed the herds. Through it all, however, the expansive Texas Panhandle continued to attract people, including cattle raisers, farmers, town builders, merchants, and the families that came with them.

The Golden Spread covers a large region, one that includes the Texas Panhandle and laps over into eastern New Mexico, southeastern Colorado, western Oklahoma, and southwestern Kansas. At its heart emerged modern Amarillo, located at a site that even before it was founded represented a crossroads for various precontact Indian peoples, later horse-mounted nomadic bison hunters, and still later whites—both Hispanic and Anglo. And, although the region attracted people from the appearance of the first humans in present-day Texas, the beginnings of Amarillo, the area's major western town, came later still—near the end of the nineteenth century. The city's future site on the divide between river drainages that formed Tule and Palo Duro canyons to the south and the Canadian breaks to the north was a spot where transportation and travel lines crossed. The future Queen City enjoyed the good fortune of its convenient location, for here in the late 1880s, with the appearance of the first railroads in the region, Amarillo was established.

2

The Founding of Amarillo

In the spring and summer of 1887 several developments occurring simultaneously brought Amarillo into being. A growing population in the area, the convergence of several northbound cattle trails at and near Wild Horse Lake, and other activity associated with the Texas Panhandle cattle industry were among them. But perhaps the most significant development was the extension of the Fort Worth and Denver City Railroad through the area around Wild Horse Lake and near the upper end of East and West Amarillo creeks. The result was that after months of political intrigue and timely land purchases, it could have been said at the end of August that "There will be an Amarillo by morning."

Foremost among the many people who were responsible for the location and early development of Amarillo were James T. Berry, Jesse R. Jenkins, William B. Plemons, Henry B. Sanborn, and, to a lesser extent, Warren W. Wetzel. They were promoters who, except for Wetzel, each wanted a town laid out on property he owned at various sites along or near the railroad. Because they held or sought title to separate tracts of land, the men did not always get along, and they either competed with one another or, eventually, joined with a competitor in trying to build a viable town on the land they owned.

Berry, or "Colonel Berry," was a real estate promoter and cattleman who had been one of the developers of Abilene, Texas. He was in the Panhandle because Colorado City merchants had hired him to represent their interests in the upper South Plains where they counted a number of customers. Worried that a new railroad might undermine their businesses, they wanted Berry to locate a town site where they might establish branch stores and thus continue, or even expand, their operations in the Texas Panhandle. In the spring of 1887 Berry chose as his town site a section of public school land the state had reserved for the support of its educational system. Located along Fort Worth and Denver City tracks and called Oneida, the place, B. Byron Price and Frederick W. Rathjen indicate, "lay just northwest of the head of Palo Duro Canyon." It was, in other words, just below Wild Horse Lake.[1]

Jesse R. Jenkins, a rancher and saloonkeeper from Tascosa, claimed a site he called Adessa. Most people called it either Ragtown or Amorilla Village. Located "in a beautiful little valley decorated with huge cottonwood trees and willows," the place, a railroad construction camp of tent dwellings established in the spring of 1887, lay where the railroad crossed Amarillo Creek on the edge of the Frying Pan Ranch. Jenkins set up a bar there and planned to move permanently to the new town, a village that in the summer of 1887 held about five hundred people, most of whom were Irish construction workers. James R. Gober remembered that Ragtown tents housed "four saloons equipped with gambling, two restaurants, two supply tents with groceries and work clothes, and several tents of the inevitable dance hall girls." It seemed to be in the strongest position for future town development.[2]

Plemons, or "Judge Plemons," a Civil War veteran and aggressive lawyer who would shortly win election as judge of Potter County, selected land about two miles southeast of Jenkins's Ragtown community. Plemons's site lay near the railroad right of way and close to a spring at the head of Amarillo Creek.

Sanborn, often called the "Father of Amarillo," was in 1887 one of the owners of the Frying Pan Ranch. When he saw the activity associated with town promotion along the Frying Pan's eastern border, he convinced his ranch partner, Joseph F. Glidden, an Illinois farmer who had patented a superior type of barbed wire, to help establish a town of their own, one that would compete with those of Plemons, Jenkins, and Berry. Sanborn and Glidden, in association with Frank Lester, an attorney, selected a section of land about two miles east of the Berry site. They called it Plains City.

Wetzel, a New Yorker who was superintendent of the Frying Pan Ranch, joined Colonel Berry's group. In fact, he may have been the person who suggested the name Oneida for the town. Wetzel, who did not support his bosses, Sanborn and Glidden, left the ranch for opportunities in Berry's town shortly after voters selected Berry's site for the county seat.[3]

But the Fort Worth and Denver City Railroad was the key to Amarillo's location. Though chartered in 1873, the railroad did not lay its first rails until early 1882 due to economic difficulties related to a nation-wide economic panic in the 1870s. Construction crews pushed the tracks westward until 1885, when financial trouble and internal disputes again slowed the line's progress. A year later, with the difficulties overcome, work started again, and this time with much more dispatch.

Railroad executives originally planned to build their line through Panhandle City in Carson County where it would intersect with the Southern Kansas Railroad, a branch line of the Atchison, Topeka, and Santa Fe. Sanborn had other plans. Wanting the railroad to run its line through the center of his Frying Pan Ranch property, he helped company engineers convince Grenville Dodge, who headed the railroad's construction arm, to redirect its tracks southward some fifteen miles. The new route extended through Washburn in Armstrong County and from there along a path that took the railroad westward just below Wild Horse Lake, across the upper end of the Amarillo creeks, and then northwestward through the heart of the Frying Pan cattle ranges.[4]

Thus, in the spring and summer of 1887 railroad surveyors marked a route through the Frying Pan. Behind them, workers graded rail beds.

And still farther behind, construction crews erected a few small bridges and laid track, advancing through Armstrong County at a pace that averaged one and a half miles per day.

To provide housing, the railroad built a short spur to park boarding cars for the construction gangs. That, remembered an old-time cowboy, was how the tent community of Ragtown came into being. The construction camp lay along Amarillo Creek on public school land. In addition to railroad workers, the busy little community attracted cowboys, gamblers, prostitutes, restaurateurs, and such barkeeps as Jesse Jenkins, Lee Cone, and Tip McDowell. That summer Ragtown may have had a population of about five hundred people. Because of its location near Amarillo Creek, as early as July, the editor of the *Tascosa Pioneer* was calling the town Amarillo.[5]

Now events moved quickly. First, because the unorganized Potter County was under the political jurisdiction of Oldham County, Wetzel led a delegation of citizens to the courthouse at Tascosa to seek home rule. On August 6, Wetzel's group supposedly turned over a petition, claiming 164 voting citizens in Potter County, to the Commissioners Court. The document, for which records no longer exist, asked for separate jurisdiction. The commissioners accepted the petition and ordered elections for county officials and a seat for Potter County to take place at the end of the month—Tuesday, August 30, 1887.

Next, Plemons, probably in exchange for supporting his candidacy for county judge, joined the influential Berry camp, which included Wetzel and several prominent merchants from Abilene and Colorado City. Berry's Oneida site, located across both sides of the Fort Worth and Denver City tracks below Wild Horse Lake, now was in a powerful position to secure a favorable election.

Jenkins did not give up, but chances for a winning vote had declined. In modern parlance, his town suffered from an image problem. Public intoxication, fighting, gun shooting, and "roughhousing" led to enough trouble that the Oldham County sheriff from Tascosa, J. M. "Tobe" Robinson, placed a deputy in Jenkins's Ragtown. The deputy, James, or Jim, Gober, a cowhand from the LX Ranch, began work on August 1. He created a "jail" in the tent city by placing leg irons around a "big center post that was well set in the ground" and attaching the irons to his prisoner. Although Gober established order, many citizens of the little community moved away, most to keep up with the railroad construction activities. Others relocated to school land along the stagecoach line between Ragtown and Tascosa, and some shifted their portable property to Berry's town site. In addition, Gober encouraged a few "hard cases" to move away.[6]

Berry, who had paid the state $1,280 for his section of school land (640 acres), was determined that his Oneida would win the election for county seat. To ensure victory, not only did he get Wetzel and Plemons on his side, but also with John Hollicott, the LX Ranch manager, he offered LX cow hands—"who comprised the majority of the electorate"—two Oneida lots each in exchange for their vote to make Oneida the county seat.[7]

Meanwhile, officials set up voting procedures. They divided Potter County into four precincts and located voting places for precinct one at Berry's site, for precinct two at M. V. Kinney's grocery store, for precinct three at the Frying Pan Ranch headquarters, and for precinct four at the LX Ranch headquarters. They also appointed election officials and presiding officers.

In mid-August 1887, Charles F. Rudolph, editor of the *Tascosa Pioneer,* listed in his paper some of the candidates for public offices. On August 13, he noted that W. D. Laird, "an exceptionally good scholar [and] sociable fellow," and John Bain, "an employee of the American [Pastoral] Company," were candidates for clerk and treasurer of Potter County, respectively. He wrote that William Ruth, a former resident of Tascosa who was an old LX Ranch wagon boss, and Jim Gober, the young cowboy already serving as a deputy law enforcement officer, sought the sheriff's badge. He announced that William Lee Wyness was a candidate for county tax assessor. A week later Rudolph wrote that Allen T. Davidson, a lawyer from Abilene and a justice of the peace in Oldham County, and Plemons, the town promoter who had Berry's support, were candidates for county judge.[8]

The elections occurred on schedule. Laird, Bain, Gober, and Plemons won, but Wyness lost to one John W. Graves. Henry H. Luckett won the vote for county surveyor, and Richard Thurmond became county attorney, as Frank Lester, the only other candidate, withdrew the day before the elections. For county commissioners, citizens voted into office Charles Gillespie in precinct three (Frying Pan Ranch) and John Seeley in precinct four (LX Ranch). M. Beaver of precinct three and Elijah "Lige" Lynch of precinct four won elections for constable. A total of fifty-three votes were cast, none in either precinct one (Berry's site) or precinct two (Kinney's store).[9]

Berry's Oneida site won the vote for county seat. Jenkins was disappointed, of course, but there was little he could do; he did not have adequate financial resources to maintain his Ragtown community. He went back to Tascosa. Sanborn was miffed, but realizing that his Plains City site was not going to win, he had left Amarillo the day before the election. But Sanborn, with support from his wealthy partner, Glidden, planned to return. He was not ready to quit.

Berry's locality, which extended along both sides of the Fort Worth and Denver City tracks, quickly became known as Amarillo. The site stretches between modern Washington and Georgia streets and south from the railroad tracks. And, although the place lay in a shallow draw, few people suspected that the low lying but well-watered prairie site was subject to flooding after heavy rainstorms.

Above the town site but on the same public school section lay Wild Horse Lake. A playa that held permanent water, the lake covered about six acres. As has been noted, it was an important landmark, watering hole, and camping place. Its location and utility, plus the railroad right of way, represent important reasons why Berry and his group of Abilene and Colorado City merchants chose the section for their town.

To plat the new town, Berry called upon Henry Luckett, the county surveyor. Starting south of the railroad tracks, Luckett numbered the east-west thoroughfares, called them "streets," and made them eighty feet wide. He intersected the streets at right angles with "avenues," which Berry named for relatives, friends, and local residents, names that the City of Amarillo changed in 1928. Luckett marked out lots in each of the gridlike blocks, and Berry made plans to sell or dispose of the lots as he had promised. In fact, he sold most of the lots a year later, on May 29, 1888, when he held a public auction for town property. At that time he got between fifty and one hundred dollars for each lot that he sold.

In the meantime, as Luckett laid out Amarillo, Judge Plemons and the county commissioners held their first meeting. Because no one voted in precincts one and two, Judge Plemons appointed H. T. "Tuck" Cornelius commissioner for precinct one and James T. Holland commissioner for precinct two. They would serve until the next election. As lumber and other building materials were at a premium, the commissioners determined that the county clerk, W. D. Laird, must work in a tent. Sheriff Gober, they decided, could use a small, wooden but flimsy jail, one in which tall people could not stand up straight. Other county officials must work from home until a permanent courthouse went up. Because no city government for Amarillo existed, the county provided for political jurisdiction and public safety in the nascent community.

Still, Amarillo attracted many citizens. Some were former inhabitants of Ragtown, whose only other options seemed to be following the railroad or "nesting" on public school lands. Others, such as Warren Wetzel, who had resigned his position as the Frying Pan superintendent, left area ranches for the new city. And some of Tascosa's citizens moved away, many to the growing Amarillo community.

As Amarillo grew, Tascosa declined. Causes for the demise of the once busiest community in the western Panhandle related mainly to economics, politics, and nature. There may in fact have been a conspiracy to undermine Tascosa, but such a charge is difficult to prove. The evidence is circumstantial, and, moreover, the editor of the *Tascosa Pioneer,* Charles Rudolph, never complained about collusion or intrigue.

Nonetheless, officers of the huge XIT Ranch were concerned about Tascosa, and the Fort Worth and Denver City Railroad supported the powerful ranch. XIT officials, led by John V. Farwell, Charles B. Farwell, and Abner Taylor of Chicago, did not want tracks laid through Tascosa, for such a circumstance might impact negatively on their agricultural operations, which lay to the west. According to Richard C. Overton, who has written about the railroad, and others, "the mighty XIT Ranch, seeking to dominate the area surrounding its three-million-acre empire, was the sworn enemy of Tascosa."[10] The ranch manager, Albert G. Boyce, laid out the town of Channing on XIT property along the railroad right of way in Hartley County, built shipping pens, and otherwise encouraged the Fort Worth and Denver City to make his town an important rail stop.

Boyce and the XIT executives wanted farmer-settlers to purchase XIT lands. As early as 1887, in fact, ranch personnel raised various farm crops and shipped them to Dallas for showing at the Texas State Fair, hoping such a display would encourage settlement. They also promoted the Fort Worth and Denver City Railroad as providing easy access to Channing and their lands.[11]

Politically, the railroad and the XIT got support from W. M. D. Lee, a rancher and entrepreneur who did not want settlers coming into his country around Tascosa, believing that "nesters and herders could not mix." Lee, angry that Oldham County commissioners planned a bond sale for money to construct a railroad bridge at Tascosa, somewhat illogically offered the Fort Worth and Denver City a town site about three miles west of Tascosa at a place deemed an easy and safe crossing of the Canadian River. When the railroad accepted, the community, called Cheyenne, boomed—for about two months, after which it died—just long enough to thwart other efforts to get the rail line to cross the river at Tascosa.[12]

Chicago investor William H. Bush, Sanborn, and Glidden also got involved. Friends, or at least business acquaintances, of XIT leaders in Chicago, the three men understood that a railroad center—what would become Amarillo—along their eastern pastures would increase their property's value. Bush and Sanborn talked with the Farwell and Taylor interests—the Capitol Land Syndicate—in Chicago, apparently agreeing to cooperate on pushing for a rail line that might be beneficial to both ranches. Sanborn helped convince Grenville Dodge of the Fort Worth and Denver City Railroad to redirect its line, moving it some fifteen miles south so that it would run through the heart of the Frying Pan Ranch. He expected that with such a rail line, "we cannot but anticipate a large enhancement of value in our realty." Bush and Sanborn also visited in Chicago and Kansas City with Atchison, Topeka, and Santa Fe leaders who were concerned that the Fort Worth and Denver City was not going to extend its tracks to Panhandle City. Presumably, the Frying Pan bosses assured the Santa Fe officials that another railroad, a short line, would soon be built to connect the Fort Worth and Denver City Railroad to the Santa Fe at Panhandle City.[13]

Finally, perhaps Tascosa's demise can be attributed to the fact that it was simply in the wrong place. First, by not building to Panhandle City, the Fort Worth and Denver City could save time and money. A route from Clarendon in Donley County through Armstrong and southern Potter counties to New Mexico near modern Texline in Dallam County would be, railway construction engineers advised, "considerably less expensive" to build and "a far shorter route." And, second, Grenville Dodge, at least, claimed that quicksand in the Canadian River at Tascosa made a river crossing at that point too difficult. The claim may have been more a serviceable excuse than a legitimate reason to bypass the seat of Oldham County, but Dodge knew that he must cooperate with Albert Boyce of the powerful XIT Ranch, whose officials did not want a railroad through Tascosa. Whatever the case, the tracks passed the city about two miles south of the town and below the Canadian River. Afterward, Tascosa declined rapidly.[14]

At the same time, Amarillo, or Berry's site, enjoyed a minor boom. In the fall of 1887 and spring of 1888 a passenger station and a freight depot went up along the tracks between Greene (Parker Street, after 1928) and Courtney (Lipscomb Street) avenues. At Fourth Street (Fourth Avenue after 1928) and Greene Avenue, Tuck Cornelius established a livery stable, where he also sold livestock feed. Several people from Jenkins's Ragtown moved over to Amarillo. Most townspeople lived in tents at first, as lumber and other materials could not yet be brought by rail; they still needed to be hauled on freight wagons from Tascosa or Clarendon. Lot sales began in the spring, and by that time full service on the railroad had begun.

The town began to develop, even if it endured some growing pains. Through the winter many people hauled wood for heating from the breaks of the Canadian River. From the prairies, some folks gathered cow chips, which made a fine, if pungent, fire. They hauled water from Amarillo Creek, and women washed clothes in Wild Horse Lake. Although life in the emerging little community was not easy, townspeople enjoyed a growing sense of permanency, something that had not existed in Ragtown.[15]

Part of Amarillo's early success came from its reputation as a cattle-shipping point. For some years, cattlemen had moved their animals by way of Wild Horse Lake to Dodge City, Kansas, about 225 miles farther north, where the Santa Fe Railroad maintained pens and loading chutes. The lake and the east branch of Amarillo Creek provided water in abundance and a good resting place for drovers moving their animals from the south and southeast. Now, with the extension of the Fort Worth and Denver City Railroad through the Panhandle, Texas cattlemen, if buyers were present, could sell their livestock at Amarillo. The railroad could then carry the animals north to the stockyards in Denver, Colorado.[16]

The railroad built a siding and temporary loading chutes west of Wild Horse Lake. But without holding pens and with few cattle buyers at the place, most drovers pushed their animals past the lake and on to Dodge City, as they had been doing since the mid-1870s. A few cattlemen turned their herds toward Carson County and Panhandle City, where they expected to find tracks, sidings, and loading chutes associated with the Southern Kansas Railroad and the Santa Fe. When they arrived, however, they discovered that construction of the railroad was ongoing and that the line had not yet reached Carson County. They then turned their animals toward Dodge City.

During the winter of 1887–88, Fort Worth and Denver City officials determined to make the Amarillo community a permanent cattle-shipping point. Influenced in no small way by Berry and his associates, who provided the land, they selected a spot on the high ground at Wild Horse Lake and ordered construction of additional sidings, corrals, holding pens, and permanent loading chutes. Their site, located east of the main tracks on twenty acres of land, would allow cattle to be loaded onto four railway cars at once.

Construction got underway in the late winter. From the east, the railroad brought to Amarillo carloads of lumber for pens and corrals, steel for track, and equipment for chutes. Workers arrived, and building moved forward. By late spring of 1888, the normally bucolic area around Wild Horse Lake just above Berry's Amarillo came alive with the activity of laborers.

As construction moved forward, cattle drovers and buyers waited for their chance to use the new facilities. In May the editor of Amarillo's first newspaper, the *Amarillo Champion,* wrote—inaccurately—that the stock pens were "within one or two miles of a hundred springs in East and West Amarillo." He wrote that "if 200,000 cattle drank at this unlimited supply each day, the streams would not be perceptibly lower." Although his numbers were high, the editor, H. H. Brookes, was correct about shipping cattle, for that spring, writes Della Tyler Key, a Potter County historian, "thousands of cattle were held around the town awaiting cars."[17]

Brookes predicted that Amarillo "would be the great cattle shipping point in Northwest Texas." He was right. But the city's emergence as a cattle market was not without difficulties. While pens and corrals went up and chutes became available with great dispatch, a shortage of cattle cars slowed shipping. "There was," according to Key, "much bickering between the railroad and the cattlemen over the lack of cattle cars." Each side blamed the other for the problem, and in the meantime herds of blissfully unconcerned cattle grew fat on the surrounding pastures.[18]

With their animals waiting two weeks or longer for loading, drovers contracted with neighboring ranchers for temporary grazing. They placed herds on LX ranges east of Amarillo, Frying Pan land to the west, and T-Anchor pastures south of the city. The Frying Pan made available "twelve or more sections of land" along Amarillo Creek northwest of the cattle pens, and several large herds grazed there. The daughter of one of the Frying Pan Ranch managers remembers, "There would be herds that looked like a thousand cattle on the hills—[well,] not much of a hill anyway." Duncan Kersey, sometimes called Amarillo's "first native," said that "frequently there would be a hundred thousand cattle, or more, pastured close to town, from twenty or more ranches, each with fifteen or twenty men to the herd."[19]

Drovers held even larger herds along Palo Duro Creek in Randall County, about eight miles southeast of Amarillo. As related by others, Mrs. Davis Tudor told a small group of historians that when she was a child, her father came home and said that he wanted "everyone of you to come with me to see a sight you'll never see again." He took the family to inspect the herds near their home in the upper Palo Duro Creek watershed. Family members, she recalled, saw a solid mass of cattle, "by count fifty thousand of them," spreading in all directions nearly as far as they could see. Seemingly transfixed on that quiet, autumn evening, they surveyed enormous numbers of "cattle as they milled about, bawling softly," and as the sun set they viewed "the smoke that spiraled upward from the many campfires, all forming a charming scene never to be forgotten."[20]

If the Fort Worth and Denver City seeded Amarillo's growth, the arrival of a second railroad secured its future. In the early summer of 1888, Grenville Dodge completed a short line, the Panhandle Railway Company, that extended from Washburn, about fifteen miles east of Amarillo, to Panhandle City. There it made a connection with the Southern Kansas Railroad, part of the Santa Fe network. The junctions at either end of the short line opened a new artery of rail traffic that gave Amarillo access to the Midwest through Wichita and Kansas City. Now Amarillo cattle buyers could ship their animals by rail to Chicago, America's largest and busiest livestock market.

Shortly afterward, write Price and Rathjen, Amarillo "boasted eleven stores, several saloons, a hotel, a restaurant, two lawyers, two real estate officers, two cattle brokers, and a population of 200." The main business district, they indicate, was near Third Street and Greene (Parker) Avenue, but "much of the commercial activity centered on the stockyards northwest of town," where the Fort Worth and Denver City maintained corrals, pens, and loading chutes. Lunch counters, saloons, brothels, and related businesses existed near the yards; a boot shop and other stores catered to drovers and cowboys from the cattle trailing crews.[21]

The most imposing building in town was the Champion Hotel. Called "one of the finest structures in Northwest Texas," the large hotel, located on the corner of Third Street and Greene Avenue, contained twenty-five rooms. But, when Berry and John Hollicott, who was manager of the LX Ranch, bought out the other hotel and town site partners, it became the Tremont Hotel. Berry and Hollicott hired A. W. McGregor to manage the place.[22]

Amarillo got a post office early in its existence. On November 23, 1887, city leaders established a fourth-class office in William Martin's large general merchandise store at Third and Greene near the Tremont Hotel. R. M. "Mack" Moore, the first postmaster, used "a few dry goods boxes with built in pigeon holes" for mailboxes. When Moore left the position a short time later, George S. Berry, son of James Berry, took over postal duties. He moved the post office to his father's real estate business located just up the street.

At the end of May 1888 Amarillo's future seemed secure. The Fort Worth and Denver City had opened its passenger and freight depots; Berry had held his big public auction lot sale; T. B. Hinkle, an agent for the W. A. Scott and J. D. McReynolds Company, had started a huge lumberyard near the depot; a drug store had opened; and a physician, C. J. Cornelius, had moved over from Ragtown. Other businesses included a short-lived hotel called the Amarillo House whose owners boasted that our "table is supplied with the best the market affords, making commercial trade a specialty"; it did not last, and the small building soon became a private residence.[23]

In addition, the county built a large courthouse. Approved in a thirty-eight-thousand-dollar bond vote and located at present-day Fifth and Bowie, the two-story brick and mortar building was impressive. According to the *American Breeder Magazine,* the "magnificent" structure, completed in June 1889, was spacious and "well-arranged," with plenty of office space and wide corridors.[24]

And, a newspaper had been established. The editor, H. H. Brookes, a pugnacious Englishmen whose fiery opinions sometimes angered Amarillo residents, often delivered papers with a gun under his arm for protection. He called his paper the *Amarillo Champion* and released the first issue on May 18, 1888, one week before Berry's big lot sale. Not unexpectedly, he promoted the town. He also indicated that an excursion train from Fort Worth would be bringing prospective buyers for the lot sale, included a plat of Amarillo, and described some of the businesses and leading townspeople.

Brookes indicated that several problems, or at least inconveniences, such as fuel shortages and the fact that water sources that had existed a year earlier had been eliminated. "The water problem," he wrote, "has been solved, for a number of wells have been sunk at a depth of 150 feet." He noted that an "abundance of pure water has been found." Moreover, he suggested that a "project is now underway to supply this city with a complete water system."[25]

Difficulties relating to fuel had likewise been resolved. Mack Moore, the former postmaster, ran a coal yard at his store on the corner of Sixth and Courtney (Lipscomb), and T. B. Hinkle sold coal at his immense lumberyard at First and Mabry (Travis) near the depot. They purchased the efficient, but dirty, black fuel from eastern sources and moved it to Amarillo on cars of the Fort Worth and Denver City.

As noted, Third and Greene, the location of the Tremont Hotel, was the heart of the town. A majority of businesses had their address on Third Street, and several businesses clustered at the intersection of Third and Green. Residential homes scattered from First Street, which paralleled the railroad tracks, to Fifth and along avenues on both sides of Greene. The outer boundaries were modern Washington Street on the east and Georgia on the west, but no residential or business structures existed that far from the city's heart. North of the tracks, near the stockyards, however, business activity was brisk.

Then Henry Sanborn reentered the picture and brought trouble—at least for Berry's group. Apparently piqued with the Berry cabal for having been denied an interest in the town site and especially angry with his former employee Warren Wetzel, Sanborn planned his own community, one that would compete with and, as it turned out, surpass the low-lying village. Securing financial backing from his wealthy partner and from Glidden's son-in-law William H. Bush, Sanborn purchased in June a section of land—the Glidden and Sanborn Addition—bordering the Berry site on the east, plus two additional sections of land, which became the East Amarillo and the Ridgemere additions. He paid six thousand dollars for the combined property. In November, his agents began platting section 169, land just north of the site Sanborn and Frank Lester had once called Plains City.[26]

Sanborn poured big money into the project. He "vowed," writes a Potter County historian, "that he would spend $100,000 to put" Amarillo on his property. Similarly, the *Tascosa Pioneer* editor, Charles Rudolph, noted that Sanborn planned to build a large hotel, to construct rows of business houses to rent, and to give away town lots to citizens who might settle on his property. While, in fact, he did give away several lots, Sanborn sold the majority of his town property. To ease the purchase of his lots he provided liberal credit. With Glidden, a lumberman named M. T. Jones (who would soon operate a lumber and coal yard in Sanborn's section), and George A. F. Parker, he established the Panhandle Loan Association. Parker, the company's secretary, set up an office in Amarillo and issued loans to people who wanted to buy lots in the Glidden and Sanborn Addition.[27]

Sanborn also hired John H. Willis, a land agent and surveyor, to plat the town. The agent, in contrast to Luckett in Berry's site, called the east-west roadways "avenues" and the north-south ones "streets." He located most of the residential lots near Third Avenue along Fillmore, Pierce, and Buchanan streets south of the railroad tracks. He oversaw the construction of wood-frame buildings to be rented for businesses, placing them along Polk Street between the railroad and Sanborn's signature hotel.

Located on the corner of Third Avenue and Polk Street, the sprawling wood-frame hotel was impressive—and colorful. Painted yellow and called the Amarillo Hotel, it cost more than forty thousand dollars to build. A two-story structure of some forty rooms, it contained common baths and outdoor toilets. A wide porch encircled two sides of the building, and Sanborn drilled a well and erected a tall windmill to provide water for the facility. W. P. Hardwick became the manager. Called "the finest hotel in the Panhandle," it opened in April 1889, and not long afterward "ranchers and cattle buyers . . . made the place their headquarters when in town." Drovers with herds awaiting shipment at the stockyards also rented rooms at the hotel.[28]

To enhance his "New Town," Sanborn persuaded Brookes to shift the *Amarillo Champion* to the Glidden and Sanborn Addition. The paper, or so Sanborn reasoned, would make his site more attractive than Berry's "Old Town," as some people were calling the original community of Amarillo. Brookes moved in January 1889—but not completely. "For a while," write Price and Rathjen, "he simply transported his press once a week from 'old town' by wagon, set up shop, and then returned home."[29]

A few other people were not as tentative and fully moved over to Sanborn's property. Tuck Cornelius, who operated a livery stable in Berry's Amarillo, was the first. On October 11, 1888, he purchased three lots on the northwest corner of Third and Tyler and soon built a new facility. In January 1889 he purchased "lots on the northeast corner of Fourth and Fillmore (301 East Fourth)," where he planned to build a home. In March, F. M. Burns and J. A. Walker, general merchants from Colorado City who operated a ranch supply store in Old Town, bought two lots in New Town on the northwest corner of Third and Polk, facing the Amarillo Hotel. Here, in an adobe building, they established their business, Burns and Walker Company. To encourage others to abandon Berry's site, Sanborn called attention to Amarillo's location in a draw that, he claimed, would flood after heavy rains.[30]

Old Town leaders fought back. They lobbied with prospective settlers and nervous townsfolk, desperately trying to prevent a major exodus to the New Town. They pushed construction of the county courthouse, improved the Tremont Hotel, and offered to donate land for a permanent schoolhouse. They briefly convinced W. R. Bright and J. T. Johnson, both of Navarro County, to establish a bank, the First National Bank, to be located in a two-story brick building near the courthouse. But the flooding that Sanborn had predicted came to pass in April 1889 during negotiations on the bank building, and plans for the bank fell apart.

In the nineteenth century, rainfall on the Llano Estacado was unpredictable. It might be a gentle and scattered rainfall, but just as often it might be sudden and heavy. Editor Brookes wrote in his paper that unexpected "and peculiar rain storms are one of the penances of the Panhandle." Such an April rainstorm, one that poured "down in torrents and streaks," flooded the low-lying Old Town community, inundating the streets and buildings situated near the bottom of the draw. Apparently, the railroad embankment crossing the lower end of the draw on the north edge of town prevented the water from running off toward Amarillo Creek.[31]

Old Town leaders surrendered. They gave up on the bank, sought their own lots in New Town, and no longer pressured citizens to remain at their site. Berry and Hollicott sold the Tremont Hotel to Sanborn, who moved the large building on skids to a site next to his Amarillo Hotel on Third and Polk. In addition, Sanborn snatched up lot after lot in Old Town and exchanged lots already purchased by others for property in New Town. He also arranged and paid for the removal of houses and business structures to his town. Clearly, Brookes was correct when he predicted, "A man with a check book is going to build a town."

Within weeks after the flood few houses or businesses remained in Old Town. Wetzel, who like Sanborn was buying up lots, still lived there, and Brookes, the feisty newspaperman, continued to live in Old Town and haul his printing press to New Town each week. The courthouse, which was finished in June at Fifth and Hollicott (Bowie Street), remained in Old Town, which meant that county officials each day rode over from Sanborn's site to conduct business. The postmistress, Martha Ingerton, a widowed former school teacher from New York, continued to operate the post office in Old Town until September, when, upon getting government permission, she moved it to a building on East Third Avenue. A small business community still existed at the stockyards west of Wild Horse Lake, and the passenger and freight depots kept people coming to the mud-filled streets of Old Town.

Old Town's dying breath came shortly after the Fort Worth and Denver City Railroad agreed to establish passenger and freight depots along its tracks near Polk Street in New Town. Then even Wetzel and Brookes gave up, and like other citizens of the Old Town community, loaded their homes on wagons or skids and hauled them east to the area centered around Third Avenue and Polk Street. Old Town was deserted—or nearly so. At the end of the summer in 1889, write Price and Rathjen, the impressive, but now forbidding, "two-and-one-half story brick courthouse" was the only building that remained, and it "stood like a lone sentinel on the prairie."[32]

Sanborn did not rest. He bought more sections of land and attached them as "additions" to Amarillo, owning as a result interest in at least five subdivisions to the city. With others, he established the First National Bank in a frame building on Polk Street. He placed the Tremont Hotel at the northwest corner of Fourth and Polk, where it became the "annex" to the Amarillo Hotel, and he retained A. W. McGregor and his wife to manage it. The lots between the two large buildings became a park, one that Sanborn fenced "to keep out hogs," landscaped with trees and shrubs and highlighted with a fountain in the center. Some early residents of Amarillo recall, "[we had] some real nice parties there in the park. It was the only place we had to go."[33]

The city grew, but clearly Sanborn did not build Amarillo alone. Area ranchers both large and small who purchased supplies in the city encouraged its economic growth. Some of them, such as O. H. Nelson, invested heavily in Amarillo. Real estate salesmen, such as James T.

Holland and John H. Willis, played key roles. H. A. Nobles, a grocery man, and his sometimes partners the Callaway Brothers built profitable businesses in the town. William B. Plemons, the county judge, directed the county's, and by extension the city's, administrative affairs. Coleman G. Witherspoon served as Amarillo's first public schoolmaster; with thirty-five students in 1889, he was a busy teacher who held classes in the temporary courthouse, one of the many buildings that had been hauled from Berry's Old Town.

Many other people got involved in Amarillo's growth. As Price and Rathjen write, druggists, jewelers, undertakers, blacksmiths, grocers, general merchandisers, and other shop keepers set up operations in Amarillo. There were livery stables, taxi services, laundries, restaurants, hardware stores, lumberyards, and pharmacies. Physicians, preachers, and bankers arrived, and lawyers were abundant. Day laborers appeared, and men, mainly, hired themselves out as brick masons, carpenters, painters, or other craftsmen. Cattle buyers, drovers, ranchers, salesmen, travelers, and others used the Amarillo Hotel and its annex. Some, mainly cowboys and transients, preferred the little, false-fronted Crescent Hotel next door to the 66 Saloon.

There were plenty of saloons. In 1890 six of them filled the area around Second Avenue and Polk Street. Anti-saloon people complained that such establishments attracted little more than "professional gamblers, tin horn men, and bums" who played monte, faro, poker, and other games of chance. Besides drinks, some saloons provided a buffet lunch, and many of them featured billiard tables. Connected to the saloons, one could often find dance halls and "parlors"—or bordellos—that provided cowboys off the range and other lonely men with female companionship. Too often, perhaps, saloons became the focus of general rowdiness and fighting and, to a lesser extent, gunplay or other violence.

More constructive activity related to Amarillo's water supply. John Murphy and J. H. Hamlin provide fitting examples. Murphy, who had come to Amarillo from Brownsville in 1887, hauled water in a wagon to city residences. For a small fee, he placed the water in barrels beside the homes. At least one woman remembered that her family "got a barrel once a week. . . . [The] barrel got full of paper and trash of every description. We would just take the dipper and dip off the trash and drink the water." Hamlin, who had dug a well and built a windmill for the Amarillo Hotel, was soon at work on other wells and mills around the city.[34]

In 1889 Sanborn and his wealthy partner Glidden created the Glidden and Sanborn Water Works Company. With offices and yards at a site between Fifth and Sixth avenues and Buchanan and Lincoln streets, the company placed several miles of pipes underground. From wells at the headquarters yard, the pipes provided water to hydrants around town; from the hydrants townspeople took what they needed. The efficient water system was well used and profitable enough that in 1890 and afterward the company drilled more wells, erected additional windmills to power them, and built pumping stations to move the water.

In 1890 Amarillo had a population of 482, more than half of Potter County's inhabitants. The main business district centered along three blocks of Polk Street, and most of the city's growing number of residents lived in homes east of there. Two major railroads, the Santa Fe and the Fort Worth and Denver City, entered the small but promising community, which had already replaced Tascosa as the western Panhandle's principal nexus. Amarillo was quickly becoming the major cattle-shipping center in western Texas, a circumstance that attracted even more people to the area.

By early in the new decade, Amarillo had become the political and economic center for a large region. It had beaten back competition from Washburn and Panhandle City. Tascosa was in decline but would hang on for a time before citizens moved the Oldham County seat to Vega. Channing, the general headquarters for the giant XIT Ranch, even after some Tascosa businesses moved there, was too isolated to attract a large enough number of settlers to offer a viable challenge to the little western town near Wild Horse Lake.

Despite so many hopeful signs for the lively little western town,

Amarillo had its problems. There was no city government, and officially the Potter County seat was still in Old Town, a mile away from Amarillo's center. The depots on Polk Street, because the land sloped down toward the west, represented difficult problems for train operators; they could not stop satisfactorily at the spot. Some powerful railroad interests in Washburn, fifteen miles east of Amarillo, in Armstrong County, remained convinced their city would surpass Amarillo as a major railroad center, and they lobbied for another railroad.

Still, Amarillo had succeeded, or so it seemed. It had been founded in 1887. Its few inhabitants had pulled through a cold winter in 1888, one that found them gathering cow "chips" for fuel to heat their tents or flimsy wood-frame homes. The community had withstood a difficult, costly, but short-lived struggle over its location before it and its citizens in 1889 moved—slid really—a mile east. Although Old Town had lasted a scant two years, the new, invigorated Amarillo in 1890 seemed ready for additional expansion. Efforts at self-government would come first.

3

Amarillo in 1900

Between its founding in 1887 and the end of the century, Amarillo more than doubled in size. During the 1890s it became the dominant city in the western Panhandle of Texas, replacing Tascosa as the region's urban center and holding off a serious challenge for leadership from Washburn and a minor one from Panhandle City. With a population of 1,442, Amarillo in 1900 stood at the threshold of a period of even more remarkable growth that few people at the time could have predicted.

The decade of the 1890s, however, was not all pleasant for Amarillo and its citizens. A crippling national economic depression, the worst since the Panic of 1873; several years of severe drought; declining prices for cattle, which were a key to Amarillo's financial health; political wars over the city's government, or lack thereof; and local battles over the nation's gold standard, money supply, Populism, and gambling and prohibition all affected social and economic life in the city and region.[1]

Henry B. Sanborn, often considered the "Father of Amarillo," was in the middle of the unpleasantness. He held financial interests in Houston, Sherman, Kansas City, and elsewhere, and he did not make Amarillo his permanent home until after the turn of the century. Although a highly successful, silver-tongued salesman, Sanborn seemingly got along with few people in Amarillo. He filed legal suits on a regular basis, and others brought legal action against him. His struggle with James T. Berry over the preferred site for Amarillo destroyed Berry financially. He forced Warren W. Wetzel out as superintendent of the Frying Pan Ranch, although other owners remained friendly with Wetzel. Disputes over the proper operation of the Frying Pan led Sanborn to sell his share of the large ranch. He fought with the city of Amarillo—in effect, his creation—over city parks, courthouse sites, and land ownership.[2]

Nor was Amarillo a particularly attractive place in the 1890s. Polk Street, the main business thoroughfare, was "a mass of mud and slush in rainy weather, which was not often, and ruts, chuckholes and dust at other times." Sidewalks were wooden. Some business owners placed the sidewalk boards parallel with their buildings and some placed them at right angles. Sidewalks were rarely level or at the same height, making a stroll along them an exercise in great care.[3]

Early in the decade the buildings, with such exceptions as the large Amarillo Hotel and its annex, were small, crudely built wood-frame structures with few windows and little insulation. The buildings were cold in winter and hot in summer. Most of them were narrow and single-storied but for impression's sake presented a two-story false front toward the street. Before most of the buildings was a hitching rack to which one tied his horse or mule. With the exception of lettering and advertising, few of the structures were painted. Little outhouses behind the buildings served as toilets. Rarely in the early years could one find trees or grass in the backyards of businesses. Instead, used wooden crates and other discarded materials, over-filled trash bins, and containers for burning trash were common. Piles of coal beside the buildings were also a familiar sight.

Far more saloons than churches existed in early Amarillo. Besides the six or so associated with the area around Second Avenue and Polk Street, several saloons occupied lots farther south on Polk and lots just off the main business thoroughfare. At Clem Yarbrough's saloon on Polk Street a prairie dog, which became a friendly and gentle "pet" of sorts, had dug a hole. Patrons of Yarbrough's little bar, especially "drunks," as James Hamlin called them, continually offered the prairie dog a swig of "red-eye," but the little fellow, wisely enough, always refused. Nearby, Bill Taylor operated a more successful saloon, in part because his bartender was a popular character. Cowboys from the nearby ranches favored a tavern called Pealan and Britman, apparently "because the bartender was attuned to their crude sense of humor"—whatever that might mean.[4]

But in the late 1890s the Amarillo Hotel contained perhaps the most popular taproom. Frank Anderson, who earlier had run a saloon at 404 Polk Street, operated the upscale bar. A charter member of Amarillo's Young Men's Business and Social Club, he leased the fancy hotel bar from Sanborn, for Sanborn's hotel manager wanted little to do with liquor. In a relative sense, Anderson's was something of a "high-toned place, patronized by cattlemen, lawyers, bankers and other pretentious customers." Anderson "ran a scrupulously clean establishment, tolerating no bums or rowdies." Eben F. "Doc" True, a portly, well-dressed veterinarian and former horse wrangler for the LX Ranch, was the bartender.[5]

But Amarillo was not without churches. Among the first preachers in the Amarillo area was J. T. Bloodworth, a Methodist Church circuit rider from Weatherford. In the 1880s, he conducted religious services—sometimes extending over a period of ten days—that included hymn singing and Bible reading at the Frying Pan Ranch. Not long afterward, in the spring of 1888, Isaac L. Mills, a Methodist circuit rider from Childress, held religious services in Old Town Amarillo. In November the Methodist Church South, the large regional body that governed Methodist activities in Texas, established a church in Amarillo, the city's first such organization.

A house of worship soon followed. Sanborn donated land on Jackson Street between Seventh and Eighth avenues for the building, and George A. F. Parker, who managed the M. T. Jones Lumber Company, provided enthusiastic and spirited leadership, direction, and materials for the wood-frame structure that went up at 701 Jackson. After Parker in 1890 convinced James E. Beasley to donate an organ, worship services became a popular Sunday activity. Parker's wife played the "fine pump organ," and Parker himself led the weekly singing of favorite hymns. The building, appropriately enough called Parker's Chapel at first, soon became known as Union Church.[6]

Other church groups were active. The Baptists, Disciples of Christ, and Presbyterians closely followed the Methodists. Like the Methodists, they held religious services in Old Town's temporary courthouse before moving to Sanborn's town site, where they worshiped in Union Church. In fact, each denomination, before it occupied its own building, took a weekly turn in leading the Sunday worship service, with people from all denominations attending.

Separate services came quickly. In 1890, for example, a small, sixteen-member Baptist congregation completed a church at 500 Pierce. Itinerant preachers, led by Thomas H. Storts, filled the pulpit in the early days. G. W. Capps was the first regular preacher, but because he lived in Deaf Smith County some forty miles away, he held services only once a month. In 1892 Bennet Hatcher from Vernon became the first resident Baptist pastor.

The Christian Church in Amarillo has a similar history. Its members worshiped in the Old Town courthouse before moving to Union Church. In August 1890 with fifteen members they officially organized their church. Thomas G. Nance, originally from Tennessee, came from Plainview once a month to conduct services, and S. K. Halan, who had settled near Amarillo, succeeded him. In 1893 H. M. Bandy became the first resident pastor, and a year later, during the national financial panic that produced a significant negative affect on Amarillo, the church secured the "Old Red Front" building, a former saloon, at 413 Polk. It proved a popular place for services while the congregation constructed a permanent building at Eighth and Taylor.

The Presbyterian experience was a bit different. In September 1890 thirteen charter members created the First Cumberland Presbyterian Church. They used the Union Church before erecting their own building at Seventh and Fillmore. A. W. Rodgers was the first pastor of the congregation. Then, in October 1890, shortly after the First

Cumberland group had organized, a second congregation of Presbyterians, only nine in number, formed the First Presbyterian Church, South. Its first building went up at 410 Fillmore. In 1906, following the merger on a national level of two large Presbyterian groups, First Cumberland became Fillmore Street Presbyterian Church, and four years later, upon moving to a location on Tenth Avenue and Taylor Street, it became Central Presbyterian Church. Within five years members of the smaller First Presbyterian had joined Central Presbyterian Church.[7]

The 1890s saw other churches organize. Episcopalians founded Saint Andrews Church, and soon other Protestant denominations and Catholics established churches. But church membership did not expand significantly until Amarillo's population explosion after the turn of the century.

Still, in the 1890s the churches represented strong, influential political and social institutions. Nearly all of Amarillo's key political leaders belonged to one of the four leading denominations, and some of them, such as George Parker, took active roles in their church. The Protestant denominations, moreover, especially the Methodists and Baptists, sought to enforce anti-gambling laws in the city and, through the prohibition of the sale of alcoholic beverages, to end liquor trafficking in Amarillo. While in the 1890s they failed on the former, their prohibition movement with the assistance of the national Anti-Saloon League and the Women's Christian Temperance Movement achieved success in 1902 when Amarillo went "dry," and the saloons closed—temporarily.

Wet or dry, life in Amarillo in the 1890s was quite simple. James D. Hamlin, who came to Amarillo in 1897, remembered life in the city as neither glamorous nor dramatic. "In town," he suggested, "the amusements were tame, unless one got drunk, gambled, or went to the whorehouses." Social activities for respectable women, he claimed, were "restricted to parties where they, with their escorts, played clap-in and clap-out, to church" functions, and "to an occasioned dance."[8]

Sometimes townspeople organized parties in the little park between the Amarillo Hotel and its annex. A good place to visit, it was one of the few places in town with trees for shade, and a bit of grass could be found in the area. Whether held in one's home or in the park, parties served mainly to get people together to enjoy one another's company. Coffee or tea when available was the preferred drink, but water and liquor were more common. Homemade cakes and breads dominated the party foods.

Dances, when they occurred, attracted many people. Often a fiddle and guitar represented the only instruments, but some people improvised with strings and tubs to produce crude base fiddles. If the dance was held outside, someone might spread a large canvas wagon cover on the ground to use as the dance floor. The waltz, polka, and schottische were among the more popular dances.

In the early 1890s some of the big ranches took their turn in organizing large parties—"blowouts," they were called. Normally held once a year around Christmas and New Year's Day, the events were polite but fancy affairs to which people went well dressed and sober but in good cheer. The LX, LS, LIT, T-Anchor, and Frying Pan each took its turn. Although people from town attended, cowboys from the various ranches dominated the guest list, and as a result men usually outnumbered women at the party by something like three to one. During the dancing that always was part of the annual occurrence, some men placed bandanas around their arm to show that they would dance the female part. Such galas began in the late afternoon as guests arrived. They continued through an evening meal and midnight snack. Dancing, which occurred between the meals, went on through the night, and the "blowout" did not end until after breakfast the next morning.[9]

Social life in Amarillo included dances, of course, but there were other events. Churches held socials of various kinds, and people entertained in their homes. The Amarillo Hotel was a favorite gathering place for staging more formal entertainment, and it hosted large weddings and dinner parties. Fund raising activities, such as oyster suppers at the Old Red Front, brought people together. Early in its history, the little community witnessed the formation of various women's clubs, and both men and women established lodges. Birthdays, anniversaries, formal openings for such buildings as the courthouse and depots, and holidays all meant celebrations and social interaction.

The most popular holidays were the Fourth of July and Christmas. Independence Day celebrations usually included barbecues, both large and small, at scattered places in town, and sometimes cowboys organized a rodeo of sorts. Public speeches and picnics were part of the celebration. In 1895 Governor Charles A. Culberson came to Amarillo for the July 4 holiday. He was to speak from a podium set under a temporary arbor built on Polk Street. Unfortunately, the summer day turned cold with rain that turned to snow for a brief time. Because everyone was cold and wet, organizers moved the event inside. Culberson, after being introduced by Judge W. B. Plemons, made light of the situation, saying, "I have always been told that you were able to produce anything on the Plains and when I see snow here in July, well, I know that you can."[10]

Christmas activities centered at the city's churches. Christmas trees were decorated. Parties and religious programs followed, and good crowds attended to enjoy singing and celebrating. During one of the early years, before their own church buildings were finished, men representing separate denominational groups hauled in a large cedar tree from Palo Duro Canyon, trimmed it, and set it up in Parker's Union Church. Women, writes Della Tyler Key, decorated the tree with cotton, popcorn, candies, and strings of cranberries. Adults surrounded the tree with gifts for children.

Other activities were also part of the Christmas cheer. One December, Charles Rudolph, former editor of the *Tascosa Pioneer,* wrote in his *Amarillo Daily Northwest* that the "Christmas ball will be at the Amarillo Hotel" this year rather than at the courthouse. He also noted that a "jovial little crowd of . . . bachelor boys . . . gathered at the Cowboy Restaurant this morning, and took a Christmas eggnog. You have no idea what a beverage those boys over there can get up." In addition, he indicated that a "string band rubbed up their fiddle et cetra yesterday evening, and put on their best clothes and went to make music for the Canyon citizens. There was a big dance at the latter town last night." In the 1890s, clearly, dances, church functions, and parties at home or at the Amarillo Hotel dominated the city's social activities.[11] Cultural activities were no less popular. In the 1890s the Texas Panhandle, although beginning to fill with settlers and townspeople, remained an isolated and sometimes lonely place. Kate Wetzel, one of the first Anglo women to live in Potter County, remembered that to stave off loneliness and homesickness, she would sometimes sit at her husband's desk, clear it off a bit, and pretend that it was the piano she had used back home in New York. She would "play and sing [her] homesickness away."[12]

But with railroads in the area, the Panhandle was not completely isolated. Touring concert groups came by train or wagon and set up their tents or rented space in larger buildings. Occupation tax records for Potter County reveal that touring shows came regularly to Amarillo. A group calling itself Davico and Fax Company staged a performance on July 8, 1889, and less than a year later, on March 25, 1890, the Oliver Fairy theater company entertained Amarillo citizens. These were stage plays, dramas with musical performances associated with them.

The concerts, dramas, and entertainment shows were well attended, and Amarillo citizens sought a permanent place to hold such events. In 1891 they established an "opera house" in the just-completed Board of Trade Building at Fifth Avenue and Polk Street. A two-story stone building some 116 feet long and 60 feet wide, it was a "large magnificent structure," called the "finest building of its kind this side of Fort Worth." The opera house spread across the second floor. The ground floor of the building held a hardware store and later a ranch supply business. On February 24, 1892, the Hewett Musetts Concert staged the first performance in the new opera house. The community used the opera house for traveling shows, concerts, Chautauqua lyceum speakers, theaters, high school graduations, and other events.[13]

Schools appeared early in Amarillo's history. In 1889 Susie Andrews and Lizzie Bain operated and taught small private schools in their homes, and during the same year county citizens voted in support of a tax initiative to establish a public school system. B. B. Hayden, who chaired the school system's board of trustees, led an effort to purchase the temporary courthouse for a school building. Then, with fellow trustees J. H. Hamlin and William Harrell, he saw that the building was moved to Sixth Avenue and Monroe Street, repaired, and made ready for students. It opened in September with thirty-five students. The trustees hired Coleman G. Witherspoon of Jacksboro as teacher at a salary of seventy-five dollars per month.[14]

Such activity encouraged local leaders to form a city government. Their plans did not go well, however, for the old animosities over town site location resurfaced and prevented the new city government from operating smoothly. Wetzel and former County Judge William Plemons, who favored incorporation of the city, represented the old Berry interests. James T. Holland, the bachelor realtor who, according to James R. Gober, had doubled-crossed Berry in his effort to become Amarillo's founding father, led the old Sanborn clique, a group that opposed the nature and extent of the incorporation. As realtors and relatively large landowners, the Holland faction also opposed what it considered high city taxes, especially during the drought and financial downturn in the region's—indeed, the nation's—economy.

From most points of view, the whole affair was a debacle. It included injunctions, lawsuits, appeals, town surveys, and more injunctions. It prevented the city government from acting effectively, and in the end it led to the temporary abandonment of municipal government.[15]

Incorporation efforts started simply enough. With a population of something over five hundred people in 1892, Amarillo seemed ready for its own government, and at the end of January the Wetzel group presented a petition with ninety signatures to the county commissioners court. The petition asked for a vote on incorporation and on the formation of a municipal government. The commissioners approved and set a general vote for February 20, a vote that by a count of 115 to 41 supported incorporation.

Shortly afterward, County Judge D. N. Quinn ordered "incorporation," set legal boundaries for the City of Amarillo, and called for city elections to be held on April 2. Events moved quickly, and on April 2,

Amarillo's voters chose Warren Wetzel mayor. They also voted into office five aldermen, a city treasurer, and John A. Williams as city marshal. When a week later, on April 7, 1892, Wetzel and his city council met for the first time, municipal government began in Amarillo.

The city council attended to its normal and often mundane duties. The members appointed secretaries, named a health officer, selected Wilson W. Gowan as city attorney, and awarded contracts. Subsequently, they chose a tax assessor, prepared budgets, located a city "dump" ground, hired a street cleaner, considered water needs, set regular meeting times, and went about the business of providing their little city a government and central administration.

By the end of June two problems had emerged. One was the physical size of the city. Amarillo leaders had extended the city limits to cover over five sections of land, which included Old Town and the Glidden and Sanborn Addition, of course. But the five and one-quarter sections also included the Holland and Mirror additions, the Plemons Addition, and the north one-quarter of section 187—some 5.25 square miles. Holland, W. P. Hardwick, Mack Moore, and other Sanborn cronies objected to the expansive boundaries. Taxes on their holdings would be large, and besides, they argued, few people lived beyond the immediate center of the city around Polk Street.

The other problem was taxes. The aldermen had determined that the city ought to assess and collect occupation, personal, and real estate taxes. Again, such relatively large city landowners and businessmen as Holland, Sanborn, Moore, Glidden, John Ryan, and M. E. Thompson would be hard hit, and they objected.

Then they acted. First, the Holland-Sanborn group encouraged T. B. Clisbee and E. S. Wiggins, who may or may not have been Holland confederates, to leave the city council. The men resigned in late June. And second, a month later Holland, Hardwick, Moore, Ryan, and Thompson filed an injunction against Mayor Wetzel and the city council. The injunction was long and complicated. It complained about the city boundaries and taxes; called for the ouster of Wetzel, the aldermen, Marshal Williams, and tax assessor-collector Sam H. Henderson; asked that the city officials "be restrained from assuming the functions, power and authority of their office"; and sought the recovery of all money paid on taxes. It claimed that the city boundaries did not represent the actual city population limits. It protested the occupation tax, saying the levy "made a penal offense for anyone to pursue [a] taxable occupation within the limits of . . . incorporation without first procuring a license." In addition, it protested the city's ad valorem tax on all real and personal property within the municipality's legal borders.[16]

Judge H. H. Wallace of the Forty-seventh District Court upheld the injunction. As a result the city council did not meet, taxes could not be collected, city employees could not be paid, and the day-to-day operations of Amarillo shut down. No one cleaned or graded the streets. No one drained water from the main roadways after a heavy rainfall. No one attended to city improvements that the alderman had been planning.

Wetzel and the city council fought back. They sought an order to vacate and remove the injunction, but at first did not get much satisfaction. Days turned to weeks, and a court battle followed. Months passed. Finally, nearly a year later, in May of 1893, the city council won and could meet once again.

The victory was short-lived. In June, a second injunction, one similar to the first, prevented the council from meeting. Again its members fought back, and in December the courts once more lifted the injunction. A short time later, on January 2, 1894, the council met to conduct city business—the first meeting since the previous June. It met again on January 17, but that was the end. A third injunction stopped city operations, and in the subsequent court battle, although Plemons—"an outstanding attorney in the court room"—and John W. Veale represented the city, the plaintiffs won. The court, "holding that a city's limits were determined by its populated area," ended incorporation and by doing so ended municipal government for Amarillo.[17]

Economics more than animus provoked the injunctions. Holland and Thompson were among the largest landholders in the five sections that the charter of incorporation named as part of Amarillo. The two men, accordingly, would be shelling out a good sum of money when both the region's economy and its weather discouraged land sales, their chief means of income. Simply put, in 1893 and 1894 they could not afford the city's taxes, particularly the "ad valorem tax of one-fourth of one per cent on all real and personal property" within the incorporated area of the city.

The 1890s economic depression, a devastating business panic, created anxiety. Millions of people across the country lost their jobs, and many others "reached bottom." The failure of the Philadelphia and Reading Railroad provided the spark that destroyed the confidence of Wall Street investors: the economic collapse that followed swept across the United States. When cattle prices dropped, Amarillo and the Texas Panhandle felt the financial pinch of hard times. Amarillo's population, which had been growing enthusiastically, leveled out, and new arrivals, who would have been buying town lots from the Holland group of realtors, no longer disembarked at the city's rail stations.

Complicating the economic downturn for Amarillo were drought and bad weather. A dry spell with below average rainfalls began in 1890, increased in 1891 and 1892, and tapered off some in 1894 as rainfall increased again. The *Dallas Morning News* in the summer of 1892, for example, announced that in the Amarillo area and southward all the way to the Big Bend crops "are hurting, cattle are suffering and rain is needed." The same paper reported in the summer of 1893 that hot winds and drought in the Panhandle destroyed crops in the area of Washburn in Armstrong County: "everything literally cooked to death" with one rancher reporting that even the "prairie dogs died by the thousands."[18]

Surely, the drought and hard times slowed Amarillo's development. The minor boom of 1888–90 ended, settlement declined sharply, and during the next several years—1892–97—the city's population growth slowed. During the period, some businesses closed and buildings along Polk Street stood empty. In one of them, the Old Red Front saloon, the

Christian Church in 1894 held its Sunday worship services, but not before members of the church brought in a fifteen-dollar organ and removed several stacks of whisky bottles.

Nonetheless, during the hard times people worked to build Amarillo. In May 1893 they and their Potter County brethren voted to move the county seat to the Glidden and Sanborn Addition. Because moving the large, two-and-one-half-story brick courthouse would not be possible, the county commissioners named the opera house as the temporary courthouse. They contracted to have desks and other furnishing moved over, and they hired men to remove the jail cells from the courthouse in Old Town and to rebuild a jail on a lot at Third and Tyler. Next, in January 1894 they rented space on the second floor of the First National Bank building for both district and county courts, and they moved the clerk's office from the opera house to the bank building. Through much of 1895, while the old courthouse stood empty, the commissioners sought a house or other buildings for use as a courthouse.

It did not happen. Early in February 1896, Amarillo and Potter County citizens in a petition to the commissioners court called for the old courthouse to be torn down and a new one built. The commissioners accepted and approved the petition, and they called for the appropriate bids to take down the empty courthouse in Old Town and rebuild a smaller, temporary building on a lot at the intersection of Fifth Avenue and Taylor Street. C. H. Black, a contractor, won the bid and completed the one-story brick building before the year was out.

Other activities marked the progress. A stage line with daily service opened to Canyon, and mail delivery to additional communities improved. Some men cut a road by plowing a furrow southwestward to Roswell, New Mexico, and others created a volunteer fire department. In addition, writes James Cox with more than a bit of hyperbole, Amarillo in 1895 remained "the largest cattle shipping station for stock in the United States. The cattle shipment from Amarillo has reached between 2,500 and 3,700 cars annually during the past four years." The large numbers, if they are correct, probably reflect efforts by ranchers

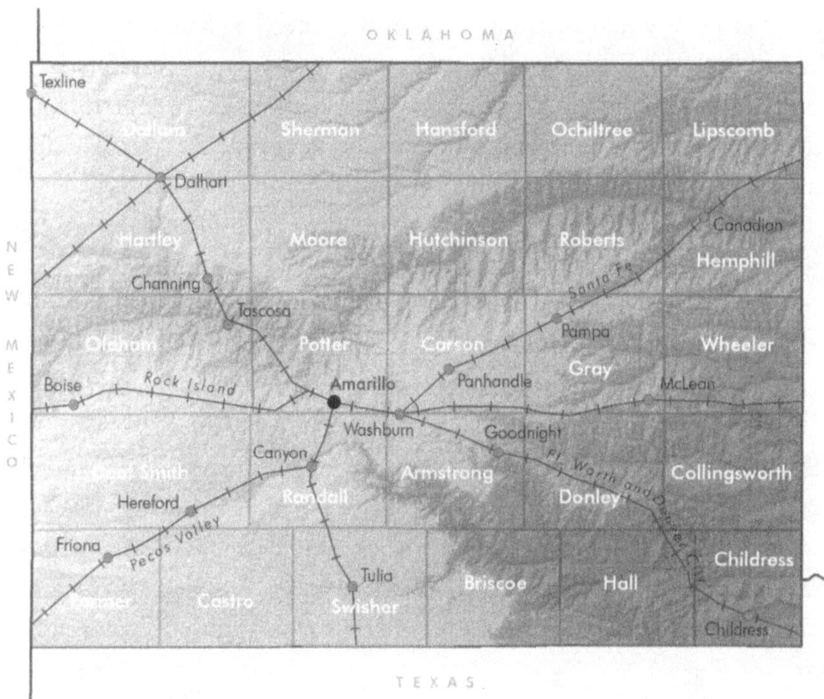

Panhandle railroads show the central position Amarillo had achieved by 1910.

to clear their dry and barren pastures of suffering livestock during the drought.[19]

More important to securing Amarillo's future was the establishment of another railroad—the city's third. Once again Sanborn and his partners were involved. Upon hearing that J. H. Hagerman planned to run his Pecos Valley and Northern Texas Railroad from Roswell, New Mexico, northeastward into the Texas Panhandle to connect with the Fort Worth and Denver City at Washburn, Sanborn and Wiley H. Fuqua of the First National Bank took action. In 1895 they went to Colorado Springs, Colorado, visited with Hagerman, and convinced the railroad magnate and Pecos Valley developer to run his line into Amarillo. At the same time, Sanborn sent attorney Sam H. Madden to Chicago, where Madden and William H. Bush, the Chicago-based owner of the Frying Pan Ranch, lobbied Santa Fe Railroad officials to connect in Amarillo with the Pecos Valley line. The Santa Fe officials agreed, but only after Amarillo citizens, led by Sanborn with Glidden's money, financed a joint terminal for the two railroads. In March 1899, the Pecos Valley line reached Amarillo, and later that year the Santa Fe moved its regional offices from Panhandle City to Amarillo.[20]

By 1899 prosperity had clearly returned to Amarillo. And with its return came a renewed enthusiasm for the city's future and new efforts toward city government. In March, the same month that the Pecos Valley and Northern Texas Railroad reached their city, Amarillo citizens voted once again to incorporate and organize a local government. During the same election they chose Rufus L. Stringfellow as mayor. B. Byron Price and Frederick W. Rathjen write that the new city "council moved more cautiously than had its [1892] predecessor and established town boundaries comprising only two square miles." The new city limits included only "parts of the Glidden-Sanborn, Plemons, Mirror, and Holland additions." No one challenged the new city government's right to exist.[21]

Amarillo in 1900 was growing. It was, in fact, an exciting place, the leading city in the western Panhandle, a railroad center, and a cattle-shipping point. Much had changed in the decade of the 1890s, but much had remained the same. Large ranches still surrounded the city—Frying Pan on the west, the LX on the east and north, and the T-Anchor on the south. Cattle drovers pushing their herds from distant ranches and cowboys off the local spreads came into town, where they patronized their favorite hotels, restaurants, saloons, and related businesses.

In 1900 the Bowery District attracted many drovers and cowboys. Located in the area bounded by First and Third avenues and Buchanan and Grant streets, the district was near the Fort Worth and Denver City depot—Union Station—that had been moved from Polk Street. Once a "fashionable" residential area, the little section of town fell into disrepute as transients, gamblers, prostitutes, and "thugs who would slug you for a quarter—or kill you for a dollar" drifted in. A few so-called legitimate businesses existed in the Bowery, but its gambling dens, brothels, and saloons made the place notorious. Ella Hill, according to James D. Hamlin, was the outstanding "madam" in the Bowery, but at least a half dozen other such houses were open. Rampant "crime and violence in the area," write Price and Rathjen, "kept law enforcement officials busy" and added to its notoriety.[22]

Indeed, the infamy of the Bowery encouraged Amarillo church leaders and anti-saloon leaguers to launch another prohibition crusade, one they hoped would close Amarillo's saloons and, by extension, clean up the Bowery District. Their emotional efforts, which drew plenty of spirited opposition, sometimes turned violent. Local officials called in the Texas Rangers to help maintain order during the explosive campaign that ended in December 1901 with a vote to end the sale and distribution of alcoholic beverages.[23]

Amarillo went dry in 1902—well, not quite. Bootleggers brought in liquor, and many saloons, rather than closing, moved to points just outside the city's limits. The Bowery changed a bit, but not much, for a short year later, after still another election over the sale and distribution of alcohol, Amarillo's citizens, perhaps having seen the folly of their ways, voted to legalize—again—the sale of liquor.

Amarillo in 1900 claimed ten attorneys, including the two influential firms of W. B. Plemons and John W. Veale and James N. Browning and Sam Madden plus six individual practitioners: William Boyce, Wilson Gowan, Dave Hill, Lon D. Marrs, Foe Lee Penry, and H. H. Wallace. In addition, Temple Houston, the son of the hero of San Jacinto and the president of the Republic of Texas, spent "considerable" time in Amarillo. Called "the ablest criminal lawyer in the entire Panhandle," Houston lived in Woodward, Indian Territory (Oklahoma), but "participated in practically every important murder trial in the North Plains."[24]

The lawyers were a solid bunch. Plemons served in the Texas legislature. Browning, an able and forceful courtroom attorney who was a popular raconteur, became the lieutenant governor of Texas. Marrs, once the county attorney, became county judge, and later he won election as mayor of Amarillo. Boyce, son of the manager of the XIT

Ranch, became the Texas attorney for the Capitol Freehold Land and Investment Company, owners of the XIT.

Although the city needed more doctors than lawyers, Amarillo in 1900 was home to only four physicians: Eli O. Johnson, John W. Pierson, Thomas F. Magee, and David R. Fly. All were community leaders. Magee, who had been practicing medicine in Amarillo for a decade, helped to organize and lead the Potter County Medical Society. Johnson contributed a room in the First National Bank to the local Women's Club for a library. Fly, "who was brilliant, knew medicine, [and] kept up with the profession," helped to establish the area's first hospital.[25]

In 1900 no hospital existed in the Texas Panhandle, but one was under construction. Many people contributed to building the hospital, or "sanitarium" as they called it. Fly, who had come to Amarillo from San Antonio, sought help at his former home from the Sisters of Charity of the Order of Incarnate Word of Saint Anthony. His close friend, James D. Hamlin, an educator who would soon become an attorney and town developer, directed a fund-raising effort, and the local drama club in one of the city's more popular funding benefits performed *Mabel Heath,* a favorite old English play, before a large audience at the opera house on Polk Street. The city's newspapers, especially the *Amarillo Weekly News,* edited by J. L. Caldwell, supported the hospital. William Bush of the Frying Pan Ranch donated two blocks of prairie land between Taylor and Tyler streets north of town and east of Wild Horse Lake and promised "active and substantial cooperation toward establishing the [sanitarium] at Amarillo."[26]

Not long afterward, in March 1901, the hospital, named Saint Anthony's Sanitarium, formally opened. Although it contained neither running water nor electricity, the two-story red brick building held twenty-five beds. David Fly became the head physician, and seven Sisters of the Incarnate Word, all from San Antonio, staffed the facility. For nearly a decade the building served as the only hospital in the Texas Panhandle.[27]

Amarillo in 1900 also contained a little college, called appropriately enough Amarillo College. Willis D. Twichell, a surveyor and educator who in 1886 had laid out XIT Ranch fence lines, started the school for the purpose of providing to local students an education beyond the tenth grade. James D. Hamlin, with a degree from the University of Kentucky, joined Twichell, and in 1897 the two men with two female colleagues began instruction in a couple of former store buildings they had moved to a block of land on the edge of town. A semester later Twichell retired. Hamlin became president of the institution and convinced some classmates from Kentucky to join him in Amarillo. The curriculum, an ambitious one, included natural sciences, history, music, physiology and hygiene, some law, and, of course, the always present classes in Latin and Greek. Never very large and always on the edge of bankruptcy, the school closed in 1910.

Amarillo at this time also supported three newspapers: the *Livestock Champion,* the *Evening News,* and the *Weekly News.* The still feisty H. H. Brookes operated the *Champion.* J. L. Caldwell owned and edited the *Weekly News,* a democratic paper that constantly found itself at odds with Brookes. The *Evening News,* a more conservative paper, battled both of its rivals for news and subscribers. All three papers were strong boosters of Amarillo.

Amarillo contained few African American citizens at the turn of the century. In fact, according to Hamlin, with exceptions "no Negroes were allowed to live, or even stop over, in some of the Panhandle towns." In one exception, the J. S. Callaway family boarded an eighteen-year-old black man named Jerry Callaway, often called "the first Negro in Amarillo." The Callaways had brought Jerry with them when they settled in the region about 1888. Callaway, who became "a giant of a man," worked at the Amarillo Hotel. A black woman, Corinne, and her daughter resided near the Bowery District, where they took in washing from gamblers and some of Amarillo's single businessmen.

The most famous exception was Matthew "Bones" Hooks, who in 1900 moved to Amarillo to take a job at the Elmhurst Hotel at Fifth and Taylor. He had come to the Panhandle several years earlier and worked on the DSD Ranch of D. Steve Donald. A highly respected and widely known bronc buster, Hooks became one of the Texas Panhandle's most famous cowboys. He broke horses on most of the ranches around Amarillo, including the LX, Frying Pan, T-Anchor, and XIT. The Elmhurst, where Hooks worked, for a time "one of Amarillo's most pretentious landmarks," eventually became the Tourist Hotel, a business that burned in 1921. Afterward, Hooks went to work as a porter for one of the railroads. About the time he settled in Amarillo, he began a practice of presenting a white flower to pioneers in the region and to "distinguished persons" in the area. In 1908, five black families, including Hooks and his wife, Anna, who also worked at the Elmhurst, lived in Amarillo.[28]

Amarillo was assuming an importance that resulted in its becoming the leading city in the Texas Panhandle. James D. Hamlin remembered that two livery stables existed, and two blacksmith shops "did a brisk business, shoeing horses, repairing broken parts of windmills, shrinking iron tires for wagons and buggies, making branding irons," and helping to keep a "horse and wagon economy going." Two hardware stores sold windmills and other farm and ranch equipment.

Four general mercantile stores handled local business and catered to the needs of ranchers from up to one hundred miles away. Hamlin remembered that the leading firm was the Walker-Smith Company, which James L. Smith had started. The Calloway Brothers and Millard C. Nobles and Henry A. Nobles also operated large stores, and Ed W. White managed White and Kirk, a firm that during World War II became the largest department store in the Panhandle.

Few specialty stores were open in Amarillo in 1900. One was called The Famous, which, although it sold various dry goods and notions, concentrated on men's clothing, or "gents furnishings," as Hamlin called them. Two young Jewish men, Phil Denitz and Joe Isaacs, ran the store. A second was Phillip H. Seewald's jewelry shop. Seewald, who had moved to Amarillo from Tascosa about 1888, "became a financial success through upright dealings." There were also two drug stores in town.

There were two financial institutions as well: First National Bank and Amarillo National Bank. W. H. Fuqua, who had operated one of the livery stables before entering real estate and banking, headed First National Bank. Albert G. Boyce, former manager of the XIT, was president of the Amarillo National Bank in 1900. It was still located in a corner of the Amarillo Hotel Annex (the former Tremont Hotel).

Although the bars and saloons sold sandwiches and light lunches, Amarillo in 1900 contained only one restaurant that featured "fine cuisine." Jack Floyd, a former freighter who had hauled goods between Dodge City and Tascosa, ran it. Housed in a large, flimsy building, the restaurant contained a round counter in front and a small dining room in the rear, but because Floyd was considered an excellent cook, it enjoyed a wide patronage, including businessmen, cattlemen and cowboys, and local gamblers. Not long afterward Warren Wetzel, the former Amarillo mayor, and his wife opened a small restaurant.[29]

Clearly, Amarillo in 1900 was a typical young, rural American town. It had struggled over its own location, over the proper site for the county seat, and over the nature of its early government. It had worked hard to acquire railroads, often the difference between life and death for a western community. Its social and cultural life was simple, but its civic leaders espoused and sought sophistication. It held a Catholic and several Protestant churches, whose key figures were often city leaders. But Amarillo was a place that also attracted plenty of tough, rough-edged characters who sought life and leisure in dark, gamy, smoke-filled, and whiskey-stained bars associated with a gambling and prostitution district.

Just as clearly, Amarillo was on the verge of phenomenal growth.

4

A City of Modern Pioneers

Between 1900 and America's entry into World War I in 1917, Amarillo expanded. Its population moved in spurts from 1,442 inhabitants at the turn of the century to 15,494 in 1920. New, fancy subdivisions appeared as the middle class prospered. Imposing homes went up along Polk Street for families of greater means. Men and women added many new businesses. The Bowery District underwent changes and then after 1911 disappeared. Local transportation improved with the construction of a streetcar system. More railroads entered the city, and civic improvements of other kinds reflected a genteel refinement.

During the period—the "Progressive Era" it is called on a national level—agriculture represented the key to Amarillo's growth. Settlers poured into the area, many of them coming by train from the Midwest. They were, for the most part, farmer-stockmen who combined cattle raising with farming on a section (640 acres) or two of land. They built successful lives for themselves and their families, and they looked to Amarillo as their marketing hub, cultural heart, and social center. They made Amarillo the "hub city of the land of modern pioneers."[1]

For the farmer-stockmen, the area's attractiveness stemmed from the Plemons Four Section Act. A state law drafted and sponsored by

William B. Plemons, Amarillo's representative in the Texas legislature, the 1895 measure was a turning point in land ownership in the Panhandle and on the Texas South Plains, for it struck a major blow to the big West Texas and Panhandle ranches.

The situation was complicated. Owners of most of the large ranches, such as the Frying Pan Ranch on the western edge of Amarillo, held title to only every other section of land within their fence lines. The state, for various reasons but mainly to support its public school system, retained title to the alternate sections, or "school lands." The ranchers at first "free-grazed" the alternate sections, but beginning in 1883 a state law required competitive bidding for leasing of the school lands at no less than four cents per acre. Within two years most Panhandle ranchers were leasing the alternate sections. The Frying Pan owners, for example, in 1886 leased 120,000 acres of school land situated within their fences, agreeing to pay four cents an acre each year on a six-year lease.[2]

The Four Section Act opened the alternating school lands for purchase. It provided that a prospective settler could acquire one section of "agricultural land" for farming at two dollars per acre and three sections of "grazing land" for herding at one dollar per acre—all for as little as eighty dollars down with four years to pay. Only actual settlers could purchase the land, and the buyers must reside on the property for three years and make some improvements, such as erecting windmills, houses, or barns, before the state would confer title. The legislation, which became law without Governor Charles Culberson's signature, was quickly amended to cut the price of agricultural land in half, thereby reducing the amount of money needed for the down payment. In 1897 another change lowered interest rates and extended the payment period for buying land.[3]

The law represented something of a turning point in Texas politics. Until the passage of the Four Section Act, Texas land legislation tended to favor railroads, corporations, and large-scale ranching operations, especially with regard to West Texas. The 1895 law suggested that the state legislature, "once sympathetic toward cattlemen," had begun to sympathize with farmer-stockmen and a growing number of rural settlers. Plemons, in fact, was "butchered" in the livestock press for his support of the Four Section Act, but a San Antonio farm publication, the *Rural,* supported him, as did J. L. Caldwell, editor of the *Amarillo Evening News.*[4]

In other ways passage of the law was timely. After 1895, for example, the national economic depression that had characterized the early 1890s was ending and the long drought of the period broke, at least temporarily. With a law that eased access to the land and farming and ranching conditions improving again, settlers, especially farmer-stockmen, moved into West Texas and the Panhandle.

Then, after 1902, farmer-stockmen overran the Amarillo region. A legal decision in 1902, *Ketner v. Rogan,* precipitated the growing rush of new settlers, for in this case the state courts declared the old "lapse-leasing" system illegal. Under the former system, cattlemen, such as the Frying Pan Ranch owners, had rented alternate public school sections within their fence lines for five- or six-year periods, re-leasing the land before the contracts expired. Such a leasing system blocked settlers' attempts to secure property. But after *Ketner v. Rogan,* grazing land leased from the state became available for purchase before it could be leased again. Consequently, when large blocks of leases expired after 1902, hundreds of thousands of acres became available to settlers for purchase.[5]

Railroads and local businesses helped prospective settlers. The railroads "furnished cars at cheap prices," writes Della Tyler Key, so that people might move their possessions, "and twice a month the Santa Fe [Railroad] ran excursion trains from Chicago into the Texas Panhandle." Upon debarking at Union Station in Amarillo, the prospective settlers met representatives of various real estate firms. The realtors conducted large tours with people riding in several wagons to outlying regions where land might be purchased. Later, at the height of the boom, such land agents as J. L. Person used automobiles and large touring cars to carry the modern-day pioneers to inspect the available farming areas.[6]

Many of the ranchers with large holdings also assisted. William H. Bush, who lived in Chicago but owned the Frying Pan Ranch, for example, distributed pamphlets about the Texas Panhandle. He also printed stationery with "William H. Bush Texas Farming Lands" and used it to write both business and personal letters. The stationery indicated that he owned "109,000 acres of very choice agricultural lands in Potter, Randall, Sherman, Moore and Wichita Counties, Texas." On the reverse side of the stationery, Bush printed a map of the Amarillo country and provided information about rainfall amounts, available railroad connections, and temperature averages. Other ranchers, including Charles Goodnight of the JA Ranch and managers of the XIT, also encouraged farm purchases.[7]

In response, farmer-stockmen with their families poured into the Texas Panhandle in a major land rush. Some of the settlers came from other parts of Texas, of course, but a large number came from the Midwest, especially the states of Illinois, Iowa, and Nebraska. The settlers included many ethnic minorities of European descent, and together the new arrivals caused the Panhandle's population to nearly quadruple before 1910. The number of farms almost doubled.

The farmer-stockmen raised both livestock and crops. They favored cattle, but they also fattened some hogs on their property. Of course, they raised horses too. In the earliest days of settlement, corn served as the staple crop, because it did not require large machines for planting and harvesting. Pioneer farmers soon added such feed crops as hay, sorghum, oats, Johnson grass, kaffir corn, and millet to provide for their livestock. A few farmers turned to winter wheat, and some ranch managers, including those at the LE, Frying Pan, and XIT, planted small tracts of fruits and vegetables. Some managers, such as the XIT boss, sent vegetables to the Texas State Fair in Dallas to show off the region's farming potential. The state fair exposure worked, apparently, for the Panhandle witnessed a land rush.[8]

The land rush impacted Amarillo. As early as 1901 the *Amarillo Weekly News* contained several advertisements from land companies and real estate firms announcing the sale of ranches and town lots. The advertisements increased in 1902 and afterward. "People are coming," proclaimed the *Evening News.* When they arrived, the people wanted to look over land, but to get to it they needed transportation. Thus, Amarillo's livery stables rented horses and wagons. Business for McKnight's Transfer and Livery Sales Company, for example, proved active enough that after 1903 it never closed day or night until the end of the 1920s. Likewise, hotels and restaurants provided lodging and food. After settlers bought the land, hardware businesses and ranch stores sold huge amounts of supplies and equipment.[9]

Many firms prospered, and some people became millionaires. Rufus L. Stringfellow and H. E. Hume "sold many hundreds of windmills and other ranch equipment to the newcomers." They "made a fortune" selling hardware, remembers James Hamlin, one of their contemporaries. Stringfellow, who was mayor of Amarillo from 1899 to 1902, later acquired the Amarillo National Bank. Seeing the Stringfellow-Hume profits, Hugh Morrow, who had worked for a competing hardware firm, organized the Morrow-Thompson Hardware Company. His firm also thrived by selling farm supplies, including windmills and related equipment.[10]

Amarillo boomed. Its population swelled, new businesses opened, and new buildings went up. Fancy new homes appeared along Polk Street south of the business center. The railroads soon opened new depots. The schools grew, the churches expanded, and the newspapers became more professional. Cultural events increased in number, and characteristic social life moved from simple "frontier get-to-gathers," holiday barbecues, and annual Christmas balls to stylish and sophisticated dinner parties, colorful parades, and amusement park festivities.

On September 7, 1903, for example, Amarillo hosted a well-attended Labor Day parade. Under warm, sunny skies, citizens of the community, dressed in "holiday attire," the *Amarillo Star* reported, filled Taylor Street to watch or to participate in the event, a mile-long parade that began mid-morning. Behind the grand marshal came Mayor Stafford Lightburne and the six city aldermen led by Millard C. Nobles. The small Amarillo concert band marched close behind, and the workers with their colorfully decorated floats—"beautiful displays," the paper suggested—followed. Printers, brick masons, painters, railroad workers, tinners, carpenters and joiners, barbers, boiler workers, and others walked Taylor Street as part of the parade. The blacksmiths came with a large float that carried a "full-fledged shop" with several of the men on it striking their anvils in chorus. The retail clerks built a "handsome carriage all in white, driven by a coachman in black and white livery, drawn by four black horses and escorted by four outriders in white shirts and black pants on black horses." That nearly all labor organizations in town participated with "magnificent floats daintily decorated in the national colors" perhaps suggests something of the booming nature of Amarillo.[11]

The Bowery District boomed too—at least for a time. Construction of the Pecos Valley Railroad from Roswell in 1898 and the Choctaw, Oklahoma, and Texas Railroad (Rock Island) across the Texas Panhandle in 1903 brought in large numbers of construction workers. Gamblers, "sharks, grafters, pickpockets," and others, many of whom were "bums" and "desperate characters," were close behind, hoping to separate the workers from their money. Several saloons, including the Palace Bar and the Stag, and brothels existed in the district where liquor "washed many a gullet and drunks lurched and stumbled along the dusty unpaved streets." At the district's peak in 1910, some nineteen saloons were operating, and the Roach Drug Company enjoyed a profitable wholesale liquor business.

Meanwhile, after 1900, the year Kirk Bryan opened his Ocean Wave Saloon on Lincoln Street, the Bowery became the toughest place in town. Fights were common and holdups not unusual. Robbery and other crimes occurred. People outside the district heard rumors aplenty of beatings, shootings, and killings. On a fall afternoon in 1906, for example, a woman and her small son, who were herding a cow home from a pasture, found on north Arthur Street the nude body of an unconscious, badly beaten young man named Earl Dockery, a railroad construction worker from Oklahoma whose uncle, W. H. Dockery, was an Amarillo realtor. The woman hurriedly sought help, and with others she took the injured man to Saint Anthony's Sanitarium, the local hospital. Dockery died a few days later, never having regained consciousness. Robbery seems to have been the motive, and several months later local authorities arrested a suspect and tried him for murder. The culprit received a life sentence.

So-called legitimate businesses also operated in the Bowery, and their owners took considerable trade away from the merchants on Polk Street. The Denver Dining Room, the Green Light Café, and the Saddle Rock Restaurant, for example, provided food at reasonable prices, as did the very popular English Kitchen. The district contained grocery stores and at least one men's fashionable clothing business. Hotels in the Bowery included the Flag, the Mason House, the Union, and the Walsh. A bit later, on the northwest corner of First and Buchanan streets, the McIntosh Hotel opened. Formerly the Tremont Hotel, or the annex to the Amarillo Hotel, the old building became a fixture in the Bowery.

Other businesses existed in the rough and tumble district. Two tough but engaging physicians, Christopher C. Savage and D. S. Ashby, located offices there, and Dr. Ashby got himself involved in a nonlethal shooting scrape with one Claude Dewey. Both men claimed self-defense. Two drug stores, including the Roach Drug Company, were present, and B. J. Steen, H. J. Walker, and Bately Matthews operated barbershops.

The Bowery's demise began in 1910. That year the Santa Fe Railroad built a new depot, one that fronted Fourth Avenue, and the Fort Worth and Denver City Railroad opened a passenger station on Fillmore Street. The old Union Station, the Bowery's "chief drawing card," closed.

The end came in 1911. With national prohibition movements gaining momentum amid the social, economic, and political reforms of the Progressive Era, citizens of Amarillo took similar action. Disgusted with the tough and rowdy character of the Bowery District, local citizens voted for prohibition in their city. Soon afterward the saloons closed, and the district began to fade away. People tore down some houses. Others moved away. Owners of the hotels and most of the other businesses quit or moved. Some of the saloon owners moved to Texico, New Mexico, from where they operated a mail-order liquor business.[12]

Still more changes came. "We grow," noted J. L. Caldwell, editor of the *Amarillo Star,* "in spite of the saloons." In 1907 the business directory in the *Daily Panhandle,* dominated by real estate announcements, listed four architects, five general contractors, two town site companies, an abstract and title company, and four real estate firms. Railroads, benefiting from the boom, advertised that low rates from and to the Midwest were available. New restaurants opened, hotels underwent refurbishing, and homes appeared all over town.[13]

Telephone service expanded. Businesses invested in telephones first, but many citizens, at least those who could afford the marvelous new convenience, followed as quickly as the phone lines were available. In May 1901, as an example, the *Evening News* added a phone line to its services. J. L. Caldwell, the paper's editor, also installed a phone at his home. Amarillo had more than one hundred phones in service at the time. More followed quickly, and the phone companies before the end of the year extended lines from Amarillo to Canyon, Panhandle, Hereford, Tulia, and Plainview. In 1911 the local phone company counted fifteen hundred subscribers.[14]

The other public utilities were also expanding. The Glidden and Sanborn Water Works Company, which had been established in 1889, grew with the city. With its growth, fewer wells were needed in the city, and as a result windmills slowly disappeared from Amarillo. City leaders extended sewer lines along Amarillo streets, and as they did fewer homes needed to maintain out-buildings for toilets. Coal provided household heat, and eventually gas became available for cooking. In 1902 a new water works plant opened and a steam-driven electric plant powered by coal from Colorado became a large presence in the town.

A few years later, an electric streetcar, or trolley, system opened. Grocery men H. A. Nobles and M. C. Nobles, lawyers John W. Crudgington and John W. Veale, and bank president James C. Paul, who also operated the Panhandle Steam Laundry Company, organized the Amarillo Street Railway Company. The firm began operations on January 1, 1908, amid a large crowd that had come to watch as operators moved four cars onto the tracks. The system's tracks extended over seven miles, stretching along Polk Street from North Ninth to South Fourteenth with branch lines running east, west, and south and looping through the Bowery District and eventually east to the west entrance of Glenwood Electric Park. Over the next few years the Amarillo Street Railway Company added lines and cars and extended its tracks, but it did not fare well financially, and a competitor, the Amarillo Traction Company, established in 1910, added to its woes. In the 1920s, with increasing competition from personal automobile use, both streetcar companies failed.[15]

Automobiles had first appeared in Amarillo in 1904. W. A. Lockett, a physician, purchased a 1903 model Cadillac. Shortly afterward Charles Tolleson bought an Oldsmobile and Charles Wolflin acquired a red Maxwell. The one-cylinder-engine vehicles could only travel up to five miles per hour, but they nonetheless attracted a lot of attention and perhaps envy. Soon other townspeople owned motorcars, and in 1909 the city registered approximately 150 automobiles.

Sue Beverley Bivins remembers an early encounter in an automobile: Bivins was riding in a car with her mother, Mrs. Harry M. Beverley, who was driving. Near the intersection of Taylor and Eighth in Amarillo, "they met a couple of girls and a boy driving a buggy and horse." The horse, frightened by the motor, "began to roll its eyes and prance." Mrs. Beverley stopped the car, but her action did not help. The excited horse "whirled round and round and broke the buggy shafts" before dashing "across the street to a house," where it tried to get in a window. Failing that, "the frenzied creature turned and ran down" Eighth to Polk Street and sought to enter "through the large double front doors" of Polk Street Methodist Church, where workmen finally subdued the excited steed.[16]

Motorized taxicabs followed private automobiles. McKnight's Transfer and Livery Company provided motorized taxi service for twenty-five cents to "any place in the city." Apparently, the taxis often transported women to Union Station, the train depot on First between Lincoln and Buchanan on the edge of the Bowery District, which closed in 1910, as most women of Amarillo did not want to walk through the saloon-filled district. In 1912 W. E. Groendyke, manager of the Ford Motor Company on Tyler Street, placed a large, black taxicab on display in his showroom. The elegant, five-passenger cab contained steel and wood racks for luggage and other materials.

C. L. Green may have put the first automobile delivery truck into service. At the time (about 1912) he owned Green Brothers Furniture and Hardware on Polk Street. Eventually, Green "painted No. 23 in large figures on the front of the radiator." Then, to add a bit of humor, he lettered on the rear of the delivery bed "Skidoo." The "23" meant "get out of the way." The term "skidoo" had no precise meaning, but was a popular phrase until the end of the 1920s. It often meant "skedaddle," and Green used both 23 and skidoo to remind people to get out of the way of his new truck.[17]

Automobile usage encouraged road and highway improvement. For years people of Amarillo and neighboring towns had sought to improve roads, build bridges across streams, and mark major roadways. In fact, in the 1890s in Potter County, voters, according to B. Byron Price and Frederick W. Rathjen, "had periodically approved bond issues for the locating, marking, and improving of county roads and bridges." And with the appearance of motorcars, automobile clubs formed on state, regional, and national levels.[18]

The automobile clubs also pushed for better roads and highways. One such club was the Colorado to Gulf Highway Association. In 1913 its leaders met in Amarillo with the local Chamber of Commerce and the recently established Amarillo Motor Club to present the organization's plans for a major highway. U.S. Highway 287 grew, at least in part, from the talks. Similarly, a national "Good Roads" program, part of the Progressive reforms of the era, led to parallel state and local organizations. Such activity encouraged Texas leaders to create the Texas Highway Department in 1917.

In Amarillo interest for improved roads mirrored the state and national interest. As the number of automobiles mounted, motor clubs formed and demands for hard-surfaced streets and roads increased. But improvements came slowly. "Not until 1900," write Price and Rathjen, "was even a single block paved with gravel." Rain, when it came, continued to turn Amarillo's streets, including many of those downtown, "into quagmires to be avoided." By 1910, however, changes had come, and in that year voters supported the laying of bricks as hard-surfaced paving on streets along twenty blocks in the downtown area.[19]

Automobile racing also became common. The Panhandle Auto Fair Association, a group of automobile enthusiasts, sponsored a series of small races over a two-day period in 1911. The *Amarillo Daily News* of August 12 proclaimed that for the races on September 2 and 4, "Amarillo is to entertain the greatest crowds in its history." The events occurred at Glenwood Electric Park, where members of the auto fair association built, or at least laid out, a racing track to accommodate automobiles. And, in fact, for a few years the races became annual sporting events.[20]

Other local sports gained in popularity. As early as 1899 Amarillo schoolboys hosted a pair of baseball games against a team from Childress. The Amarillo team, which won both games, did not treat their guests well, however, and as a consequence visiting representatives did not invite the Amarillo team for a return set of games in Childress. Less than a month later, in July, the Amarillo team hosted a series of games against Roswell.

Organized football had come to the city by 1904. In that year Amarillo High School, whose team was called the Yellow Jackets, played a game against boys from Dalhart High School. For several years, however, most football games, when they were played, were makeshift affairs, played "without uniforms, supervision, rules or official sanction." Finally, in 1909, Andy Anderson, the high school music teacher, organized a football team, coached the players, and arranged an abbreviated playing schedule that included a game against Clarendon College—a contest the Amarillo High School team won. In

1912 the local team was playing a regular schedule, and a year later, after defeating a powerful Lubbock High School team, Amarillo claimed "the championship of the Panhandle." On December 8, 1913, Amarillo High School, representing Northwest Texas, played a game in Austin for what people in the Panhandle considered the state football championship. Sponsored by the Interscholastic Athletic Association, which was a forerunner of the University Interscholastic League, the game pitted Amarillo High against a team from South Texas.[21]

Basketball was also a favorite sport. At Amarillo High School officials formed teams and arranged games for both boys and girls. Jennie Lee Hedrick and Mrs. C. M. McCullough as early as 1905 organized two local teams that played one another outside in front of what have been described as "large crowds." In 1907 the Amarillo High School girls played teams from Canyon and Canadian, and upon winning both games, claimed the Panhandle championship. The team was disbanded for a couple of years after that, but before 1911 it had been reestablished. Indeed, in 1911 the girls were battling Hereford High School, which had won the Panhandle championship in 1909 and 1910, and Canyon High School for supremacy.[22]

Sports were not Amarillo's only amusement. On the city's east side, several entrepreneurs, led by John Crudgington and brothers H. A. and M. C. Nobles, in 1908 established Glenwood Electric Park. An amusement park with a carousel, roller coaster, racetracks (for dogs, horses, and later automobiles), a two-story opera house, a zoo, and other attractions powered by electricity, the place became a popular diversion for both rural and city folks. After the Amarillo Street Car Company extended its tracks to the park's west entrance, the place was easy to reach. The park hosted reunions of Confederate veterans and family picnics.

Glenwood Park also became a fairground, at least temporarily. County events were held there, and the place became the center for larger area fairs. A regional fair begun in 1901, for instance, had struggled in its early years on land west of the city, but in 1906 its organizers, who included Henry Sanborn, abandoned their effort as a financial failure. They tried reviving the fair in 1907 as a street carnival and regional exhibition. The effort lasted only one season. The idea did not die, however, and in 1911, when interest in a regional fair increased again, several meetings were held to organize an "All-Panhandle Fair." R. B. Masterson assumed a key role. Organized in 1913 as the Panhandle State Fair on grounds of Glenwood Electric Park, the annual event attracted enough people across the Texas Panhandle that leaders built horse and cow barns, hog and sheep sheds, and various exhibit buildings. Several people gave money to support prizes. William H. Bush of the Frying Pan Ranch, for example, provided money to support the Boys' and Girls' Kaffir and Milo Maize Club of Potter and Randall Counties. Although discontinued after the United States entered World War I, the fair for about five years was a popular annual event.[23]

Intellectual activities existed in Amarillo. One of them was the monthly meeting of "Just Us Girls," or "J.U.G.," as the women called their study club. Organized in the fall of 1900 with thirteen members who at that time met weekly in the home of Floriede Ware, the group expanded during the early years of the new century. Its members discussed literature, history, philosophy, religion, and contemporary political events. At its January 1910 meeting, for example, the group studied seventeenth- and eighteenth-century British literature. They did it in systematic fashion. One member presented a brief sketch of England in the eighteenth century. Another spoke on a topic that compared the literature of the two centuries. A third member described the "Queen Anne" period in Britain. And, finally, the entire group engaged in a broad discussion of English literature over the two centuries.[24]

J.U.G. played a key role in establishing the Amarillo Public Library. In 1900, as its members initiated various study programs, the group determined to collect books to facilitate program preparations. The effort led to the library, a club organization at first but one that expanded rather quickly to a full-fledged public institution. At a special guest meeting in the spring of 1902, J.U.G. members collected thirty-three books. Shortly afterward, Margaret Willis, an elementary school teacher, "donated a set of ninety books which had been given her by William H. Bush to use as she wished." The club members placed the books in a home near downtown, and on October 4, 1902, opened their little building to the public. Subsequent moves took the library to the First National Bank building, a house on Fillmore, and a house on East Fifth. By 1910 the library had moved to the old city hall and contained three thousand volumes.[25]

The Grand Opera House, built in 1907 and located in the six hundred block of Polk Street, hosted live theater, public lectures, concerts, and other performances, including vaudeville shows. On January 5, 1910, for example, it hosted the Teal Musical Comedy Company, a touring group. The little company staged *Papa's Boy,* a musical play, before a sold out audience. In fact, season after season Amarillo citizens attended packed performances of various kinds at the opera house.

Churches too hosted various cultural galas and musical performances. Christmas and Easter cantatas were favorite cultural and religious events in Amarillo, and to avoid competing with one another's concerts, many of the larger churches cooperated in scheduling some of the most popular performances. Accordingly, for the 1909–10 season the Fillmore Presbyterian Church delayed its "Christmas" cantata until early January—the same night, as it turned out, that the Teal Musical Comedy Company staged *Papa's Boy.*[26]

Vaudeville shows at the Grand Opera House played on a regular basis, and touring tent shows of various kinds came through town. In 1911, in addition to the Grand Opera House, Amarillo claimed three small vaudeville houses that doubled as motion picture theaters. The Miller Brothers 101 Ranch Show from Oklahoma, a rodeo touring company that was in competition with Buffalo Bill's Wild West Exposition, played in Amarillo on a regular basis well into the 1920s. Each year, the skillfully run 101 Ranch Show held a parade to drum up business and, as part of its promotional activities, challenged local young men to various "daring dos." In 1911, in answer to the show's challenge, Buck Yarbrough rode a buffalo—but only after a well-publicized second try.

Unexpected trouble followed a similar touring company, the Sells-Floto Show. According to the *Daily Panhandle,* a "big fight" between show people and local citizens broke out. The "fracas," the paper reported, "grew out of the visit of a party of Amarillo men, including several prominent citizens, to the show grounds." Rather than going "to the main entrance and purchasing admission in the usual way, the visitors, without invitation, pushed into the tent for performing horses." When show people tried to stop "the citizens," a melee followed. After order had been restored, local police officials ordered Charles Saunders of the Sells-Floto Show and Lee Bivins, a prominent rancher of Amarillo, to "answer complaints filed in justice court last night charging them with simple assault." The court ordered the two men to pay small fines.[27]

To restore order in face of such incidents, Amarillo maintained a small police force. A city marshal handled most of the law enforcement activities, and according to the *Amarillo Daily News,* the force included four deputies. In December 1913, when a new city government went into operation, Amarillo's police force included a chief and five deputies.

Sometimes citizens took matters into their own hands. Although in 1905 stockyards and loading chutes had been removed from near Wild Horse Lake and established at a railroad siding east of the city, Amarillo remained a large cattle-shipping point with livestock awaiting shipment still held in significant numbers around the city. As a result there were days—perhaps many days—when the strong odor of wet manure hung heavy in the city's air. At the same time, at least before the city council passed laws to prevent it, some people kept hogs, horses, and chickens in their backyards, a practice that added to the offensive smell. In addition, a few people made a practice of dumping dead animals, including hogs, on the east side of Amarillo. People in east Amarillo warned that anyone attempting to use their neighborhood as a dumping ground for dead hogs or other garbage would find the equivalent of shotgun quarantine in place.

Perhaps Georgia O'Keeffe was Amarillo's most famous resident to complain about livestock odors. O'Keeffe lived in the city from 1912 to 1914, and while she may not have appreciated the smell of wet manure, she loved the place from the moment she got off the train at the Santa Fe depot. The fiercely independent, modernist painter who "pioneered the use of overtly vaginal imagery" spent two years teaching art at Amarillo High School. Called unusual and controversial, she lived in the Magnolia Hotel, played poker and dominoes with cowboys, wore men's clothes and shoes, and cut her hair short, in a man's style. She took long walks onto the flat plains, marveled at the wide, open spaces and big blue sky, and rode south to Palo Duro Canyon, a place that helped inspire her use of pinks and yellows and pastels in her paintings. After two years in the city, she resigned her teaching position over pedagogical issues related to required textbooks.[28]

Two years later, having accepted a teaching position at West Texas State Normal College in Canyon, O'Keeffe was back in the Panhandle. From September 1916 until February 1918 she taught art and home economics to college students during the week. On weekends she took her customary long walks out of town or rode to Palo Duro Canyon. Because of a lingering health problem related to influenza, she asked for and received a medical leave in early 1918. O'Keeffe departed Canyon shortly afterward and did not return to the region to teach.

Although relatively unknown in the art world in 1918, O'Keeffe within a decade of leaving the Texas Panhandle had become famous and wealthy. Her charcoal drawings, watercolors, and oil paintings suggest, according to the critics, an artist of imagination, one with a masterful technique with lines, shapes, colors, and values. She developed into a major figure among modernists. Eccentric and unconventional, but "a gifted teacher," Georgia O'Keeffe remained as controversial in the larger world as she was in Amarillo.[29]

When O'Keeffe lived in Amarillo, the place was changing from a town to a city. It counted seven public schools that enrolled twenty-three hundred students. Two private schools, Lowery-Phillips on South Polk Street and Saint Mary's Academy on the twelve hundred block of Washington, enrolled another two hundred students. Amarillo College had failed a few years earlier, but Draughans Business College taught post–high school students. Eight hotels served travelers, cowboys, and businessmen. City leaders boasted of public sewer and water systems, electric lights, electric streetcar and telephone systems, two daily newspapers, and three elegant and "thoroughly modern" railroad depots. Nineteen churches held religious services each Sunday. For recreation the city claimed two parks: Ellwood (or City) Park and Glenwood Electric Park, plus the Grand Opera House and three motion picture and vaudeville theaters.

During O'Keeffe's two short sojourns in the Panhandle, agricultural enterprises dominated the Amarillo economy. Cattle raising remained significant, of course, but farming, particularly wheat growing, was gaining in importance. Businesses, both large and small, spread away from Polk and Taylor streets to other sections of the city. The Bowery District had disappeared, but "suburbs" spread city expansion into new areas. Businessmen's and service clubs were plentiful. They included the Chamber of Commerce, which dominated business activities, and several lodges: Masonic, Eagles, Elks, Moose, Odd Fellows, Woodmen of the World, Pythians, and others.

Women organized their own clubs. In addition to J.U.G., several special interest societies, such as literary, library, women's suffrage, and study clubs, existed before 1910. They took such names as the "Shakespeare Club," the "Alternate Thursdays Club," and the "Mothers' Club." Most clubwomen came from a white, middle-class, Protestant background, and most were about forty to fifty years old. Their social and intellectual organizations often led to civic improvement, and clearly they provided knowledge and a training ground for female leadership. Active organizations in the period allowed Amarillo—indeed, all American—women to play larger, important roles in the Progressive Era.

In 1913 sixty women from fourteen separate Amarillo groups organized the City Federation of Women's Clubs. The new group sponsored a variety of projects related to the beautification and sanitation of

Amarillo. In one such project, according to Price and Rathjen, after the Federation agreed to pay children five cents for every one hundred dead flies they collected, one young person gathered thirty-one quarts full of the decaying winged insects. When it could, the Federation sought to involve its members in such local political issues as temperance, women's suffrage, and public education.[30]

Political issues shifted over the years, but in many ways they mirrored state and national events. Prohibition, for example, was a serious question in the early days of the century, and it came to Amarillo, as noted, in 1911. Progressive Era reform issues that included more efficient health care, better roads, women's suffrage, public health, and parks and recreation also improved Amarillo's quality of life. Reform in the way urban governments operated proved to be a major Progressive goal, and on the important issue Amarillo was a national leader.

In 1913 Amarillo became one of the first cities in the nation to adopt a council-manager form of government. The mayor continued to preside over council meetings as he had previously over meetings of the city alderman, but now the city manager, by providing expertise in government affairs, supposedly improved efficiency in the city's support offices. Under the new system, then, the city manager and his staff handled day-to-day operations. In December 1913 J. N. Beasley became Amarillo's mayor. Voters elected Charles A. Fisk and Lee Bivins city commissioners, with Sam J. Brown as secretary. The first city manager was M. H. Hardin.

As Amarillo's form of government changed, the city's downtown area changed. Fires were partly responsible. The worst fire occurred on May 22, 1901, when one quarter of the city's businesses went up in flame. On Polk Street alone, seventeen businesses burned, and nearby "every house that caught fire was leveled." The problem was two-fold: wood-frame buildings and high winds. The fire began, or at least it was discovered, at 11:00 p.m. Many people rushed to help, but the volunteer fire department with its bucket brigades stood little chance. Some two hundred men fought the blaze, and a thousand people watched as the buildings burned. In the weeks and months afterward, businessmen replaced their burned-out, wood-frame buildings with rock and brick structures.[31]

Other fires caused the disappearance of old landmarks. According to Della Tyler Key, one "of the most spectacular fires in the history of Amarillo" destroyed the Olympic Theater, formerly the Grand Opera House in the six hundred block of Polk Street, on the evening of Thanksgiving Day 1919. Some eighteen hundred people were attending a live performance of *Micky* at the theater, when about 6:30 the manager, Ross D. Rogers, discovered the blaze. He got everyone out safely, but with extremely cold weather and high winds, firemen could not extinguish the flames. In the morning, all that remained of the three-story building were the walls, and "fifty foot icicles hung from" them. Three months later, the burned-out north wall fell onto the Green Brothers Furniture Store, and the east wall fell into the alley at the rear of the post office building.[32]

Fires altered Amarillo's landscape. And, unfortunately, spectacular fires provided bookends for Progressive Era change in Amarillo. City growth and expansion, urban reform of all kinds, civic improvements, new governmental systems and operations, public school improvements, and similar developments between 1901 and 1919 had helped Amarillo reshape itself into the dominant urban center of an expansive rural area. In 1920, as a result, people of the Texas Panhandle stood in the middle of a long period of economic growth.

5

Economic Development, 1910–1930

Between the beginning of World War I in 1914 and the beginning of the Great Depression about 1930, Amarillo grew at a steady, sometimes spectacular, pace. Fueled by expansion in the Panhandle oil and gas industry, its importance as an urban marketing hub and regional service center attracted new residents who moved into Amarillo to take advantage of new jobs and career opportunities.

It wasn't all growth, however. Some sectors of the economy faltered, and Amarillo's business activity, like that of the nation's at large, sputtered a bit after World War I before enjoying a period of unprecedented growth in the 1920s. Panhandle agriculture in the 1920s suffered. Depressed prices, expensive mortgages, and lower demand for their products hurt wheat growers and cattle raisers. Many of them failed. Their condition worsened in the 1930s, and on the Great Plains blowing sand and dust in the Depression decade added to their troubles.

The agricultural woes threw Amarillo off balance, for it was a city dependent upon a healthy farm and ranch economy. But, a new business phenomenon, consumer spending, and then oil and gas production in the Texas Panhandle compensated for the agricultural slump. Oil field workers, pipeline builders, refinery operators, truck drivers, and others took the economic place that cowboys, farmer-stockmen, and farm and ranch hands had held in Amarillo.

The shift had started before World War I. In 1909, for example, Panhandle farmer-stockmen produced wheat on some 82,138 acres. They also raised corn, sorghum, sudan grass, oats, and rye, sometimes in "immense fields of waving grain." In fact, as we have seen, thousands of people were pouring into the region to take up crop farming, particularly with a view toward raising wheat.[1]

Winter wheat proved most popular. Growers sowed the popular cereal grain in the early fall. After their young crop was out of the ground and green until about the time of the first hard freeze, many of them grazed cattle on the wheat. In the spring as warm weather returned, the crop recovered. Growers harvested their wheat early in the summer.

At first hard red wheat dominated the fields. Varieties included turkey, crimson, and kharkof, each of which had come from Russia with immigrants to Canada and subsequently to the Great Plains and the Texas Panhandle. Later, on recommendations of agricultural specialists, growers turned to semi-hard types. Some farmers experimented with spring strains, but according to Garry L. Nall, "spring wheat did not do well," and most wheat producers stayed with winter varieties that could survive with only a little rainfall.[2]

Wheat production expanded—and for good reason. Crop yields reached an average of fifteen bushels per acre in some years. Wheat prices in 1910 averaged about one dollar per bushel. In response, local ranchers sold and leased land to pioneer farmers who broke the sod for wheat planting. The Frying Pan Ranch, for example, located along Amarillo's western border, urged its farmers and leaseholders to plant wheat. It also encouraged settlers who had acquired school land within Frying Pan borders to try wheat, hoping the pioneer farmers would then lease the ranch's alternating sections.

The plan worked. In 1912 James Bush, the Frying Pan manager, moved from Amarillo to present-day Bushland, located along the railroad about fifteen miles west. There, he directed additional efforts to plow up land for wheat. In short order, thousands of acres of former Frying Pan grazing lands became wheat fields, and the Frying Pan abandoned cattle raising on its Llano Estacado properties to concentrate on leasing lands for farming.

Other ranches followed suit. The XIT, the T-Anchor, and the LS, for example, leased or sold land to farmer-stockmen who raised a few head of cattle, but planted extensive fields of wheat. Production rose dramatically, and in 1912 the Santa Fe Railroad shipped from the Texas Panhandle "a total of 2,850 cars containing 2,850,000 bushels" of wheat.[3]

Then during World War I (1914–18) came even greater expansion. With their fields and crops ruined by war, European armies and civilians needed food, especially meat and bread. Prices soared, and in the United States livestock and grain production shot up to help meet the demand. Wartime demand, writes Nall, increased the price of wheat "from ninety cents per bushel in 1914 to $2.71 three years later."[4]

There followed what some have called "the Great Plow-Up." From north to south across the Great Plains, American farmers turned more and more to wheat, especially after 1917 when the U.S. government guaranteed to producers a minimum price of two dollars per bushel of wheat. On the southern plains, farmers expanded wheat production by some thirteen million acres, "mainly," writes Donald Worster, "by plowing up 11 million acres of native grass."[5]

Farmers in the Texas Panhandle participated in the boom. Wheat acreage increased rapidly during the war as growers plowed additional acres for wheat. They also pressed "into service for wheat" land on which a year or two earlier they had cultivated grain-forage and row crops. Wheat acreage increased each year during the war and with mild weather and plentiful rainfall output likewise expanded.[6]

At the end of the war in 1918, growers in the Panhandle raised wheat on nearly six hundred thousand acres. By that time, wheat, representing nearly a quarter of all small grains in cultivation, had become the Texas Panhandle's major farm crop. In 1919, as a result of a shortage of railroad cars to haul away the large crop, wheat producers west of Amarillo "piled tens of thousands of bushels of wheat on the ground near bulging storage facilities" at present-day Bushland and the little rail siding at Soncy, located between Bushland and Amarillo.[7]

The wheat industry brought changes to Amarillo. Additional storage facilities appeared in the city, and new rail sidings left the main tracks at the new or expanded grain elevators. The growing industry required people to operate the grain elevators, haul the wheat, and load the railcars. Other businesses also felt the growing economic impact of an expanding wheat industry.

Like wheat—even more so than wheat—oil and gas production changed the fortunes of Amarillo, but not until after World War I. News of petroleum discoveries in Bexar County in 1886, at Corsicana in 1894, and elsewhere, especially at Spindletop in 1901, caught the attention of a few people in Amarillo. One of them was a man named Blackshear, a semi-invalid clerk in Elmer Roach's drug store. Blackshear remembered James D. Hamlin, "entertained the crazy notion that there was oil under the land abutting the Canadian River." Accordingly, Blackshear often borrowed "a team and buckboard and [drove] north on [prospecting trips]." Having read about oil and gas seeps that led to petroleum discoveries in southeast Texas, Blackshear sought similar seeps along the Canadian River. He was unsuccessful in finding oil and gas in the Texas Panhandle, but he was right about its presence there.[8]

An oil and gas field 120 miles long and about 20 miles wide, covering 1.5 million acres, stretched across seven Panhandle counties. Mainly lying north of the Canadian River, the great Panhandle Oil and Gas Field, one of the largest such fields in the United States, reached from present-day Wheeler in the east to present-day Dumas in the west. Most of the field's oil could be found, write Price and Rathjen, "along the northern slope of an underground geological formation known as the Amarillo Mountains, while the gas-bearing strata extended over the southern two thirds."[9]

Other than Blackshear's speculations, however, oil in the Panhandle attracted little attention—at first. But conditions changed. A combination of state and federal geologists, continuing oil discoveries in southeast Texas and elsewhere, and Panhandle entrepreneurs were responsible. Geologists such as W. F. Cummins and Charles N. Gould had examined the region to check on its water resources. Although they had prepared reports and maps, they had made little note of potential petroleum holdings in the Panhandle. Nevertheless, their reports may have encouraged Blackshear's explorations, and later Gould's reports caught the attention of Amarillo grocery man Millard C. Nobles.

At the same time, oilmen drilled new wells. By doing so they found petroleum across a stretch of land in southeast Texas, including Sour Lake in 1902, Humble in 1905, and Goose Creek in 1908. Then in 1911 others opened a major oil field at Electra just below the Red River in Wichita County. The excitement, the chances for wealth, and the great economic booms that followed the opening of each new field did not go unnoticed in Amarillo.

In response, several Amarillo-based entrepreneurs got involved. In 1914, for example, William H. Bush of the Frying Pan Ranch wrote from Chicago to former Sanborn aide William S. Rule, asking about the possibilities of oil in the Texas Panhandle. Rule circulated the letter to such Amarillo businessmen and ranchers as Lee Bivins, R. F. Stringfellow, and Watson Gurney.

But Millard C. Nobles took the lead. In 1916, while visiting with Gould, Nobles inquired about the possibilities of oil in the Panhandle. Gould, remembering his geological reports about water in the region, suggested that an area in northeast Potter County seemed promising. A few months later, Nobles, his brother Henry, Gould, and another businessman investigated the Canadian River country north of Amarillo.[10]

Encouraged by their findings, Nobles and several other men in April 1917 formed the Amarillo Oil Company. Capitalized at ten thousand dollars, the company leased some fifty thousand acres of land along the Canadian River. Most of the leased property was on ranch land belonging to Lee Bivins of the LX Ranch and Robert B. "Ben" Masterson of the JY Ranch. Shortly afterward, the company hired the Hapgood Drilling Company of Oklahoma to push down a well at a place called John Ray Butte on Masterson's property.

Weeks and months passed. But Hapgood workers, or "roughnecks" as oil field workers were being called, methodically set up their oil rig, punched open a hole, and drilled deep into the ground. Finally, after spending about seventy thousand dollars in drilling costs, in mid-December 1918, just a month after the armistice ending World War I, the work paid off. A well, called Masterson No. 1, write Price and Rathjen, "roared in from a depth of 2,605 feet, yielding fifteen million cubic feet of gas per day." The drillers found no oil, but they brought in several additional gas wells. Natural gas was beginning to find a market in cities, such as nearby Amarillo, as a home heating fuel.[11]

The gas wells spurred additional interest in the Panhandle's petroleum potential. Geologists, wildcatters, oilfield workers, and speculators of all kinds sought the elusive, wealth-making mixture of hydrocarbons. Moreover, the opening of huge oil fields on the Rolling Plains west of Fort Worth, such as Ranger in Eastland County in 1917, Burkburnett in Wichita County in 1918, and Breckenridge in Stephens County in 1919, encouraged Nobles and his Amarillo Oil Company to continue their explorations.

Meanwhile, even as the speculation in gas and oil attracted attention, people in Amarillo—as elsewhere in the world—got caught up in World War I. The war, which had started in Europe in 1914, by the end of 1915 had become a struggle of gigantic proportions, characterized by trench warfare, barbed-wire entanglements, mechanized armaments, air combat, and thrusts and counterthrusts—a conflict unprecedented in its enormity. Millions of civilians and many millions of soldiers died in the fighting. In 1917 the United States entered the war.

The war brought changes to Amarillo and to the larger Texas Panhandle. In May of 1917 the U.S. Congress passed a national conscription law that required all young men to register for selective service in the nation's armed forces. From the registration lists, the armed forces drafted men to serve in the military. Others volunteered. The government also mobilized its National Guard forces, including the First Texas Cavalry, Troop B, of Amarillo.

Troop B, in fact, as early as April had received orders to mobilize. On the day the men were scheduled to depart Amarillo, "a grand parade formed at Seventh and Polk to escort the boys" to the Santa Fe railroad depot. Called "the greatest parade ever before held in Amarillo," the men of Troop B marched down streets lined with hundreds of school children and "thousands of spectators" who cheered as the National Guard force passed on its way to board three special railway cars.[12]

With scores of men departing Amarillo, more women joined the local work force. In growing numbers they took positions as clerks, secretaries, and saleswomen. Some went to work in manufacturing and administration positions traditionally reserved for men. White and Kirk, the large department store that liked to claim it was Amarillo's oldest retail business, hired additional women, as did the local hotels and restaurants. Women also joined the staff of the *Amarillo Daily News*, and others took control of small family businesses.

Women also joined men in establishing the Amarillo Red Cross. Over one hundred people attended the organizing meeting on June 12, 1917, in the Christian Church, and they pledged $450 to use for operating costs. The attendees also laid plans for a permanent organization and named Allen Early, Mrs. A. Eberstadt, and E. C. Seaman to the executive board.[13]

Meanwhile, wheat production boomed. Behind national food administrator Herbert Hoover's exhortations that "food will win the war," Panhandle growers dramatically increased their already expanding wheat acreages. Concomitantly, at a time when to keep up with such wartime demands they needed to enlarge their operations, wheat producers found that many young men and boys, such as those of Troop B of the First Texas Cavalry, had left the farms to join the American armed services. To compensate for the smaller pool of employees, farmers all over the Great Plains, including the Texas Panhandle, bought more tractors, bigger plows, and larger planting and harvesting equipment, which actually helped them run their operations more efficiently. They borrowed money to finance the purchases, which often included additional land. In effect, the war created a large and growing debt structure for farmers.

After the United States entered the war, anti-German and anti-Italian sentiment appeared. In some places it became nearly hysterical, as some schools discontinued the teaching of German and orchestras discontinued playing Richard Wagner and Ludwig van Beethoven compositions. Anti-German discrimination in shops and factories was common. In Amarillo, however, few outward signs of hostility occurred. There may have been some problems in the Hereford area where Italian prisoner-of-war camps existed, but the anti-Italian feelings do not seem to have spilled over into Amarillo.

Like Americans elsewhere, the people of Amarillo became involved in the war effort. They bought bonds to help finance America's participation in the war. They planted victory gardens to raise their own food; saved leftovers from the dinner table to be used later; and participated in Hoover's "Wheatless Mondays," "Meatless Tuesdays," and "Porkless Thursdays." They adopted, when they could, "Heatless Wednesdays," and they went along with the government's program to fix prices and regulate the economy.

The war also contributed to a global pandemic. The disease—the "Spanish Influenza"—killed twenty-two million people worldwide and about six hundred thousand people in the United States. It lasted about nine months, erupting suddenly in the spring of 1918 and ending only after the onset of cold weather. Those people afflicted by the disease, nearly one quarter of the U.S. population, suffered coughing, chills, fever, body aches, vomiting, dizziness, labored breathing, nosebleeds, and profuse sweating. To avoid the Spanish Flu, many people during the contagion took to wearing surgical masks, avoided contact with others, and no doubt prayed often and fervently.

In Amarillo, the flu epidemic struck young adults at a higher rate and exacted a heavier death toll than with children or elderly people. N. S. Griggs, a local mortician, indicated that at one time he was conducting between one and six funerals for victims every day. Graveyard headstones in many local cemeteries provided mute evidence of the numbers who died of the Spanish Flu.[14]

At the peak of the Spanish Flu epidemic, World War I ended. Fighting stopped with an armistice agreement on November 11, 1918, and as news of the armistice spread, celebrations across the nation were instantaneous, noisy, and enthusiastic. In Amarillo, the local paper carried a large headline that read "Germany Fully Crushed." Flags appeared in every business and on every automobile in the city. A large public gathering was held on the Potter County courthouse lawn. Rev. G. S. Tumlin served as master of ceremony. Mayor Lon D. Marrs spoke at the morning gathering, as did several local church pastors. In the afternoon, churches held special religious services of thanksgiving. In the evening, according to the *Amarillo Daily News,* "Polk Street became a scene of unsurpassed animation" with a grand street parade downtown.[15]

The war's influence extended beyond the end of the fighting. On January 14, 1919, women representatives of the Athenaeum Club of Amarillo asked city commissioners W. R. Cazzell and J. R. Trolinger to direct the city to plant commemorative trees in Ellwood Park. They wanted a tree for each Amarillo soldier who had died in the war, and they wanted a marker noting the soldier's birth, death, and date of service.

The American Legion was also a byproduct of World War I. Ernest O. Thompson, an Amarillo veteran of the war, played a founding role in the organization. In March 1919 he attended an informal caucus of soldiers who were planning the group in Paris, and in May he was a delegate to the organizing meeting in Saint Louis, Missouri. Soon afterward, legion posts sprang up across the United States. In Amarillo, World War I veterans, led by Thompson, established the David T. Hanson Post No. 54, American Legionnaires. Founded on July 1, 1919, with ninety charter members, the post made Thompson its first commander. Hanson, for whom the post was named, was an Amarillo physician serving in the medical corps in France when he died in October 1918 while trying to rescue an injured soldier. For his gallantry Hanson received, posthumously, the Croix de Guerre.[16]

With the war over, Amarillo on July 4, 1919, held a large Independence Day commemoration. Once again veteran Ernest Thompson led the organizing committee. The group planned several activities and encouraged thousands of people to participate. It arranged a baseball game between a team from Dalhart and the Amarillo Elks, one of the popular local "nines." Dalhart won the game 2–0. The committee also got the local Boy Scouts to hold field demonstrations at Glenwood Park. In the afternoon Thompson's group staged a parade with "representatives of every organization in the city." Some fifteen thousand people, more than the population of Amarillo, watched the parade. In the evening the Amarillo Concert Band played for a "couples dance" on Sixth Street between Polk and Taylor. More than a thousand couples participated. The next day, the *Amarillo Daily News* wrote that the popular Fourth of July celebration, "which is perhaps the biggest project of its kind ever attempted here, was a success in every detail."[17]

After the war ended, the United States brought its soldiers home as quickly as possible. The government had no significant plans for reconversion to a peacetime economy. In the Texas Panhandle, the lack of any plans made little difference—at first. The wartime boom—the one that had encouraged the expansion of the Panhandle wheat industry—continued through 1919 and early 1920 before slowing demand destabilized western agriculture. Prices collapsed. In an eighteen-month period, wheat went from $2.50 a bushel to less than $1.00. To make up for lower prices, farmers planted still more wheat. Surpluses piled up, causing prices to remain low.[18]

In Amarillo, however, new gas and oil discoveries kept the wartime boom alive. Large companies, smaller wildcatters, independent oilmen, oilfield workers, and others helped elevate the local economy. In 1919, for example, businessman Eugene S. Blasdel, rancher P. H. Landergin, and banker W. H. Fuqua formed a partnership, negotiated oil and gas leases for the Four Sixes Ranch in Carson County, and convinced the Gulf Production Company to drill for oil. In its first effort south of the Canadian River, the company tapped into a gas field; but on May 2, 1921, at a second site, it struck oil at a depth of just over three thousand feet. The well yielded about 175 barrels of oil per day.

The company then turned its efforts to the land north of the Canadian River. On the Dial Ranch in Hutchinson County it struck oil again. Although production in that location was only 135 barrels per day, the discovery encouraged several other oil company operators to test the underground formations.

In the meantime, the Panhandle Pipeline Company built lines to deliver gas and petroleum to Amarillo. It completed its first gas pipeline to the city in the fall of 1920, and soon afterward the Amarillo Gas Company, still dominated by the small group of local businessmen headed by M. C. Nobles, was selling the product to city businesses and homeowners for heating and cooking fuel. Expansion continued throughout the 1920s.[19]

As the number of pipelines expanded, the number of refineries and processing facilities likewise increased. Natural gas plants appeared in Amarillo and across the Panhandle Oil and Gas Field. Plants to extract carbon black, an important compounding ingredient, from natural gas sprang up. In 1923, to take advantage of the abundant gas reserves in the area, the American Smelting and Refining Company built a facility in northwest Amarillo. From mines in Arizona, Colorado, and New Mexico, the company brought in zinc ore and refined it into zinc. The plant expanded in the 1920s and afterward until it covered a five-block area and employed some five hundred people.[20]

A helium plant appeared just west of Amarillo. The U.S. Bureau of Mines, seeking to extract helium from natural gas, secured leasing and drilling rights to gas fields northwest of Amarillo, and in 1927 the bureau selected a plant site about seven miles west of Amarillo and on the Rock Island Railroad at Soncy. Two years later the plant went on line, and by the end of 1929 Amarillo had become known as the "Helium Capital of the World."[21]

Roy Roddy, an Amarillo reporter, wrote in 1941 that the helium plant at Soncy was "the only helium [extracting] plant in America." The plant, he boasted, turned out "practically the entire supply of the world." Under the supervision of C. W. Seibel, the plant employed nearly five hundred people, many of them highly trained scientists and technicians who had come to Amarillo from a helium plant the government had closed near Fort Worth.[22]

Helium extraction was part of the larger oil boom. Large-producing wells began to come on line in 1925 and 1926. Perhaps the most important of the early oil wells was one called Smith No. 1 in Hutchinson County. S. D. "Tex" McIlroy, founder of the Dixon Creek Oil Company, decided to deepen the well, which produced about four hundred barrels a day. In 1926, his drillers, write Price and Rathjen, punched into "a vast reserve that yielded an astounding 10,000 barrels per day."[23]

Madness followed. Thousands of roughnecks rushed to the Texas Panhandle. Scores of small businesses opened to serve both oil field needs and the oil field workers. Dozens of oil companies formed. Speculators arrived. The activity was frantic, and a few shrewd entrepreneurs, such as A. P. "Ace" Borger, built new towns amid the oil fields. The Panhandle Oil and Gas Field, as indicated earlier, became one of the largest in the world, and the amount of oil produced increased twenty-five fold—from one million barrels in 1925 to twenty-five million barrels the next year.[24]

Amarillo benefited tremendously from the gigantic boom. Oil companies located their headquarters in the city. Pipelines reached from the oil fields to carbon black and helium plants near the city. The Amarillo Gas Company provided natural gas to the city's residents. New housing subdivisions opened. New businesses appeared, and older ones grew larger. The country club expanded. Job opportunities increased. The population increased. Bank deposits increased. Wealth proliferated.

Amarillo became an exciting place. Construction work moved into high gear as new homes and new businesses appeared, and from January to April 1926 the city issued nearly four hundred building permits. The city's population nearly tripled during the 1920s, growing from approximately 15,500 people in 1920 to 43,132 ten years later.

In downtown Amarillo, oil money helped create a skyline. The offices of Shamrock Oil and Gas Corporation, Magnolia Petroleum Company, and Phillips Petroleum Company looked upon the city and distant horizons from new skyscrapers. The Amarillo Hotel in 1927 completed a tower of twelve stories, and in 1928 the fourteen-story, six-hundred-room Herring Hotel opened. The Capitol Hotel, which in 1927 was under construction at Fourth and Pierce, expanded before it opened. Its owner, Ed R. Mayer, a longtime Amarillo business and political leader, announced on June 17 that the building would be enlarged with a twelve-story addition. In early 1930 at Ninth and Polk, the Santa Fe Railroad opened a new general office building, one with two fourteen-story towers.

Adding to the excitement was the appearance and expansion of an airport and flying service. It had started in 1920 when Fred Hinds, with two thousand people watching, landed a little Curtis Canuck plane in the city. Afterward, civic leaders Lee Bivins, W. K. Whipple, and H. E. Fuqua established the Panhandle Aerial Service and Transportation Company. The company, according to Della Tyler Key, did not fly regular schedules, but it provided air service for charter trips and planes "for barn-storming, stunting at [fairs,] and other occasions in the Panhandle."[25]

Flying operations soon began to evolve. In 1923 Bivins and Harold English moved the airport to a place seven miles east of Amarillo. In 1927 one A. J. Edwards arrived from California to open headquarters for an airmail service between Los Angeles and New York City. Amarillo, he argued, stood almost in the center of a route that would make refueling stops at El Paso and Oklahoma City. In 1928 the airfield, covering about 640 acres, became known as Bivins English Airport, and a year later, after Bivins's death, Thornton Oxnard from New York joined English. They established the Amarillo Airport Corporation and opened flying service to Dallas and Denver, with connections to other parts of the country.

The city also got involved. Under the leadership of Ernest O. Thompson, whose key role in veterans' affairs had catapulted him into the mayor's office, Amarillo built a municipal airport in 1929. Citizens approved a bond sale totaling one hundred thousand dollars, and the city government used the money to buy land and other equipment and erect a large brick and steel hangar and a twenty-five-hundred-feet-long asphalt landing strip. The city leased the airport to the Texas Air Transport Company. But problems and lack of service forced Amarillo only a year later to abandon the facility as an air terminal. Others afterward operated it as a private flying field.[26]

Adding to the excitement was Route 66. The famous highway, billed as the "Main Street of America," connected Chicago with Los Angeles, a distance of 2,448 miles. It ran across the Texas Panhandle from Shamrock on the east to Glenrio on the west, passing through Amarillo along Sixth Street (Sixth Avenue after 1928). Although commissioned in 1926, the long road, the dream of Cyrus "Cy" S. Avery of Oklahoma, had been in the planning stages for years. In fact, as Michael Wallis writes, "when the highway became official" in the mid-1920s, some eight hundred "miles were already paved."[27]

In 1921 a long stretch of Sixth Street became the first paved roadway in Amarillo. As mentioned, a portion of Route 66 later followed the commercial street in the San Jacinto Heights neighborhood. But in the early 1920s highway promoters, led by the Amarillo Improvement Company, were calling the busy east-west route—at the time a part of the newly designated U.S. Highway 60—the "Ozark Trails Highway." Along the part of Sixth Street that had been paved, they placed large signs so indicating the roadway's name. But "Ozark Trails Highway" did not stick, nor did a later name for Route 66: "Will Rogers Memorial Highway."

As time passed and the city's population grew, the route of U.S. Highway 66 through Amarillo shifted. Particularly, it changed after World War II. For a time it left Sixth Avenue in west Amarillo to follow Bushland Avenue. And in north Amarillo it came from the east along Amarillo Boulevard East. Later still, the highway department moved Route 66's northwest Amarillo location from Sixth Avenue to Amarillo Boulevard West. In 2006 most historic maps show the famous road coming in from the east along Amarillo Boulevard East (the old U.S. Highway 60 and 66 route), shifting south on Fillmore Street, and turning west again on Sixth Street (Sixth Avenue) to Bushland Avenue from where Route 66 left the city.

In Amarillo, the importance of Route 66 became clear on June 20, 1927, when some five hundred members of the U.S. Highway 66 Association converged on the city. They came to promote their highway, to get federal aid for construction costs and rights-of-way, and to cheer on the additional paving projects. Mayor Lee Bivins gave a welcoming address to the assembled delegates, some of whom had come in car caravans and with marching bands. Although representatives of all eight states through which the highway ran were present, most delegates came from Oklahoma, Texas, and New Mexico. The association convened in the morning, finished most of its business in the early afternoon, and concluded its meeting with a banquet at the Amarillo Hotel in the evening.[28]

The association, which had been formed in February, was ambitious. In one of its more colorful projects, the association determined to get a well-advertised cross-country footrace to follow part of Route 66. C. C. "Cash and Carry" Pyle, a fantastic promoter of general sporting events, was planning a marathon from Los Angeles to New York City for 1928. Pyle also planned to spend fifty thousand dollars on prizes for the race, and both Amarillo leaders and the U.S. Highway 66 Association wanted the racers to come through towns, including Amarillo, along Route 66. They were successful.

Another project encouraged highway improvement, particularly the paving of roadbeds. Paving stretches of Route 66 in the 1920s meant a macadamized roadway, in which workers prepared a well-packed and well-drained roadbed and onto it placed gravel with a bituminous binder. The road builders obtained gravel from Jack Hall's ranch northwest of Amarillo and from a large pit on Lee Bivins's ranch about eight miles north of the city. And in 1927, about the time of the Route 66 convention, people saw Sixth Street, from Georgia to Bellview streets, paved with brick.[29]

Concrete roadways came later. In 1929, for example, no portion of Route 66 was paved with concrete. "In 1930," remembers Marita Bumpers, once a café owner in Shamrock, Texas, workers had not "put 66 through." When traveling west along the dirt and gravel route to Amarillo, she says, "We had to stop four separate times to open barbed wire fence gates at the big ranches." But even then, both state and federal governments were in the process of grading and constructing a good highway. "It was something," Bumpers acknowledges, "the first time we got to go to Amarillo on the pavement" of Route 66.[30]

"America's Main Street" in Amarillo ran through the San Jacinto Heights neighborhood. In the 1920s the northwest subdivision was something of a suburb. Homes, rooming houses, small businesses, family restaurants, and grocery stores spread out through the neighborhood.

The San Jacinto Heights neighborhood also housed the Amarillo Natatorium. Built in 1922 as a large indoor swimming pool at the intersection of Georgia, McMasters, and West Sixth, "the Nat," as it was called, was unusual in its design. It "looked," writes Tom Snyder, "like an architectural Appaloosa horse—with a graystone Moorish-Camelot front half joined to a porthole-dotted steamship posterior." As a swimming pool, the Nat did not succeed. In 1926, however, the same year that Route 66 was commissioned, new owners floored over the pool and reopened the place as a ballroom. It became the city's most important nightclub. In the 1930s and 1940s it hosted the big bands of Louis Armstrong, Count Basie, Benny Goodman, Harry James, Guy Lombardo, Rudy Vallee, and Paul Whiteman. Friday was high school night. Owners gave over such evenings to teenagers who danced to the music of smaller and less-known groups. Later still, the Nat hosted such rock and roll artists as Elvis Presley, Buddy Holly, and Bill Haley.[31]

Meanwhile, after 1926, West Sixth Street through San Jacinto Heights attracted new businesses that catered to travelers along Route 66. Curio shops, tourist courts, gasoline stations, and restaurants opened along the roadway. The growing activity encouraged local folks to patronize Route 66 establishments, further adding to the excitement of the place.

Thanks in part to John Steinbeck's tragic tale *The Grapes of Wrath*, published in 1939, U.S. Highway 66 became larger than life. The socio-political novel stirred the American conscience, and more than half a century later it is read, as Daniel S. Burt writes, "not as a piece of literary or social history, but with a sense of emotional involvement and aesthetic discovery." Steinbeck's descriptions of life along the road for 1930s migrants, especially the long-suffering Joad family, brought attention not only to Route 66 but also to the plight of Great Depression refugees. The highway became the "Mother Road." In 1946, after good times returned, Bobby Troup's "Get Your Kicks along Route 66" was recorded by many talented musical artists. It ensured the exaggeration. So much, in fact, that years later others could say, as Stanley Marsh 3 of Amarillo did, "The old road has a certain romance that no other highway in the world possesses."[32]

In the 1920s the romance of the road lay largely in the future. The times, nevertheless, represented exciting years for Amarillo—and for much of the United States. The twenties were boom years, fueled by a developing consumer-goods industry that had not existed earlier. Moderately priced items like hand cameras, cigarette lighters, wristwatches, vacuum cleaners, washing machines, and linoleum, for example, became available. Expansion of telephone and electrical power systems, plus reliable and affordable automobiles and the invention of the radio helped to transform American society.

Amarillo citizens enjoyed the new creature comforts. The city also maintained its World War I economic and population growth, and Route 66 made it a crossroads for coast-to-coast travelers. Amarillo became the urban center for the large and prosperous Panhandle oil and gas industry, and its old economic foundations of cattle and wheat seemed to have survived the "poverty of overabundance" that marked the early years of the 1920s.

Indeed, the wheat industry continued to expand, but in the long run bumper crops proved seductive to those who invested so much in the agricultural business. Panhandle wheat growers, according to the *Amarillo Daily News,* in 1927 put two hundred thousand more acres into production than they had the previous year, meaning that they planted over 1.3 million acres to wheat. The yields also remained high, and in 1929 Panhandle farmers produced forty-two million bushels of wheat. Each fall storage facilities along the railroads bulged with grain, and nearly every year storage operators piled tens of thousands of bushels of wheat on the ground. Soon, however, such scenes would seem fantastic as wheat prices crashed and the great farms in the early 1930s blew away like so much dust.[33]

The economics of cattle raising mirrored those of wheat. That is, between 1912 and 1919 prices doubled, and cattlemen increased the size of their herds. Although their income improved for a time, cattle raisers saw their debts increase as they borrowed money to expand herds and purchase feed and equipment. Overproduction characterized the 1920s, and as with livestock men elsewhere in the country, Panhandle operators saw surpluses mount, markets unravel, and prices decline.

But for a while longer at least, Amarillo boomed—especially after 1926. Price and Rathjen note that in the half decade after "Tex" McIlroy and his Dixon Creek Oil Company deepened the Smith No. 1 well near the future site of Borger, "some 114 companies, representing a capital investment of about twelve million dollars, formed in Amarillo." Older businesses remodeled and expanded.[34]

Residential districts grew. Toward the southwest part of town, the "highly restricted" Wolflin subdivision filled with large homes, and in 1926 the city replatted the Bivins Addition. Contractors built "a great number of new homes" in the Glenwood subdivision, "one of the oldest additions in Amarillo," and nearby Edgefield, one of the most recent additions, expanded with fancy houses. North Amarillo grew with "four or five room cottages," and the Old Town neighborhood changed with "unusual new growth" that made it seem "like a new place." Additional homes also appeared in such older subdivisions as the Roberts Place, the Summers, and the Country Club.[35]

Home of Hartwell Tucker Cornelius. Cornelius built the house in 1887 around a plank-floored ...nt at 319 Parker in Old Town; using logs, he moved it in 1889 to 303 East Fourth Avenue (Fourth and Fillmore) in the Glidden-Sanborn Addition. (Courtesy Amarillo Public Library)

Henry B. Sanborn. (Courtesy Panhandle-Plains Historical Museum)

he Amarillo Hotel was built in 1889, just two years after Amarillo was founded. It was located Third and Polk streets. The original thirty-room structure was built by Henry B. Sanborn. ourtesy Amarillo Public Library)

he 1889 Potter County Courthouse was the second one built in the county. (Courtesy Amarillo ublic Library)

Amarillo, c. 1890. The windmill stands where the front of the J. Marvin Jones Federal Building today, and the man is standing in the center of present-day Courthouse Square. (Upper right-hand corner is torn in original photo; courtesy Amarillo Public Library)

Views of original Amarillo Stock Yards near Wild Horse Lake in 1890s. Courtesy Southwest Collection, Texas Tech University, Lubbock.

James D. Hamlin. (Courtesy Panhandle-Plains Historical Museum)

Amarillo's Polk Street in 1900. (Courtesy Panhandle-Plains Historical Museum)

Lon Marrs. (Courtesy Amarillo Public Library)

Members of the Just Us Girls Club Library Committee in 1903. In the back row are Florieda Ware Vaughan, Iva Nobles, and Truly Wors Bailey. In the front row are Bernice Trigg Owens, Mamie Trigg Owens, and Carrie Brower Richardson. In 1902 the J.U.G. Club created what eventually became the Amarillo Public Library. (Courtesy Amarillo Public Library)

The home of Warren W. Wetsel, an early Potter County settler, was built in 1903 at 1101 South Pierce Street. (Courtesy Amarillo Public Library)

ɔis house was built for Henry B. Sanborn in 1903. It was originally located at 600 South ɩchanan Street and was later relocated to 1311 South Madison. (Courtesy Amarillo Public brary)

The home of Lee and Mary E. Bivins, built in 1905, became the Mary E. Bivins Memorial ɩibrary, serving the city of Amarillo from 1955 to 1976. (Courtesy Amarillo Public Library)

Amarillo in 1907. The water tower stood at the two hundred block of Fillmore at the site of the city's Water, Light, and Power Company plant. The domed building in the left center background is the old county courthouse located in the five hundred block between Taylor and Fillmore. (Courtesy Amarillo Public Library)

The Grand Opera House as it appeared before 1919. (Courtesy Amarillo Public Library)

marillo's Polk Street in 1910. (Courtesy Panhandle-Plains Historical Museum)

'he Lowrey-Phillips football team in 1911. (Courtesy Amarillo Public Library)

Lee Bivins. (Courtesy Panhandle-Plains Historical Museum)

The old post office building was constructed in 1914 and served as the main post office for Amarillo until 1939, when a larger building was erected at 207 Fifth Street. It was later renamed the Coble Building. (Courtesy Amarillo Public Library)

he Olympic Theater, at the corner of Seventh and Polk, previously known as the Grand Opera ouse, was destroyed by fire on Thanksgiving night, 1919. (Courtesy Amarillo Public Library)

Northwest Texas Hospital opened as Amarillo's first public hospital on March 22, 1924. The hospital relocated in 1982. (Courtesy Amarillo Public Library)

The Nat swimming pool at the intersection of Georgia, McMasters, and West Sixth, was built in 1922. Five years later it was floored over to become the Nat Ballroom, where the likes of Benny Goodman, Rudy Vallee, Guy Lombardo, Count Basie, and Roy Orbison played. (Courtesy Amarillo Public Library)

e tall building on the left of the photo is the White and Kirk department store, which was ablished as a grocery store by Dr. M. W. Cunningham in 1890. (Courtesy Amarillo Public brary)

ust clouds envelop buildings and automobiles in the Texas Panhandle. (Courtesy Amarillo ublic Library)

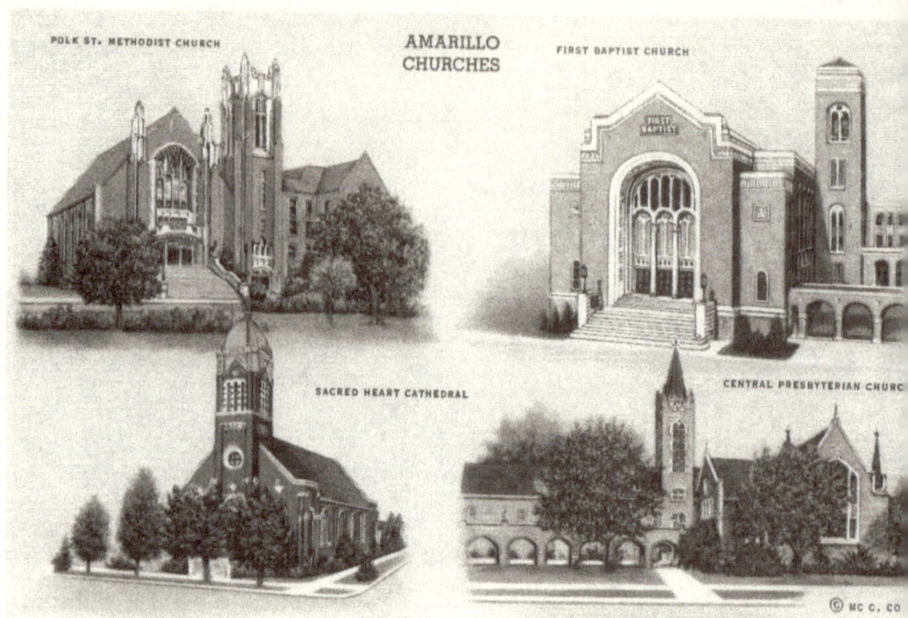

Amarillo churches shown on a color postcard. (Courtesy Amarillo Public Library)

Amarillo High School, 1210 Polk, from a color postcard. (Courtesy Amarillo Public Library)

Partly in response to the expanding city, public transportation received a boost. Gasoline-powered buses appeared, replacing the failed electric streetcar systems. In fact, the Amarillo Street Railway Company, which had dominated public transportation in the city, had stopped running its cars as early as 1923, and its tracks had been taken up the next year. The Amarillo Traction Company, which ran a second line from the San Jacinto Heights neighborhood to connect it with the main city network, quit in 1926. Yet its leaders, dominated by W. W. Lynch, sought a franchise to operate a city bus system, and on March 27, 1927, they received a charter.

Others operated bus lines too—at least briefly. After the Amarillo Street Railway Company abandoned public transportation, local businessman Ed Cantrell opened a bus service in the area near downtown. In 1925 Frank Doerfler and Joe Doerfler came to Amarillo from Oklahoma and established a bus service. Because their route covered much of the territory served by Cantrell's line, neither the Doerflers nor Cantrell prospered.

But Lynch's Amarillo Traction Company, which became the San Jacinto Bus Company, succeeded. The company operated buses over a large route that looped through the city east and west of Polk Street on Third, Fourth, Sixth, Seventh, and Eighth avenues. The company expanded in the late 1920s and maintained a steady business through the hard times of the 1930s. In 1938 the San Jancinto Bus Company, with S. D. Spillers as superintendent, operated eight buses, employed fifteen people, and claimed an annual payroll of twenty-five thousand dollars.[36]

Meanwhile, bus service into and out of Amarillo was gaining popularity. Highway construction, including Route 66, encouraged entrepreneurs to establish public transportation networks to communities not serviced by railroads. Bus lines appeared in the 1920s, and Amarillo quickly became a hub for much of the Texas Panhandle. In response to growing business, various lines supported the idea of a central terminal in the city, and on June 19, 1927, Union Station opened as a headquarters for bus lines serving the public out of Amarillo.

Clearly, the 1920s represented a time of growth and expansion in Amarillo. The population increased rapidly, making Amarillo the largest city in the greater Texas Panhandle–South Plains area. A fantastic building boom accompanied the growth. Oil and gas discoveries of major proportions impacted not only Amarillo but also much of the state of Texas. Employment expanded, and with money to spend, people in Amarillo, as well as the rest of the country, engaged in a nascent consumer economy that placed emphasis on home conveniences and even luxury items.

The twenty years after 1910 represented an exciting, but often challenging, time for Amarillo. The pressures of World War I, the Spanish Flu, and a fluctuating agricultural economy brought unease and concern, but the concomitant development of a large oil and gas industry promoted population growth, urban expansion, and a sense, at least, of prosperity and excitement. Some of the excitement is reflected in the city's social and cultural milieu—the Jazz Age—in the 1920s.

6

The Jazz Age in Amarillo

Flivvers, flappers, Fords, and fanatics all characterize the Jazz Age in America. So too do fast-paced and exciting new dances such as the Charleston. Prohibition and bootlegging, the Ku Klux Klan and religious fundamentalism, radios and movies, speakeasies and sexual license, and Mah Jong and crossword puzzle crazes also characterize the period. It was a time for heroes and a time for flagpole sitters. It was a golden age for sports and for business. And jazz music, coming out of the nightclubs and bars of the French Quarter in New Orleans, gave the 1920s a name.

Amarillo was not left out. Business boomed in the city, especially after 1925, including the automobile and construction sectors—the industries that fueled national prosperity in the 1920s. Entrepreneurs opened radio studios in the city and expanded Amarillo's newspaper operations. The local movie theaters attracted an increasing number of viewers. Speakeasies, those illegally operated taprooms and taverns, "clandestinely" existed on Tyler, Polk, and Taylor streets and probably elsewhere in the city, and many people not only knew their location but also patronized them. Some local folks built and operated whiskey stills in their homes, and, if newspaper reports are correct, many people engaged in the bootlegging of alcoholic beverages. Amarillo, like many other Texas and southwestern—as well as midwestern—communities, was home to a large Ku Klux Klan organization.

In some ways the 1920s represent the formative years of modern American society. During the decade, as George E. Mowry and others have pointed out, the country first became urban, particularly in its ideals and temperament. Old habits and patterns of thought broke down as the country's social goals and aspirations, which since the Civil War had been determined by an educated and economic elite, came to reflect the tastes of the common folks who preferred popular culture, mass production, and, for lack of a better term, consumerism. The 1920s was a time of cultural conflict. It was a transition period, one in which Americans had not quite given up old patterns and attitudes but were beginning to embrace new ideas about religion, marriage, liquor, immigration, and moral standards. It was a period when the rise of the city to the central position in American life challenged the supremacy of rural, small-town America. It was a business-dominated age.[1]

Many business and ranching leaders owned some of the finest homes in Amarillo. Along South Polk Street with its small but attractive esplanade, some of them built veritable mansions, creating what others called "Silk Stocking Row." Benjamin T. Ware of Amarillo National Bank, John Monning of the Monning Mill and Elevator Company, former lieutenant governor John N. Browning, XIT Ranch manager Albert Boyce, Ray Wheatley of Amarillo Bank and Trust, Jefferson Davis Shuford of the Fort Worth and Denver City Railroad, cattleman John M. Shelton, W. H. Fuqua of First National Bank, and Avery Turner of the Santa Fe Railway Company were among them.

The Lee Bivins home was typical. Built at 1000 Polk Street, the elegant three-story, tall-columned house featured wide curving porches, high dormers, broad stairways, and many rooms. A windmill in the backyard provided water from a well until city water lines were available. Bivins, his wife, Mary, and their family lived in the house until Bivins's death in 1929. Mary stayed until the early 1950s before moving to a smaller home. The large Bivins home eventually housed the Amarillo Public Library and later still the Amarillo Chamber of Commerce.

John and Pat Landergin built a huge, neoclassical revival–style residence at 1600 South Polk. Two and one-half stories high, the white-columned mansion of some fifteen thousand square feet included an elevator. With its tall windows, curving drive, and fine interiors, the magnificent home, built in 1913, was for years an Amarillo showcase. Don and Sybil Harrington bought the home in 1943.

Other wealthy and affluent businessmen built palatial homes on neighboring streets. Businessman-banker J. L. Smith, for example, lived at 1101 Taylor Street in a large, two-and-a-half-story home with long porches that wrapped around the big brick structure. At 2304 Van Buren, "Colonel" Cornelius Taylor Herring, who operated the Palo Duro and Herring Hotels, owned one of the city's most magnificent homes. Lawyer-judge-banker John W. Veale lived in a large white house at 1300 Madison, and Mrs. W. R. Curtis built a beautiful home at 1626 South Washington.

On the edge of the city, near what became Western Street, William H. Bush of the Frying Pan Ranch in 1914 constructed a large home. Although it was among the first houses in Amarillo to be wired for electricity, electrical power was not available at the brownstone dwelling until the early 1920s. Situated on a small hill with a grand view of the country around it, the magnificent home, according to the *Amarillo Daily News,* became the scene each summer "of the season's outstanding social events in Amarillo."[2]

Business leaders dominated Amarillo's political and social activities. Local businessmen, including Colonel C. T. Herring, John B. Gilvin, R. B. Masterson, and Ernest O. Thompson, for example, led efforts to revive the old harvest-season fair that had folded during World War I. They formed the Panhandle Fair Association in 1921 and with others attended meetings in Tulia, Hereford, and elsewhere to consider the proper city in which to locate the fair grounds. At the meetings they encouraged delegates to support Amarillo, over Lubbock and smaller towns, as the best site.

The men also talked up the fair in Amarillo, and they got the Board of City Development (BCD) to back them. Indeed, the BCD called a special meeting on the fair issue. At the meeting on March 16, 1922, in the Amarillo City Hall, F. M. Ryburn reviewed some of the discussions and regional meetings that had been taking place, asked those in attendance—about forty Amarillo men, including preachers, physicians, and businessmen—to join the fair association, and discussed proper funding for the renewed fair with its location in Amarillo. The attendees considered various proposals, funding ideas, fairground sites, and related issues, but they took no action.

Because the meeting was encouraging, C. T. Herring, Ross D. Rogers, and others continued to push for the fair. They moved slowly, but a year later, on May 22, 1923, they convinced the city commissioners to allow them to use the streets around the new Municipal Auditorium for a fair. Then, on June 23, with events moving more rapidly, they established the Amarillo Tri-State Fair, capitalized at ten thousand dollars. Herring became president of the fair, and John W. Crudgington, John B. Gilvin, and J. C. Fain served as officers.

The first Tri-State Fair began on schedule on September 25. Lasting six days, the fair attracted people from across the Panhandle. Tents on Buchanan Street and south of the auditorium held exhibits from some thirty-five counties. Other exhibits were on display in the foyer of the auditorium. Booths of several kinds lined the streets. While the number of people who attended is not known, leaders proclaimed the fair "a great success."

A few months later, in January 1924, the Potter County government secured a tract of land for the fair's permanent grounds. Purchased from John Crudgington for $25,820, the site in east Amarillo stretched between Third and Tenth streets. Comprising nearly 130 acres, it served the Tri-State Fair well. Improvements to the grounds were made, especially in the 1930s, and the annual event grew in size and popularity, attracting people from New Mexico and Oklahoma as well as the Texas Panhandle. Some eighty years later, the fair remains a popular annual event.[3]

The same businessmen who had reinstated the fair pushed the city to establish a tourist camp in Amarillo. They had two goals in mind.

First, as personal automobile travel increased after World War I, the need for overnight lodging facilities grew. Motor courts and motels were still a few years off, and downtown hotels did not always fill the growing niche for short-term hostelry, but a tourist camp could provide accommodations for people passing through the city. Second, place the camping facilities on the fairgrounds so that revenue from the tourist camp could be used to defray expenses of the annual Tri-State Fair.[4]

Judge John W. Crudgington took the lead. He proposed that the Panhandle Fair Association rent to the city twenty-nine acres of the fairgrounds at no charge providing that the city improve the camp grounds with lights, water, electric power, and gas lines. City manager Jeff D. Bartlett opposed the idea, for the site was too far from the city and the cost of constructing sewer lines to the grounds would offset other gains.

Bartlett, under urging from city commissioners and the Crudgington group, agreed to find an alternative site. He did, selecting a site in Old Town Amarillo bounded by Fourth and Fifth and Mabry and Hollicott streets. The city leased the old courthouse block from Potter County for a period of fifteen years.

Shortly afterward, a local construction firm, Brodie and Mackey, went to work. It built a community center on the block, plus a "keeper house" and four cook houses. It constructed a five-feet-high board fence around the site, and it laid out roads, paths, and camping places. The camp opened on June 17.[5]

Some of the tourist camp and Tri-State Fair promoters were members of Amarillo's Ku Klux Klan. The immediate post–Civil War Klan, which for the most part was aimed at African Americans and carpetbaggers in the South, had died in the early 1870s. After the turn of the century and during World War I, a new, reoriented Klan appeared. Directed at immigrants, Catholics, Jews, blacks, and communists as well as what it saw as "un-American" institutions, ideas, and ideals, the revived Klan gained prominence in Texas in the fall of 1920. It spread quickly across the state in 1921 and reached a peak in membership in 1922 with nearly two hundred thousand dues-paying followers.[6]

In Amarillo, about four hundred men belonged to the Ku Klux Klan. Organized on August 10, 1921, the local group was number 141 in Texas. Dr. W. H. Virgin was the first Exalted Cyclops, or "E.C." Business leaders, physicians, druggists, engineers, and preachers joined the organization, but the names of less educated and less financially secure men of the community dominate the membership roll.

Members of the Amarillo Klan paid a $16 initiation fee and annual dues of $6. They purchased their robes and hoods for $6.50 and at inflated prices bought literature and equipment for klavern—as a local unit was called—activities. Although in some ways a vicious racket based on the initiation fees, annual dues, and equipment costs, the Klan, many people believed, was a movement to protect old-line Anglo-Saxon stock, Protestantism, Gentiles, and rural ideals from the encroachment of "foreigners," Catholicism, Jews, and urban sins.[7]

In Amarillo, Klansmen engaged in the "usual" Ku Klux Klan activities. They held secret meetings with secret passwords and secret grips. They donned their expensive white robes and hoods, held parades, moved about at night, lit large fiery crosses, made threats, and flogged victims. Lieutenant Governor T. W. Davidson sent a small group of Texas Rangers to Amarillo in 1923 to investigate some floggings, and authorities arrested an Amarillo Klansman, T. W. Stanford, for "whitecapping" (threatening a person while disguised) E. T. McDonald, a Potter County resident. Stanford received a two-year prison sentence, which a criminal appeals court overturned.[8]

Seldom favorable to the organization, the *Amarillo Daily News* nonetheless covered Klan activities in Littlefield, Floydada, and elsewhere in West Texas and in New Mexico. It also described Klan affairs in Amarillo and in such "downstate" cities as Dallas, Houston, San Antonio, and Waco. Neither J. L. Nunn, the paper's publisher and general manager, nor David M. Warren, the managing editor, were members of the Klan, and apparently they held little sympathy for its activities. Some of their employees, however, including Horace C. Anderson and G. W. Camp, joined the secret organization and attended klanklaves (Klan meetings).[9]

In Amarillo on April 25, 1922, Robert L. Henry spoke favorably of the Klan. A candidate for the U.S. Senate, Henry, a Waco resident, was on a campaign tour through the Panhandle and northwestern portions of Texas. "I believe in the tenets of the Ku Klux Klan," he told a receptive audience in the district court room of the Potter County Courthouse, "and I belong to it." Arguing that he "believed in 100 percent Americanism," he urged those at the meeting to back "the principles for which the Ku Klux Klan stands," principles that include protecting "the virtue of our young womanhood; . . . [expanding] the religion of Jesus Christ; . . . [keeping] the negro in his proper place; . . . [and driving] the bootlegger and the moral degenerate from among us." The large crowd, according to the *Amarillo Daily News,* was enthusiastic.[10]

Though H. E. Fuqua introduced Henry before his speech at the district court, it is unclear whether Fuqua was a member of the Amarillo Klan. His name does not appear on the membership roll for December 31, 1923, but four Fuqua men from Wildorado, west of the city, were members of the local klavern. In fact, several Wildorado men, including two Protestant ministers, belonged to the group. Burton Roach and Less Whitaker, Potter County sheriffs, were members. Henry L. Ford, the county attorney; Neil S. Griggs of the Griggs Funeral Parlor; three of the Blackburn brothers from Blackburn Brothers Furniture; R. D. Kirk of White and Kirk Mercantile; Ben Masterson Jr., the son of the wealthy rancher-oil man R. B. Masterson; W. A. McIntosh, superintendent of schools; J. R. Snyder, the chief of police; three mayors or future mayors of Amarillo (Ernest O. Thompson, Ross D. Rogers, and Lon D. Marrs); and three leaders of the Amarillo National Bank belonged to the local Klan.[11]

The long membership roster for the Amarillo Klan is revealing. It suggests that some business leaders may have coerced their employees, perhaps under some work-related threat, to join the organization. The Panhandle and Santa Fe Railway, for example, counted a very large number of members in the Klan, ranging from yard and maintenance workers to clerks and office personnel. Several employees of both the

Great West Mill and Elevator and the Amarillo Laundry Company were members, but just as often Klan members were owners of small businesses, independent salesmen, and lawyers and physicians who were in effect small businessmen. Undoubtedly, some men, who perhaps wanted little to do with the organization, joined the Klan as a result of strong but subtle social and political pressure.[12]

In any event, after 1923 the Amarillo Klan declined quickly. People became disgusted with its intimidation, its violence, its secrecy, and its politics. Once they realized that the Klan was more a business scheme to make money for its national promoters than a movement to preserve core beliefs and traditional values, members left the organization. Not even the somewhat comforting fraternal nature of the Klan—at a time when fraternal organizations were highly popular—could save it. The Amarillo klavern fell apart in 1924, and in 1928 the Texas statewide organization counted only about twenty-five hundred members. The Ku Klux Klan did not die altogether, and into the twenty-first century it continues to be a nuisance in Texas and elsewhere.

In the early 1920s many Klan members supported the national prohibition of alcoholic beverages. Made law by the eighteenth amendment to the U.S. Constitution and instituted by the October 1919 Volstead Act, which defined an alcoholic beverage as one having 0.5 percent alcohol by volume, Prohibition was a flop. The speakeasies, bootlegging, and bathtub gin that followed in the wake of the national prohibition, suggest not only difficulties in enforcing the no liquor mandate but also Americans' unwillingness to submit to unpopular legislation. That racketeering, prostitution, and related felonies grew in number in the 1920s may imply that prohibition also spread vice and crime.

In Amarillo, prohibition had been law since 1912. Thus, not much changed with the Volstead Act. Bootlegging whiskey from New Mexico had been common, but now "rum runners" shifted their operations to sources in El Paso and in Juarez across the Rio Grande in Mexico. Several citizens produced liquor of various kinds in their homes, but, according to David L. Nail, at least two whiskey stills operated on

South Washington Street and a gasoline station at Fifteenth and Washington served as a common and convenient retail outlet for liquor—illegally, of course.[13]

In the early 1920s, the *Amarillo Daily News,* established in 1909 by J. E. Nunn, William Askew, Robert Underwood, and John Crudgington to support their temperance ideals, reported arrests associated with Prohibition-related activities. On April 13, 1922, for example, it noted that Sheriff Burton Roach arrested A. B. Thrift and his wife and Walter Willmering and his wife for "having intoxicating liquors in their possession for sale." The sheriff noted that the arrest, which occurred in southwest Amarillo, represented "the biggest liquor haul ever known in this part of the Southwest." He and his men netted "approximately two hundred and twelve quarts of whisky, some pints, a few packages of champagne and forty gallons of alcohol, with a total value of approximately $8,000." In a well-camouflaged hole behind the house at which the arrests were made, they uncovered a second large stock of liquor, which according to the labels on the bottles, came from England, Canada, and Mexico.[14]

For several years some men hauled liquor from El Paso to Amarillo. In one instance Tom Maddox, Frank Winkler Jr., and Earl Difendorff stole an automobile from F. E. Ezell's Amarillo dealership, drove the vehicle to El Paso, loaded the big sedan with liquor, and returned to Amarillo to sell their contraband. Although they ditched the car upon their return, the men made several similar trips, each time carrying in a stolen automobile a cargo of whiskey and other alcohol valued at nearly fifteen thousand dollars. Difendorff quit the illegal wholesale business in 1922, but after authorities in 1924 arrested Maddox and Winkler, he testified at their trial. The state found Maddox and Winkler guilty of violating its liquor laws.[15]

At the same time it convicted Maddox and Winkler of bootlegging, the state arrested P. J. Johnson and his wife for manufacturing and selling alcoholic beverages. When arrested on the north side of Amarillo, the Johnsons were carrying ten gallons of "booze" in their automobile, and in the kitchen of the Johnson home at 2004 Taylor Street local police officials discovered a whiskey still. They also found five barrels of mash in a closet of the home and ten additional gallons of alcohol. The court released Johnson, a Santa Fe Railroad Company engineer, on a fifteen-hundred-dollar bond and his wife on a five-hundred-dollar bond.[16]

Speakeasies became rather popular. Indeed, they had existed in Amarillo since local option laws had closed saloons in 1912. But in the 1920s there was a difference. Old-fashioned saloons and corner bars with swinging doors once were largely all-male establishments. Some speakeasies, or "night clubs," as the more fashionable ones were called, even if they did not operate at night, attracted a growing number of women. Women who had never entered, or even thought about entering, a bar or corner saloon before Prohibition, could in the 1920s be found in a nightclub or cabaret.

Because they engaged in the liquor trade, speakeasies were all technically illegal establishments and they all operated behind relatively closed doors. But some were more luxurious establishments that required "memberships" and provided jazz music, lively dancing, fancy dining, and relatively innocent amusement. A few became centers of depravity, housing gambling operations and prostitutes.

Amarillo in the late 1920s was home to at least four "houses" of prostitution. One, writes Nail, existed in the Verdun Hotel, one stood on Tyler between Second and Third streets, another faced the Army-Navy store on Fourth Street between Polk and Taylor streets, and a fourth operated in the three hundred block of South Johnson Street. Raymond Swindell, a physician who regularly gave the prostitutes medical examinations, claimed the houses "were all operated by the same madam." Apparently the "madam's" businesses became even more successful in the Depression years of the 1930s, for then she added a full-time accountant to keep track of her growing business.[17]

According to James D. Hamlin, Prohibition in Amarillo created "strange bedfellows." Hamlin, an Amarillo educator, lawyer, county judge, and town developer, was a hard drinker and a strong anti-Prohibitionist who spoke and voted against the local sumptuary laws.

At a political meeting in Hereford where pro- and anti-Prohibitionists publicly debated for their cause, claimed Hamlin, four of the "pro" speakers lined against him "were rather heavy drinkers, and had many times shared a convivial bottle with me." Before the speaking began, one of them, in fact, asked Hamlin as a courtesy "not to make any personal allusions to me and to the fact that I have many times overindulged." Because he "got so drunk before the rally that he had to be taken home," another of the "pro" speakers, so Hamlin said, "did not appear on the improvised rostrum."[18]

In addition to promoting such brazen hypocrisy, Prohibition helped to encourage some odd new fads and fashions. One of these was the "flapper," younger women who, having adopted the 1920s styles of short hair and short skirts, revolted against convention and custom. Flappers painted their cheeks and lips red and patronized the local nightclubs and taprooms where they listened to jazz music, danced to the lively strains of the Charleston, and dared to smoke in the company of men.

One-piece swimming suits were part of the new fashion, and flappers in Amarillo bought them off the racks at White and Kirk Mercantile. They wore the suits to favorite swimming holes at city lakes, at "the circles" near Cliffside northwest of the city, and in Palo Duro Canyon. Flappers, the "modern" women of the 1920s, planned to wear the daring suits at the large new swimming pool, the Natatorium, built in 1922 in San Jacinto Heights, but the plans fell apart when the Nat's ownership outlawed the new swimming attire.[19]

Although not a flapper, Melissa Dora Oliver-Eakle was a modern woman. An 1879 graduate of Georgia Female Seminary for Women, Oliver-Eakle was one of Amarillo's most influential and colorful entrepreneurs. Upon arriving in the city in 1895, she went to work for Callaway Brothers Mercantile. Not long afterward, she took over management of the large firm, which later became the Amarillo Mercantile Company. She platted a new subdivision, the Oliver-Eakle Addition, that extended the city south and west in an area that later included Amarillo College and Memorial Park. In the 1920s she built the ten-story Oliver-Eakle Building, one of Amarillo's first skyscrapers, at Sixth and Polk; in 1947 it became the Barfield Building. "To help disguise the fact that she was a women in a business world ruled by men," Oliver-Eakle often used the name M. D. Oliver-Eakle.[20] A businesswoman of considerable skill and success, Oliver-Eakle was also a generous philanthropist. She provided money to her church, for city parks, and for cultural activities, and she supported local education.

Amarillo held its share of other "modern" women. In 1921, for example, Mrs. S. L. Seay and Mrs. J. I. Kendrick won election to the Amarillo Board of Education. They were the first women to serve in such capacity, and "everyone admitted that they were well-qualified to serve." They helped to oversee a school system that in 1925 enrolled 4,750 children with a high school graduating class of 100.[21]

Amarillo education in the 1920s began to take on modern characteristics. New schools opened, and athletic and such other extracurricular activities as marching bands and University Interscholastic League events increased in importance and popularity.

In 1922 a large and beautiful new high school—built at a cost of $416,290—opened on Polk Street at the site that had recently held W. H. Fuqua's magnificent home. The older school building, Tyler Street School, located next door, became Central Junior High (later renamed Elizabeth Nixson Junior High School). At the new high school, Oscar Wise organized a band. It started with twelve members, and T. B. Kennedy served as senior class director.

That same year the high school football coach, Astynaxs S. Douglass, nicknamed his team the "Golden Sandstorm." The name stuck, but fans shortened it to the "Golden Sandies." Although baseball was the favorite sport in the early 1920s, football at all levels of competition, especially high school and college, gained in popularity through the decade, and in Amarillo in the 1930s high school football became king.

Private and parochial schools witnessed mixed progress. The Lowery-Phillips School in University Heights had closed in 1917, but Saint Mary's Academy, the pioneer Catholic school of Amarillo, enjoyed success. Founded by Sisters of the Incarnate Word in 1913 but led by the efforts of David Fly, F. M. Shaughnessy, and David Dunn, the school opened in 1914. Located at 1200 South Washington Street in a strikingly beautiful three-story brick building, it was a girls' school at first but in the 1920s became an elementary school for both boys and girls.[22]

Another important parochial school was Saint George's College, a Catholic boys' high school. Bishop Robert Rudolph Gerkin directed work that led to its opening in 1928 at 1800 North Spring Street in east Amarillo. A year later, after Katherine E. Price provided a large gift of money to support it, the school became Price College. It also began to enroll girls, and in the 1960s it enrolled both junior and senior high students under the name Alamo Catholic.

Education for minority students made some headway. As early as 1913 a school for Mexican American children existed. Mrs. A. K. Mendoza was the principal. In 1919 educational leaders opened at Tenth and Arthur streets a Catholic school for Hispanic students, and in 1930 the district constructed a school, Dwight Morrow Elementary School, in east Amarillo to serve Mexican American students.

In 1914 a school for African American students opened at First and Jackson streets in the North Heights community. Named for the great abolitionist and diplomat Frederick Douglass, the school enrolled mainly elementary students. In 1925 S. C. Patten was both a teacher and the principal. Three years later, in 1928, the district constructed a new school at the site and named it S. C. Patten School. It served black students in all grades.[23]

Higher education did not come to Amarillo until late in the 1920s, although not for lack of effort by community leaders. Amarillo had in 1910 lost to Canyon in its bid for a teachers' college—what became West Texas A&M University. It also misfired in its efforts in the early 1920s to secure an agricultural and technological college—what became Texas Tech University in Lubbock.

Having failed twice to secure a state-supported institution, Amarillo leaders moved to get a private parochial school established in the city.

Thus, led by George W. Shearer, a presiding elder in the Methodist Church, they began negotiations in the spring of 1924 with the Board of Education of the Northwest Texas Conference of the Methodist Episcopal Church for moving the church-supported Clarendon College to Amarillo. They convinced many people in Amarillo to sign a petition in support of the school, which they called the University of Amarillo, and arranged a formal meeting with the board of education. On May 2, President J. Winford Hunt of McMurry College in Abilene and George Slover of Clarendon College with other members of the board attended a public meeting in Amarillo.

Although participants reached no decisions about the college's removal, negotiations continued and seemed to go well for Amarillo during the next few years. Mayor Lee Bivins donated a plot of ground he owned and fifty thousand dollars to secure the school, the Northwest Texas Conference's Board of Education in 1927 authorized the school for Amarillo, and an official of Clarendon College moved to Amarillo to oversee the transfer. The removal did not happen, however, and plans for the five-hundred-thousand-dollar University of Amarillo fell apart.[24]

But Amarillo got a college. This time city leaders determined to build their own tax-based institution: a two-year community college. They moved quickly after negotiations with the Methodist Church ended, and on July 16, 1929, when local citizens voted approval for the institution, Amarillo College became a reality. Attached to the Amarillo school system and thus under the jurisdiction of the Amarillo Board of Education, the school with B. E. Masters as president opened in the fall of 1929 with seventy-seven students who each paid a tuition fee of one hundred dollars. Seven instructors held their classes in the east wing of the Municipal Auditorium. The Great Depression slowed college development and enrollment in the early 1930s, but late in the decade, with a permanent campus in the southwest section of the city—the Oliver-Eakle Addition—between Monroe and Washington streets and Twenty-second and Twenty-fourth avenues, a building program began, and enrollment expanded.[25]

Amarillo also got a second hospital. Northwest Texas Hospital, the city's first public medical facility, opened on March 22, 1924, in the twenty-three hundred block between West Sixth and Seventh streets (avenues after 1928) in northwest Amarillo. A private room with a bath cost six dollars per night, but for a double room the hospital charged four dollars. From the beginning the community facility was a busy, often overcrowded place, and as a result the Potter County Hospital Board considered expanding the hospital's size. When extra funds became available through the federal government's Public Works Administration program in the late 1930s, the board voted to build a seventy-five-bed addition, which opened in 1940.

Churches, like the hospitals, expanded in the 1920s, especially after the population boom that characterized the second half of the decade. The larger, mainline churches, including Polk Street Methodist, Central Presbyterian, and First Baptist, built new and modern worship centers. Central Presbyterian occupied its impressive new building at 1100 Harrison on Easter Sunday, April 17, 1927; Polk Street Methodist completed its beautiful five-hundred-thousand-dollar structure on February 26, 1928; and First Baptist dedicated its magnificent new church at Thirteenth and Tyler streets on August 31, 1930.[26]

At the same time, other churches appeared. In its weekly "Sunday School Reports," the *Amarillo Daily News* in 1924 listed four Methodist and four Baptist churches plus the older Central Presbyterian and First Christian churches. Its listings also included Saint Andrew's Episcopal, First Church of Christ Scientist, Trinity Evangelical Lutheran, the Salvation Army, and others. Saint Mary's remained the leading Catholic church.[27]

A "Mexican Mission" church opened in 1927. Its leaders conducted regular Sunday services for Spanish speakers in Amarillo. A Reverend Garcia, assisted by Deacon A. W. Nunn, led the mission chapel in the early days of the church, and F. E. Romo succeeded Garcia, but Reverend Manuel de la Cruz was also active at the mission.[28]

Pastors Flournoy and Menogan led African American churches, one of which may have been the Baptist San Jacinto Chapel. Like their white counterparts, black church leaders from time to time in the 1920s brought in revival leaders. The timely events attracted many whites as well. On one occasion, James A. Stout, a leading revivalist, spoke at the Olympic Theater to a crowd that "overtaxed [the] capacity" of the place. Stout also led fifty jubilee singers in a "rendition of plantation melodies [that] was highly enjoyed by the vast audience."[29]

A Jewish congregation likewise grew in the 1920s. Formally organized in 1913, the assembly, with A. Eberstadt as the first president, met in the Webster Building downtown briefly, but its members moved the meetings often, holding them in the Oliver-Eakle Building, Christian Science Hall, the Central Presbyterian Church, and elsewhere. Sometimes rabbis came from Fort Worth, Dallas, or Denver, but at other times such members as Louis Jacobson, Sid Braunig, and L. Gilman occupied the pulpit. With its membership increasing, the congregation behind the building committee chairman Wolf Herring moved to erect its own synagogue, and on November 10, 1929, the members dedicated Temple B'nai Israel at 2224 Taylor Street. Perry Nussbaum, a graduate of Hebrew Union College in Cincinnati, served as the first resident rabbi.[30]

Cultural life in Amarillo in the 1920s was surprisingly sophisticated. Chautauqua speakers and vaudeville performers still appeared in Amarillo. The Fair and Mission theaters hosted many of the events. Emil F. Myers, who with his wife, Lila, had founded the Amarillo College of Music in 1915, continued to teach classical music, both vocal and instrumental. He also sponsored and promoted in Amarillo many touring music company performances. Myers, wrote John McCarty, "spent years of dedication to bring fine music and great performers to Amarillo."[31]

But when the Grand Opera House on Polk Street burned down in 1919, Amarillo lost its most popular venue for such events. Townspeople, as a result, encouraged the city government to construct a new and larger facility. Indeed, they supported with enthusiasm in 1920 a three-hundred-thousand-dollar bond issue to build an auditorium, municipal building, and library, and in 1922 construction began.

Opened in 1923, the large Amarillo Municipal Auditorium with its distinctive architectural style covered the five hundred block between Buchanan and Lincoln streets.

The Amarillo Municipal Auditorium housed the Panhandle Music Festival. A weeklong series of events directed by Emil Myers, the music festival featured New York–based musicians some nights and local musicians others. In April 1923, for example, Albert Salvi, called the "world's greatest harpist," filled the Municipal Auditorium, and for its 1924 season the festival sold fifteen hundred season tickets. In 1928 the Panhandle Music Festival included tenor John McCormack, Hungarian piano virtuoso Gottfried Galston, and one of the Western world's most celebrated operatic sopranos, Ernestine Schumann-Heinck.[32]

The auditorium was also home to the Amarillo Symphony Orchestra and the Amarillo Little Theater. Sophie Meyer of the *Amarillo Daily News* in 1922 started the little theater as a club, and in the late 1920s the group numbered nearly three hundred. Sometimes the theater's plays attracted twelve hundred people. Grace Hamilton and the city's Philharmonic Club founded the orchestra in 1924 with an ensemble of twelve pieces. It grew in size and popularity until its performances became perhaps the city's principal cultural attractions.[33]

Popular entertainment was also plentiful. Movies attracted citizens to the Fair, State, San Jacinto, Capitol, and Rialta theaters. Gloria Swanson was one of Amarillo's favorite movie stars in the 1920s, but after "talkies" and especially after Al Jolson's *The Jazz Singer* (1927) appeared, local citizens turned to other favorites. Dancing occurred at the several venues, including the Amarillo Country Club, and the Nat Ballroom provided dancing lessons.

Radios, one of the new phenomena of the 1920s, were enormously sought after for entertainment and other purposes. Although developed slowly after 1895, their practical use and popularity increased with chaotic suddenness after stations KDKA in Pittsburgh and WWJ in Detroit in 1920 began regularly scheduled broadcasting programs. Only two years later, by the end of 1922, some 508 broadcasting stations existed in the United States, and three million American homes had radios. By the end of the Jazz Age, the radio industry had become a billion-dollar business.

Amarillo's first radio station was WDAG. The station provided some news, sold advertisements, and covered a few special events, including a 1924 Easter Sunday service with music and R. N. MacCallum preaching from Saint Andrew's Episcopal Church. In the first couple of years that it operated, the station featured music programs of various kinds. In 1924, for example, a reporter for the *Amarillo Daily News* noted that the "Derden's Kiwanis Orchestra gave radio fans a splendid program." The Derden School of Music provided the orchestra and selected the orchestra music. The reporter also noted that Virginia King and Rust McQueen, local singers, performed vocal solos. By 1924 the station had begun to list its programs in the local newspaper.[34]

The Harley Sadler Show was also a favorite in the 1920s. A traveling tent exhibition of vaudeville and variety acts, the Harley Sadler Show appeared in Amarillo each summer for about fifteen years. In the 1920s Sadler employees pitched a huge green tent on the prairie on the east edge of town. People drove out in their automobiles, and according to the local newspaper, cars raised "dust as they came to park helter-skelter around the tent." Because "seating at the show was on a first-come-first-serve basis," many people "arrived two or three hours ahead of time to get in line" for tickets. The show declined in popularity in the mid-1930s, but before its demise it was the largest touring group in the Southwest, having surpassed such traveling competitors as the Miller Brothers 101 Ranch Rodeo and the Arthur Names Show.[35]

The 1920s was a golden age for sports. Spectator sports took on a central role in American life. Americans had long enjoyed sporting activities and participated in organized sports, but the twenties were, as Frederick Lewis Allen suggested, the "ballyhoo years."[36] Americans became fascinated with Babe Ruth hitting sixty home runs for the New York Yankees, Bobby Jones winning all the major golf tournaments, and the enigmatic "Big" Bill Tilden sweeping his opponents from the tennis courts. On a national level perhaps the biggest change was in college football, where fans, including those who had not attended college, crowded into huge new stadiums going up around the country.

The *Amarillo Daily News* covered major sporting events, and prize fighting was one of them. It reported, for example, the July 2, 1921, fight in New Jersey between Jack Dempsey and the handsome Frenchman Georges Carpentier in the first "million dollar gate" in boxing. The paper both previewed and reviewed the two Dempsey–Gene Tunney matches in 1926 and 1927 in greater detail, suggesting, perhaps, that people in Amarillo, as throughout much of the country, had become during the decade enamored with professional boxing, a sport once outlawed in Texas.

In local papers more column inches were given to baseball than to any other sport. Amarillo citizens followed the major professional teams carefully, but they likewise monitored the progress of local baseball teams, including semi-professional, high school, and town teams. Names and league affiliations for the town teams changed during the decade, but the sport's following in Amarillo remained solid. Glenwood Park had a baseball diamond, but after 1926 such local teams as the Elks, Greys, and Metros played at Metro Park.

On the high school level in Amarillo, football, which perhaps had surpassed baseball in popularity briefly prior to World War I before sliding back, began again to claim its place as the dominant sport. The high school football coach provided a colorful nickname, the Golden Sandies, and fans of the local team attended the games in Amarillo and followed the team to its games in Lubbock, Canyon, Hereford, and elsewhere, usually taking the train but sometimes packing into automobiles for the trip. The team played its first night game in 1922, using spotlights for illumination and a football painted white.[37]

Perhaps the biggest local sports hero of the period was Cal Farley, a professional wrestler. Professional wrestling had begun in the city in 1909, but a year later, when a participant broke his neck in a match, local promoters stopped the activity for a time. In the 1920s, after it had started again, Farley became the local favorite. He took on "all comers" but wrestled often in the Fair Theater against Billy Landos, a big bruiser from Oklahoma. A wrestling match in the 1920s usually consisted of two or three "falls," with the match winner needing to defeat his opponent in two of the falls. A single fall might last up to an hour and a half. Farley defeated such other wrestlers as Dutch Mantell, Bert Willoughby, Frank Brown, Blacksmith Pedigo, Jack Reynolds, and Gus Sonnenberg.

Farley became a business leader and philanthropist. In 1939, with support from several friends, he started Cal Farley's Boys Ranch at Old Tascosa. The place served as a residence to boys from broken homes or young men "in need of a second chance" in life. In 2004 over 350 children lived there.[38] He started the Maverick Club to provide activities for young people after school. In 1945 he organized Kids Incorporated, a program that offered sporting events for young people not involved in school activities. In 2005 Kids Incorporated, which directed youth leagues in soccer, basketball, football, softball, and baseball, plus cheerleading, celebrated its sixtieth anniversary.

The Jazz Age in Amarillo represented a time of prosperity, expansion, and physical growth. Activities in the city often mirrored events on the state and national scene. Radios and automobiles created a new energy about life, and a dozen or more newfangled, modern home appliances powered by electricity together with an expansion of personal credit helped to develop a new culture of consumerism and the acquisition of "goods." While many folks engaged in agriculture may have struggled through some difficult financial times, for many others the decade was an exciting time, full of ballyhoo, granted, but flush with wealth, success, and good fortune.

Unfortunately, the affluence and excitement that characterized Amarillo in the Jazz Age did not survive the stock market crash in 1929 and the subsequent depression of the 1930s.

7

Amarillo and the Great Depression

The excitement and expansion that characterized Amarillo in the 1920s came to an abrupt end in the 1930s. The New York stock market crash in 1929 and the subsequent economic downturn that produced the Great Depression resulted on a national level in bankruptcies, bank failures, agricultural depression, large-scale unemployment, soup kitchens, bread lines, and related problems. The economy in Amarillo also suffered from economic maladies, although to a lesser degree.

Causes for the Great Depression are not hard to find. Agricultural and industrial overexpansion had resulted in surpluses that reduced prices to figures too low to earn a profit. Moreover, high tariffs in the 1920s hurt foreign sales of farm products and manufactured goods. Bankruptcies and unemployment followed. Easy credit and installment buying, a new phenomenon in the 1920s, had encouraged a consumer culture that worked well until unemployment increased, resulting in faltering automobile sales and residential construction and in slowing of consumer spending. A corresponding decline in purchasing power brought further cutbacks in business. Caution became the watchword. Buyers held out for lower prices, orders declined, and wages fell—or ceased altogether as unemployment rose.

The great stock market crash, dramatized by "Black Tuesday" on

October 29, 1929, did not cause the depression—at least directly. But, it weakened confidence among investors, businessmen, and consumers, fueling additional cutbacks in producing, buying, and hiring. Corresponding reductions in capital investment and in consumer spending fed on each other, creating the downward spiral in the economy of the early 1930s.

The Great Depression did not strike evenly across the country. Western farmers and ranchers had been suffering a financial crunch since the early 1920s. They continued to be hurt, but the Depression hit northeastern and midwestern manufacturing and business centers first. It spread to other sections of the country. Unemployment, bankruptcies and business closings, bank failures, soup kitchens, stock market declines, and financial and economic hardship characterized the Depression.

Mortgage foreclosures also were extremely common. Some families lost their homes and farms, forcing them to move in with relatives. Some of the dispossessed took to living in so-called Hoovervilles, shacks of tarpaper and galvanized iron, old packing boxes, and abandoned cars. Named for President Herbert Hoover and usually located near the city dump or along an isolated railroad right-of-way, Hoovervilles also attracted penniless vagrants, migrants, and others "down and out on their luck." Some of them were hoboes, aimless drifters who rode freight trains on the sly from one end of the country to the other. As time passed, hoboes included women and children among their ranks. To "hobo" became an American institution of sorts.

And the Depression lingered. Earlier downturns in the economy, such as in the 1890s, had usually hit bottom after six months or so and then came slow but gradual improvement. The recovery might take a few years, but signs of improving business activity were visible. Such a downturn and recovery occurred in Amarillo in 1907. This time, however, the economic depression continued to deepen. For four years, there were no signs of improvement.

Indeed, conditions got worse. Unemployment in the United States grew until it reached figures of well over 20 percent of the workforce.

The stock market continued down. By March 1933 stock values on the New York Exchange had dropped to less than one-fifth of their level in 1929. Personal incomes declined by more than half. By the end of 1932, some nine thousand banks had closed, hundreds of factories and mines had shut down, and thousands of farms had been lost: foreclosed for debt and sold at auction.

In Texas people living in larger cities such as Houston and Dallas noticed the effects of the Depression before other sections of the state. But farmers, already suffering from low returns on cotton, wheat, and cattle, saw the prices of their products decline even more. At first, some newspaper editors denied that a depression existed, but soon reports of unemployment and business failures indicated that the Great Depression had reached the state.

For the Amarillo economy, growing oil surpluses complicated business activity. In 1928 Texas produced some 256.8 million barrels of oil, more than any other state and nearly 20 percent of the total for the entire world. Then in October of 1930, the huge East Texas Oil Field, stretching from Upshur County in the north to Cherokee County in the south, opened and swamped the state in oil. A boom followed in East Texas, but it did not last, for overproduction drove down the statewide price of oil from a dollar a barrel in 1930 to as little as eight cents a barrel in 1931.

Then, rather suddenly, Amarillo found itself in the Depression. Although perhaps not as hard hit financially as some places, Amarillo nonetheless felt the pinch of an economy turning sour. Some businesses closed. Unemployment increased, reaching about twelve hundred families in early 1931. Wages dropped. The tax base declined. Some people went hungry, and by the fall of 1932 the local Community Chest, the city's chief welfare agency, had for lack of funds reached a point of closing. To reduce expenses, the Amarillo school system cut salaries, reduced the number of teachers, and closed temporarily the one-year-old Lee Bivins Elementary School.

Blacks and Hispanics, Amarillo's principal minority groups, were among those who saw their wages and their incomes cut. Hispanic men, mainly Mexican Americans, worked in the cotton fields south of Amarillo during the harvest season and took various jobs—often meaning whatever was available—in the city during other times of the year. African Americans numbered about sixteen hundred in Amarillo in 1930. A sizeable portion of the adult black population, men and women, worked for Amarillo's railroads and hotels, and they too saw their wages and hours cut and sometimes their employment eliminated. Many Hispanic and African American women who worked as domestic servants lost their positions when their employers lost income.

Thus, for blacks and Hispanics in Amarillo the Depression experience was not unlike that of some of their white neighbors. Their children too often went hungry and suffered from malnutrition and related health problems. People from unemployed households paid their physicians with homegrown vegetables or home-produced canned goods. For lack of money to buy new shoes, they and their children wore shoes fitted with cardboard soles. People patched old coats, darned old socks, repaired torn shirts, and saved old clothes for the younger kids.

But life went on. The Amarillo Rotary Club met each Friday for its luncheon at the Amarillo Hotel. The Lions, Elks, and other service organizations continued their weekly gatherings. Schools remained in session. Baseball—from sandlot and high school to professional—continued to be popular in the summer, and during the autumn months football grew in popularity. Women's clubs remained active. People attended concerts, went dancing at the Nat Ballroom and elsewhere, visited the local movie theaters, held dinner and card parties, celebrated birthdays, observed both secular and sacred holidays, picnicked at the city parks, and traveled out of town when they could. Those people who could afford the relatively high costs bought and sold such major items as homes and automobiles.

Moreover, with a huge Panhandle trade area Amarillo was able to sustain, at least in a relative sense, an active commercial position. In January 1931, for example, the city issued, according to David L. Nail, "fifty-five building permits totaling" $519,610. The fifty-five permits represented a figure that was "the fourth largest number in the state" for the month. And although the city could not afford to pave streets in the new subdivision, the Bivins Addition on the southwestern edge of town added several new homes during the Depression.[1]

Still, the Depression brought changes. Some businesses, such as Hub Clothiers, closed, at least temporarily. Soup kitchens, particularly one sponsored by the local newspaper—the *Globe-News*—appeared. The Junior Welfare League opened the Rose Bowl Tea Room at 410 Polk Street to support a relief project for indigent young people, including African American, Hispanic, and Anglo children.

With tax revenues down, the city made changes in its operations. It cut some construction projects, such as repairing and paving of roads. It cut its portion of the budget for the Board of City Development, an agency designed to advertise and promote Amarillo. For the fiscal year 1929–30, for example, the BCD received an appropriation of one hundred thousand dollars. The city cut it to seventy thousand dollars the next year, and in March 1932 Mayor Ernest O. Thompson requested that the BCD slice its budget for the fiscal year 1932–33 to twenty-five thousand dollars. The board, as a consequence, could no longer function and began to shut down. Faced with similar budget difficulties, the self-supporting Chamber of Commerce, which had for years operated on an irregular basis, also foundered. The result was that by the summer of 1932 Amarillo had neither a Board of City Development nor a Chamber of Commerce.[2]

Sometimes the changes were more dramatic than substantive. Along West Sixth Avenue in San Jacinto Heights, for example, a grocer to advertise his produce started what came to be called the "Chicken Follies." To announce his daily specials, the man threw live chickens off the roof. Their wings clipped, but otherwise "market-ready," the birds fell "with all the flight characteristics of a feathered rock." The follies attracted cheering crowds along the grocer's portion of Route 66.[3]

In the same neighborhood the Depression inspired the Pig Hip Sandwich shops. O. R. Tingley, the "Pig Hip King," worked in the tiny

San Jacinto Pig Sandwich shop of John Dinsmore in 1930 when the owner indicated that he was about to close his business. The Depression, he admitted, had cut too deeply into sales to continue his 2704 West Sixth Avenue sandwich operation. The younger Tingley did not want to give up, and accordingly, the two men, claiming that their meat came only from the "finest blue ribbon pig's hips," launched the Pig Hip Sandwich. Shortly afterward, Tingley bought out Dinsmore, renamed the struggling business the Pig Hip Sandwich Shop, and grew the colorfully named food service. Claiming "the meat is cut from the hip (the tenderest part of the pig) of fine Texas hogs," Tingley expanded, locating a stand at 501 Pierce and later opening similar shops in Borger and Tulia plus in two towns in Oklahoma: Minco and Anadarko.[4]

Nonetheless, the Great Depression was severe and prolonged. Its economic stagnation ruined businesses, destroyed farm operations, and increased unemployment. Likewise, its seemingly unending nature ruined dreams, destroyed personal values, and increased fear and self-doubt. A common belief in America in 1930, for example, was that people succeeded through their own efforts, their own hard work, thrift, and application. Logically, then, they failed through their own shortcomings. That people who remained employed during the Depression held onto such an article of faith is understandable. But even men and women who through no fault of their own had lost their jobs perpetuated the myth. People lost not only their income but also their self-respect and their self-confidence.

People in Amarillo and elsewhere across the nation needed help and assistance. They needed hope and inspiration. The help and hope came slowly and by degrees.

Herbert Hoover was president of the United States in the early days of the Depression. At first Hoover believed that private business and industry must provide the help and stimulus to pull the country out of its economic slump, and accordingly, his administration did little beyond trying to promote a culture of coming recovery. Soon enough, however, Hoover realized that the federal government must get involved, or the country might slip into complete economic chaos.

During the four years, 1929–33, that he was the chief executive, Hoover did more than any previous president to help an economy in dire circumstances. He called business and labor leaders to Washington for conferences and talks at the White House, where he asked owners to keep the mills and shops open and union representatives to forgo wage demands and strikes. He tried to reassure the American public. He established public works programs that were designed to provide jobs. He got the Federal Reserve System to ease its credit policies. He convinced Congress to lower taxes and the Federal Farm Board to step up its loans and increase its purchases of farm surpluses.

As the economy continued to worsen, Hoover and Congress took unprecedented steps. In 1932 they created the Reconstruction Finance Corporation (RFC) to aid banks, railroads, insurance companies, building and loan groups, and farm mortgage associations. They passed the Glass-Steagall Act to improve bank credit by broadening the definition of commercial loans that the Federal Reserve could support. For homeowners, they passed the Federal Home Loan Bank Act to establish a series of discount banks for home mortgages. Congress passed and Hoover signed the Emergency Relief and Construction Act, which gave the RFC $300 million for relief loans to states, authorized loans of up to $1.5 billion for state and local public works, and appropriated $322 million for public works.

Amarillo citizens participated in relief projects. One of them created Thompson Park. The seven-hundred-acre plot on Amarillo's north side had long been used as a city dump ground, but in 1930 the city, behind Mayor Ernest O. Thompson's leadership, converted the place into an expansive playground. Workers, using the city water department's ditching machines, dug huge trenches—some of them twelve feet deep and one thousand feet long—through the grounds and then pushed tons of old cars, abandoned junk, and other trash into the trenches. Using other equipment, the workers, writes James A. Clark, "ploughed under and covered over" the material. Then, using city draglines, workers built a dam across the lower end of a draw in the park so that "the first rain would provide a mammoth lake."[5]

At the park, the city also hired workers to dig holes in which to plant trees, paying the hole diggers a dime per hole. Each worker carried a "hole card," which supervisors, led by city landscaper J. D. French, punched each time a hole was completed. After his card had been punched ten times, a worker could redeem the card at City Hall for a dollar. The men dug some ten thousand holes. The city then bused Amarillo school children out to the site, which Mayor Thompson was calling "Municipal Park," to plant trees in the holes. Under the direction of city forester Temple Robinson, the children planted trees, and on each tree teachers placed a metal disc with the name of the child who had planted it. "Twenty years later," writes Clark, "those children would hold picnics in that park with their own children under their own trees."[6]

Other improvements followed. The city constructed an elaborate irrigation system to water the trees, and a few months later it built a swimming pool at the park. Budgetary constraints delayed other improvements, but in 1940 the city built Ross Rogers Golf Course, an eighteen-hole layout in Thompson Park, the name given to Municipal Park after Mayor Thompson left office. Additional changes came after World War II.[7]

The Depression encouraged other parks, or at least some park improvement. Not far from the large Thompson Park, in a section of Amarillo that housed predominately African American families, the city "built an elaborate playground." It also built a playground in an area where many Hispanic families resided. By 1938 Amarillo had seven parks: Ellwood, Glenwood (East Park), Sanborn, Thompson (North Park), San Jacinto, Bivins, and Oliver-Eakle. Five of the parks contained playground equipment used by an estimated twenty thousand children per year.[8]

To help with unemployment relief, Mayor Thompson also took advantage of the federal government's RFC loans. In 1932, shortly before leaving office, he named local attorney James O. Guleke, Wilbur C. Hawk of the Globe-News Company, and W. H. Fuqua of the First National Bank to head Amarillo's RFC committee. With assistance from

Fred DeCoster of the Community Chest, the RFC group instituted various work programs that over time employed some thirteen hundred people, including blacks, whites, and Hispanics—but it may be that fewer employment opportunities per capita went to minority groups.

RFC projects in Amarillo were often make-work programs. They included, according to Nail, refurbishing the Tri-State Fairgrounds and Butler Field, the high school football stadium. The projects also comprised the repair of "streets, curbs, and gutters in all parts of the city, beautifying parks, and assisting in the maintenance of school buildings." The "most extensive RFC project in Amarillo was the enlargement and renovation of Llano Cemetery," the city's ninety-two acre public burial ground. Workers at the east side cemetery repaired and constructed roads, excavated an ornamental lake, constructed buildings, planted grass, and laid sewer lines.

RFC funds came with restrictions. Each worker, for example, could receive only one dollar per day. Nor did RFC funds provide for supervisory expenses or equipment costs. Still, they represented a way to get people in Amarillo to work. At Llano Cemetery, writes Nail, to employ as many people as possible, the RFC supervisors adopted a "scheme [that] provided for each man to work six days and then lay off two weeks." The system, which included several staggered shifts, not only allowed directors to rotate work among some two hundred citizens every three days but also spread employment among many people.[9]

Some RFC funds went to women. The local committee cooperated with the Amarillo Red Cross to sponsor a sewing room. Located on the fifth floor of the Potter County Courthouse, the room employed about twenty-five women. The ladies produced quilts, made and mended clothes, and even distributed flour—some eleven thousand sacks of which the RFC provided—after it became available to them in September 1932.

By the fall of 1932 the people of Amarillo, indeed of all America, had had enough of Herbert Hoover as president. Unfairly, they blamed the Depression on him and his Republican Party. But rightly, perhaps, they believed Hoover and his administration had not done enough to help pull the country out of the Depression or aid the suffering of the American people.

Indeed, the Hoover administration had pretty much abandoned farmers. When in mid-1931 the government quit buying surpluses, already-low farm prices slid further. Wheat, for example, one of the major farm products in the Texas Panhandle, dropped in 1932 to thirty-eight cents a bushel, and cotton before the 1932 harvest sold for five cents a pound. Other farm prices fell in a comparative fashion, and livestock prices, especially cattle, declined. During the first four years of the Depression, nearly one million farms fell to mortgage holders.

Thus, in the November 1932 election, Franklin D. Roosevelt, the Democratic candidate from New York, swamped incumbent President Herbert Hoover. On the national level, Hoover carried only six northeastern states, representing 59 electoral votes; Roosevelt, who got 472 electoral votes, received some 7 million more popular votes than Hoover. In Potter County, citizens went for Roosevelt by a count of 5,324 votes to 961. It seems that the bulk of Amarillo's small group of Hoover supporters, led by Judge J. W. Crudgington, came from old-fashioned, diehard Prohibition advocates who did not like Roosevelt's stance on the manufacture of beer and light wine.

During the four months between Roosevelt's election and his inauguration, the economy hit bottom. Government policy drifted during that bleak winter of 1932–33, and partly as a result, unemployment rose even higher and misery and destitution spread. Panic struck the U.S. banking system, forcing banks to close one after another as people moved to withdraw their money. Perhaps a majority of the nation's banks had shut down operations by the end of Hoover's administration. In some states, beginning in Michigan, the governors declared a euphemistic "bank holiday," thus preventing so-called runs on bank deposits and stopping the closings. In Texas, Governor Miriam A. Ferguson, back in office for the second time, closed the state's banks on March 2, 1933, and three days later Roosevelt, in one of his first acts as president, declared a four-day national banking holiday. The American banking system shut down.

To deal with the crisis in Amarillo, banking and business leaders met. Led by Dean Kirk, president of the Retail Merchants Association and an official of the large White and Kirk clothing firm, they sought ways to deal with customer accounts and, as they could make no bank deposits, protect their cash incomes. Their plan called for greater use of credit buying and for regular customers to write checks for the amount of purchase. Another business group, the Clearing House Association, opened a money changing facility at the former National Bank of Commerce building on Polk Street.

Amarillo's mayor, Ross D. Rogers, announced that the city would cooperate with the banks and businesses as best it could and in addition provide greater vigilance in the downtown area. Rogers also planned to cooperate with the county sheriff's office, led by Bill Adams, in maintaining a larger security presence in the city's heart and in keeping downtown streetlights illuminated past the usual midnight shut off.

Meanwhile, beginning on March 2, the four Amarillo banks remained closed for two weeks. During the period, federal examiners inspected the banks, declared them financially sound and solvent, and set in motion procedures—the "paperwork," if you will—to allow reopening. Then, on March 15, after what seemed an eternity, the banks—Amarillo National Bank, First National Bank, American State Bank, and Amarillo Bank and Trust—reopened. Amarillo bankers were expecting large crowds on that Wednesday 9:00 a.m. opening, and they were not disappointed. But rather than coming to withdraw their money, the people of Amarillo stood in long lines to deposit nearly $1,435,000.[10]

With the banking crisis over, President Roosevelt moved in dramatic fashion to counter the Great Depression. Having called Congress into special session beginning on March 9, Roosevelt moved quickly. There followed the so-called Hundred Days, March 9 to June 16, in which Congress, at Roosevelt's urging, passed one major piece of legislation after another "with a dizzying speed unlike anything seen before in American history."[11] Two of the laws, the Beer-Wine Revenue Act that amended the Volstead Act to permit the sale of beverages with an alcoholic content of 3.2 percent and the Economy Act to cut certain government expenses, fulfilled campaign promises.

The others, which were more significant and far-reaching, launched the Roosevelt administration's legislative initiative—the New Deal. As part of the New Deal, Congress created government programs for relief to unemployed persons; for recovery from industrial, agricultural, and marketplace stagnation; and for reform in the financial, social, and business structures of the economy—the three Rs of the early New Deal. Over time New Deal measures created the Social Security program, empowered labor unions, aided homeowners and farmers, protected bank deposits, established ideas about minimum wages and maximum hours and about regional planning, encouraged land and resource conservation, protected stock market investments, regulated business and industry, and provided jobs.

The New Deal reached quickly into Amarillo and the Texas Panhandle. Local committees to handle federal relief and other programs in the area formed. T. C. Johnson, for example, chaired a committee that aimed at finding relief work sites in the area. Johnson, Wilbur C. Hawke, James O. Guleke, and several others who wanted a park in Palo Duro Canyon saw the magnificent place as one of the work relief sites, and accordingly, in 1933 the Civilian Conservation Corps (CCC), one of the most popular of all New Deal measures, set up camps in the recently established Palo Duro Canyon State Park. Before the summer was over, some six hundred CCC workers, earning forty cents per hour and living in one of four camps, were building a road into the deep gulf. CCC work on additional roads, buildings, and water crossings continued for several more years.[12]

CCC workers also planted trees in the New Deal's Prairie States Forestry Program, or shelterbelt project. Created in 1934, the project was aimed at building a series of farm and ranch shelterbelts on the Great Plains and, of course, putting people to work. Trees and shrubs planted in such belts would, it was believed, ameliorate the ground winds that picked up dirt and dust and carried them away. The shelterbelts would also provide protection for wildlife and beautify empty homesteads. CCC workers and others planted more than 222 million trees from North Dakota to Texas.[13]

Other projects put people, including CCC members, to work. Workers constructed dams, built roads and buildings, created and improved parks, and prepared recreation areas or access to them. The Buffalo Lake compound, located in Randall County, was one such facility that federally employed workers improved. The lake attracted fishermen, swimmers, boaters, campers, and others, and it offered great facilities until 1978, when a flood damaged the area causing officials to close the place as a recreation spot.

In Amarillo, the New Deal's Federal Emergency Relief Administration (FERA) carried on work begun with Hoover's RFC. Thus, Amarillo citizens employed under FERA grants continued working on streets, curbs and gutters, and in schools, the Llano Cemetery, and the Tri-State Fairgrounds.

The federal government's Public Works Administration (PWA), which concentrated on large projects, also employed Panhandle citizens. Created in June 1933, it built roads and highways in the Amarillo area and constructed buildings and dams. It also employed men in repair and replacement of seven miles of water mains in the city, most of which were in the downtown area, and in completing a huge water storage facility at Eighth and Crockett. The water project gave some two hundred men work and doubled the city's capacity to store water.

Another New Deal agency, the Civil Works Administration (CWA), was a stopgap effort to provide work through the winter of 1933–34. Although Gaines Whitsit directed Amarillo's office, the CWA was a federal operation. It employed, according to B. Byron Price and Frederick W. Rathjen, some "2,000 people in Amarillo at rates ranging from thirty to fifty cents per hour." At Amarillo High School, the CWA offered adult education classes at night, and by day under John E. Roland's supervision it operated a canning factory in an old laundry building on West Sixth Avenue that "processed about 1,300 cattle."[14]

The CWA also built roads. Under the urging of a group of lobbyists headed by Clint Small, James Guleke, Wilbur C. Hawk, T. E. Johnson, and other Amarillo leaders, the federal government committed some $7.5 million for Panhandle road building. CWA workers received portions of the grant to widen State Highway 5 north of Amarillo and Highway 33 south of the city. They improved streets in the Country Club and Ridgemere sections and conducted citywide clean-up campaigns. Most dramatically, perhaps, they paved "Jerico Gap," an eighteen-mile section of Route 66 east of Amarillo, the last "unpaved portion of [the highway] between Amarillo and Chicago."[15]

One of the most imaginative of the New Deal efforts to increase employment was the Works Progress Administration (WPA). Begun in 1935, the WPA, as the PWA and CWA before it, created a large number of jobs in construction and maintenance positions, but it also provided work for unemployed teachers, students, actors, historians, artists, writers, and other intellectuals in nonconstruction activities. While it undertook some very large activities, the WPA aimed mainly at putting people to work—even make-work, or "boondoggle," activities that some critics referred to as "leaning on shovels" and leaf raking. Nonetheless, in Amarillo WPA workers built curbs and gutters in the San Jacinto and Country Club additions, helped to construct the post office and downtown federal building, repaired county roads and bridges, and contributed to improvements at Northwest Texas Hospital. WPA monies helped to fund archaeological digs in the Panhandle and construction activities at the Panhandle-Plains Historical Museum in Canyon.[16]

Amarillo business leaders also participated in other New Deal efforts, including the National Recovery Administration (NRA), one of the most dramatic—as well as controversial and ambitious—of the recovery programs. The NRA, created in June 1933 in the National Industrial Recovery Act, established codes of "fair practices." That is, businesses and industrial operations that participated in the NRA accepted various regulations and agreed to a uniform system of wages and hours, meaning, presumably, higher wages and shorter hours.

In Amarillo, Rolla E. Townsend of the Amarillo Credit Association headed up NRA activities. He designated some sixty-one different business groups for the city, including, for example, cafés and restaurants, laundries, clothing stores, automobile dealerships, construction companies, grocers, gasoline stations, banks, and hotels. He asked each group to organize, to collect its own codes and regulations from state and federal agencies, and to conduct its businesses within NRA guidelines. Further, he pressed each group to select representatives to serve on a central enforcement committee headed by Mayor Rogers.

Cooperation was quick and mainly positive. Although some businesses could not or would not cooperate, most local companies joined the NRA program. Upon joining, they could place a large placard with the NRA's "Blue Eagle" emblem and its "We Do Our Part" slogan on it in their windows and in their advertisements. The Blue Eagle reminded citizens of each business's efforts at securing economic recovery.[17]

In Amarillo, the plan worked—at least for a time. The *Amarillo Daily News* reported that the NRA codes and regulations helped create almost five hundred new jobs. The Phillips, Gulf, and Magnolia oil companies, for example, by August 3, 1933, had established, respectively, twelve, fourteen, and sixteen new positions. Tire companies in town, led by the Goodyear and Goodrich dealerships, added new men, as did the Sears and Roebuck and Montgomery Ward stores. In some operations, such as the local Coca Cola bottling plant, people who held part-time jobs began working full time. Employment increased, and wages went up. Prices rose as well, but with improved purchasing power the economy began to improve.[18]

As the economy began to recover, complaints against NRA code restrictions and NRA enforcement procedures mounted. The honeymoon was over. Besides, neither agricultural nor domestic employees were covered, effectively denying many Hispanic and African American workers NRA benefits. Thus, when two years later in May 1935 the Supreme Court declared the NRA and its codes unconstitutional, few people mourned.

In Amarillo, most of President Roosevelt's New Deal's reform efforts were welcomed and lauded. The 1933 Home Owner's Loan

Corporation, which allowed refinancing at lower mortgage rates, for example, saved many city homeowners. The Emergency Farm Mortgage Act of 1933 provided for the refinancing of farm mortgages. The Social Security Act of 1935 proved to be one of the most enduring and eventually one of the most popular of all New Deal reform measures. The Banking Act of 1935 strengthened the Federal Reserve System. The 1935 Wagner National Labor Relations Act, although not as significant for Amarillo as the other bills, ensured workers the right to organize unions and bargain collectively.

Clearly, by 1935 the national economy, while still in a depression, had begun to improve. Likewise, in Amarillo, although unemployment remained relatively high, economic and business activity was picking up. The banks were sound; most businesses were stable; wheat, cotton, and cattle prices were increasing; and, perhaps most important, people's confidence had returned. Moreover, the Great Depression in Amarillo had never been as bad as it had been in larger, eastern and northern cities.

Not everything was plush. During the Depression era, people living in Amarillo and other cities and towns or on farms and ranches of the Great Plains suffered from a long period of terrible drought. Rainfall amounts dropped to an average of 9.96 inches in 1933 and 1934, and for the twelve years between 1929 and 1940, writes agricultural historian Garry L. Nall, "rainfall failed to reach the normal 19.67 inches at Amarillo" nine times.[19]

High winds—some of the "strongest winds in memory"—accompanied the drought, and wind gusts, which frequently reached thirty to sixty miles per hour, picked up dry soil and swirled it skyward to create dust storms that blew over much of the Great Plains. Indeed, sometimes the dust blew eastward all the way to the Atlantic Ocean.[20] There were many such "black dusters," as people often called the storms. Citing weather bureau reports, Donald Worster counts 179 small dust storms in 1933. The Soil Conservation Service, listing dust storms in which visibility was cut to less than a mile, notes 14 in 1932, 38 in 1933, 22 in 1934, 40 in 1935, 68 in 1936, and 72 in 1937. Many rural residents cite the sand storm on March 3, 1933, as "the worst I ever saw." In Amarillo, writes Nall, "residents experienced 192 dusters in the three years between January 1933 and February 1936."[21]

For Amarillo, the dust storm of April 14, 1935, was the most dramatic. It rolled across the Texas Panhandle from the northwest and struck Amarillo in the mid afternoon. Because it was Sunday and a pleasant afternoon, many people were home and outside. They saw it coming as it churned and twisted toward them in a solid mass of black that reached sixty or more feet in the air. Pushed by winds that may have gusted to over sixty miles per hour, it "looked as black as tar paper, boiling over, all crumpled and wrapping around itself."[22]

The dust storms were ecological disasters. They carried away millions of tons of topsoil, ruined crops, and created erosion problems of scarring proportions. They heaped sand and dirt, much like drifted snow, along buildings and fence lines. They produced pneumonia and aggravated such respiratory problems as emphysema and bronchitis. They covered homes and businesses, inside and out, with sand and grit, although, granted, such a circumstance was more an inconvenience than a disaster. After the storm of April 14, 1935, Robert Geiger, an Associated Press reporter from Denver, coined the term "Dust Bowl," a name he applied to the southwestern Great Plains, including the Texas Panhandle, where the number and severity of the dust storms were large.

But life continued. On July 4, 1933, for example, Amarillo citizens celebrated the American Independence Day. Hard times notwithstanding, some three thousand people attended a "giant" two-day picnic at the Jack Hall Ranch northwest of the city. Sponsored by the local American Legion Post, the affair included camping, swimming, and dancing. Baseball games, horseshoe pitching, and other activities took place, and after dark the picnic directors put on a large fireworks display. Earlier in the evening, the Amarillo Country Club and the Nat Ballroom also held free dances to celebrate the occasion.[23]

The Amarillo public schools opened on September 10, 1933, with nine thousand students enrolled. Although functioning under a greatly reduced budget, the system operated twenty-two school buildings and employed 276 teachers plus several administrators and other personnel. The large and beautiful Amarillo High School, about eleven years old in 1933, stood along the thirteen hundred block of Polk Street. Central Junior High (later named Elizabeth Nixson Junior High School) was nearby.

The Amarillo High School football team won the Texas state championship in 1934. Coached by Blair Cherry, who later joined the University of Texas Longhorns, the team also won the state's University Interscholastic League (UIL) title in 1935 and 1936, marking three consecutive years as champions. The Golden Sandies continued to be strong through the second half of the 1930s, and in 1940 the team, coached by Howard "Bull" Lynch, again won the state UIL championship. In 1943 *Look Magazine,* a popular national publication, claimed, "The Golden Sandies of Amarillo High School are the most famous schoolboy football team on earth!"[24]

Across Polk Street from the junior and senior high schools was the Double Dip Drive-In. Opened in 1930 by Sam Stinson and J. E. Jenson, the place quickly became an Amarillo institution. After a year Stinson bought out his partner, expanded from selling home-frozen ice cream to five- and ten-cent hamburgers, soft drinks, and other lunchtime favorites of the high school students from across the street. For forty years, the Double Dip remained the most popular place in Amarillo for students to eat lunch, meet friends, and "hang out."

Like the Double Dip, Amarillo's churches kept busy. Although collection plates seldom filled and budgets fell, church attendance held steady or even increased during the Depression years. The city in 1933 counted at least twenty-five active churches. Baptist and Methodist congregations dominated the number of churches, but one could find a wide range of Christian denominations, including Christian Scientist, Assembly of God, Seventh Day Adventist, Unitarian, Episcopal, Lutheran, Catholic, Christian (Disciples of Christ), Presbyterian, Latter Day Saints, and Church of Christ. A Jewish congregation, Temple B'nai Israel, worshiped each week as well.[25]

Some of the Protestant churches sponsored a visit to Amarillo by Sister Aimee Semple McPherson, the famed Los Angeles evangelist. On February 1, 1934, McPherson spoke twice at the Municipal Auditorium. In her afternoon talk, titled "Milk Pail to Pulpit," she reviewed her life and defended herself from recent morals charges that critics had leveled at her. She titled her evening speech "America Awake." Dynamic, colorful, and theatrical, McPherson's appearances were always popular, and in Amarillo large crowds attended both of her presentations.

In popularity, the annual "Mother-in-Law Day" event surpassed McPherson's visit. Started in 1934 by Gene Howe of the Amarillo Globe-News Corporation, the mother-in-law jubilee began as a tongue-in-cheek affair after Howe inadvertently had offended his mother-in-law in his newspaper. The idea, which had been hatched in 1933, grew as Amarillo women, led by Mrs. C. C. Cunningham, Mrs. N. S. Griggs, and Mrs. L. O. Thompson, got involved, and on January 23, 1934, Howe through his "Tactless Texan" newspaper column announced that Mother-in-Law Day would be celebrated on March 5, a day that coincided with the annual, well-attended Amarillo Fat Stock Show celebration.[26]

The event quickly gained national attention. Political satirist and rodeo performer Will Rogers talked on his national radio program about Amarillo's Mother-in-Law Day. Other radio broadcasters gave it notice. Paramount and Universal film studios sent camera crews from Hollywood to record the day's festivities; they planned to use some of the filmed material for news features that were a characteristic part of movie theater showings. The Associated Press sent reporters. Eleanor Roosevelt, wife of the president, sent greetings, and mothers-in-law from as far away as Illinois and New York came to Amarillo to join the fun.

On the appointed day, people from across the Texas Panhandle arrived in the city. Mothers-in-law registered at the Amarillo Hotel and received sweet pea corsages. The high school band led a parade, in which two thousand marchers participated, south down Polk Street to the Paramount Theater. Some six thousand people watched the parade.

At the Paramount, leaders hosted a reception at which they awarded various prizes, and Howe unofficially named his mother-in-law, Nellie Donald, whose hurt feelings had started it all, "the stateliest and most beautiful."[27]

Four years later, in 1938, Howe's fifth Mother-in-Law Day celebration was truly a national event. Eleanor Roosevelt, who had agreed to participate, ride in the parade, and speak in the evening, was the special attraction. An estimated 125,000 people attended, overwhelming Amarillo's population of less than 50,000 inhabitants. Five state governors participated, and Governor James V. Allred of Texas made the day an official state event. The city's banks closed, and the city hired extra policemen. Highway patrolmen on motorcycles also arrived to direct traffic and maintain order. During the annual parade, Roosevelt at the head of the procession rode in an "Eleanor Blue" Buick, and upon completing the route, she watched the rest of the colorful pageant from a reviewing stand. There were parade floats, and on one of them—165 feet in length and shaped like a ship's hull—some 591 people, most of them mothers-in-law, rode down Polk Street and passed Roosevelt's place on the reviewing stand. Shortly afterward, local officials, led by the Mayor Rogers and Gene Howe, presented the First Lady with a bouquet of over five thousand roses—"the World's Largest Bouquet." Because it weighed twenty-five hundred pounds, workers used a crane to lift it from a truck to the reviewing stand.[28]

Meanwhile, in 1935, Amarillo hosted another large and colorful event: the Forty-fifth Annual Confederate Veterans Reunion. The weeklong affair began on Monday, September 3, and ended with a grand parade of veterans that stretched for two miles through the downtown district on Friday. Some seven hundred veterans and "thousands of delegates" from such related organizations as the Sons of Confederate Veterans and Southern Memorial Association attended. Carl Hinton of the recently reconstituted Amarillo Chamber of Commerce led the planning committees, and Wilbur C. Hawk of the Globe-News Company organized funding activities. Amarillo housed and fed the aging veterans, most of whom were eighty to ninety years old, in Amarillo High School and turned the campus into something of an army field camp, with a hospital tent and other facilities. CCC workers, Boy Scouts and Girl Scouts, United Daughters of the Confederacy, and other groups provided various kinds of assistance.

The event was a major undertaking. Texas governor James V. Allred welcomed the convention delegates, and the governor of New Mexico was present to welcome the visitors to the Southwest. Downtown hotels housed many of the nonveteran visitors, and the Amarillo and Herring hotels served as headquarters for registration and official business of the organizations. Banquets, meetings, dances, and dinners were all part of the reunion activities. Amarillo also hosted a large barbeque in Palo Duro Canyon, and bands, some from as far away as Lamesa and Slaton, Texas, and Clarksville, Arkansas, played at a bandstand on the high school grounds. But the chief musical attraction was the U.S. Marine Corps Band. It provided music for a grand ball on Wednesday night and gave a concert on Thursday evening at the Municipal Auditorium, where officials turned away enough people that the band agreed to a second concert at the football stadium, twelve-thousand-seat Butler Field, on Friday evening after the reunion had ended. Some forty thousand people lined the downtown streets for the stirring parade that ended the reunion on Friday morning.[29]

Although such events as the Mother-in-Law Day celebration and the Confederate Veterans Reunion helped local businesses, Amarillo's larger economy in the 1930s rested on foundations of oil and agriculture. While the local petroleum industry improved in the late 1930s, Panhandle agriculture continued to suffer. "Between 1935 and 1940," write Price and Rathjen, "the number of farms in the [Texas] Panhandle declined by nearly twenty-five percent." Property values dropped and hundreds of thousands of acres went out of production. In the 1930s perhaps twenty thousand farmers and their families in the region left their homes.[30]

Then, rather suddenly, World War II lifted Amarillo and Panhandle agriculture out of the Great Depression.

8

World War II and Afterward

On December 7, 1941, the people of Amarillo, as elsewhere in America, upon hearing the news of the Japanese attack at Pearl Harbor in Hawaii, reacted first with shock and fear and then with stunned anger. The two-hour air and bombing attack sank or disabled nineteen American naval vessels, destroyed about 180 planes at neighboring Hickam Air Field, and left 2,400 American servicemen and civilians dead and 1,178 wounded. Quickly afterward—in fact, the next day—the United States declared war on the Empire of Japan and three days later found itself at war against Germany, Italy, and other Axis powers.

Amarillo supported the war effort. Many local and Panhandle citizens enlisted in the armed services, some bought government savings and defense bonds, others willingly enrolled in military-related jobs, and all accepted the war-induced material shortages that followed. The city's small airfield expanded, and with Amarillo's blessing the U.S. Army in 1942 created the Amarillo Army Airfield. With the air base the federal government also established the Pantex Army Ordnance Plant, and the next year the huge Excell Helium Plant, some thirty-one miles north of Amarillo, underwent construction. Both the *Amarillo Daily News,* led by its editor John L. McCarty, and its sister paper, the *Amarillo Evening*

News, led by Wes Izzard, in editorials, opinions, and news articles backed the country's participation in the worldwide conflict.

World War II had begun in Europe in 1939. Dozens of countries became involved, but in its early years the war pitted mainly England and France and their allies against Germany and Italy and their allies. For different reasons at first, the Soviet Union and the United States, among the leading military powers of the day, remained out of the expanding hostility, but through the long months of 1940 and 1941 a whole series of military and diplomatic events inexorably brought them into the deadly conflict. For the United States, the surprise attack on Pearl Harbor was the culminating event.

After the Pearl Harbor attack, the reaction in Amarillo was typical. The *Amarillo Daily News,* recognizing that citizens of its city, like others all over the United States, had been divided on the proper course of action vis-à-vis the European strife, proclaimed: "At last we have unity. We are aroused. We have the will to win." As in other parts of the country, so also in Amarillo, the attack on Pearl Harbor closed off arguments about American neutrality in the war. It forced Amarillo citizens to look beyond their state and nation and to view a world far from the Texas Panhandle's Golden Spread.[1]

Moreover, the attack launched Amarillo into a period that transformed the city's social and intellectual landscape. "Prior to World War II," as an example, "the Texas Panhandle was redneck country," argues Bishop Leroy T. Matthiesen, "insulated from the remainder of the world." But the war, Matthiesen writes, "drew young men from the East coast to Amarillo . . . by the thousands and sent Panhandle volunteers and draftees to the world outside." The combination, he concludes, made the citizens of Amarillo "more tolerant of people who differed from them."[2] Amarillo's African American and Hispanic populations increased during the war, with blacks taking residence, when they could find it, on the north side and Hispanics moving into homes on the southeast edge of downtown.

Even before 1941, Amarillo's economic landscape was changing. The city's population had increased from 43,132 inhabitants in 1930 to

51,686 ten years later, making Amarillo in 1940 the eleventh largest city in the state, well ahead of such other Southern High Plains cities as Lubbock and Plainview. In the late 1930s building permits increased as construction expanded. In 1935, for example, in the middle of the Great Depression, the city issued construction permits that totaled only $336,943, but in 1940 permits reached $2,589,856. In 1940 the city boundaries extended south into Randall County and approached Western Street in the Country Club section. Amarillo contained 728 acres of parks, dominated by Ellwood, Thompson, Sanborn, and Glenwood.[3]

Oil and gas production continued to be high. In 1940 the average daily output from the large Panhandle Oil Field, write B. Byron Price and Frederick W. Rathjen, "amounted to twenty billion cubic feet of gas and just more than 80,000 barrels of oil." Similarly, in 1941 the region's share of the nation's carbon black production stood at 98 percent, and the Amarillo helium plant just west of the city accounted for nearly all the country's production. In addition, the busy oil and gas industry—including drilling, constructing, transporting, storing, refining, piping, and selling—employed thousands of people and had kept Amarillo a bit ahead of the Depression.[4]

In 1940 Polk Street still dominated Amarillo. Called "America's best-lighted main street," it remained the city's business hub. The large and majestic Paramount Theater, which was a special place to see a movie, anchored the south end of Polk, and the State Theater dominated the north end. At night well-lit storefronts and multi-colored streetlamps made "the Drag," as it was called, a colorful place, especially on busy Friday and Saturday nights. Farther south near the high school, the Double Dip Drive-In remained among the most popular teenage attractions.[5]

For adults, several attractions existed downtown. The elegant Paramount Theater, "one of the great showplaces of the Southwest," was one of them. It contained "magnificent chandeliers, . . . gigantic oil paintings[,] . . . and a cathedral-size electric pipe organ with three consoles." Another was the opulent Capitol Hotel. Built in 1928 by oilman

Ed Mayer, the six-story, 145-room hotel featured plenty of marble, "intricate carvings, ornate light fixtures, and expensive murals." One could relax in the marble-lined coffee shop or wait in the spacious lobby and perhaps catch a glimpse of one of the celebrities who stayed at the hotel, including Wendell Wilkie, a 1940 U.S. presidential candidate, and entertainers Lawrence Welk, Arthur Rubenstein, and John McCormack. Or one might spend an evening in the posh Old Tascosa nightclub, located in the basement of the large Herring Hotel—still the city's convention center. A favorite dining, dancing, and entertainment spot in the 1940s, the nightclub featured a western motif with murals that local artist Harold Bugbee created.[6]

But automobile traffic and cross-country highways were changing Amarillo. U.S. Highways 60, 66, 87, and 287 all came through the city, making Amarillo, as one advertisement boasted, the "Hub City of the Land of Modern Pioneers." To accommodate travelers stopping overnight, the city in the early 1920s built a modern camping ground in the Old Town area. Not long afterward, entrepreneurs, such as Lela Mae Barnum, who in 1926 opened her fashionable business at 811 North Fillmore, built roadside stopping places, auto courts, and tourist camps. At 806 North Fillmore, H. E. Smith in 1939 established Smith's Motel, the first place in Amarillo to use the "motel"—short for "motor hotel—designation. U.S. Highways 60 and 66, which merged for several miles on Amarillo's northeast side, attracted most of the motels.

To cater to the increasing highway traffic, other entrepreneurs opened roadside cafés, restaurants, gasoline stations, and other businesses, sometimes in conjunction with the motor courts. Pueblo Cibola, "one of the finest tourist courts in the Southwest," was a good example. It had opened in 1935 at the northeast city limits on U.S. Highways 60 and 66 and advertised itself as being "surrounded by beautifully-landscaped grounds" and combining "ultra-modern accommodations with the charm of early Pueblo Indian architecture and furnishing." By 1939 it had added a gasoline station to its grounds.

In 1940 Cleo Scamahorn opened the Capitol Garage and Service Station along Northeast Eighth Avenue on Route 66. Attendants sold gasoline to cross-country travelers and performed minor repairs to their automobiles. A small café attached to the garage was part of the trendy operation. A tall, neon imitation oil derrick on top of the garage revolved to call attention to Scamahorn's business, which advertised itself as a "truck stop."

Closer to downtown, Sam D. Hanes owned and operated the Amarillo Auto Clinic. A large full-service garage located at 400 West Seventh Street, the clinic dispensed gasoline, sold tires and batteries, and provided engine tune-ups on all makes of cars and trucks. In 1940 Hanes sold gasoline for sixteen cents a gallon, and his teenage son, who later took over the business, might repair or replace automobile engine valves on a six-cylinder vehicle for $12.50.[7]

As automobile travel and truck transportation increased, travel by train diminished. Railroad track mileage, which had reached a peak in Texas in 1928, began to decline in the 1930s, and the economic impact of the Great Depression further added to the growing woes of railroads and businesses dependent upon them. In Amarillo, for example, at the Santa Fe Railroad depot the famous Harvey House dining room, which had opened in 1910 and which for nearly three decades was the city's elite eating spot, with its carefully groomed and neatly dressed Fred Harvey waitresses, closed January 31, 1940.[8]

The year 1940 was not always good to Amarillo. Besides the Harvey House closing and the decline in rail service, the city on November 23 and 24, endured a destructive ice storm, perhaps the worst such storm to strike the city. Freezing rain began on the twenty-third, making streets slippery and driving dangerous. As the cold rain continued, ice formed on trees, shrubs, buildings, and automobiles, and it clung to the city's utility wires, including telephone and electric lines. As the ice thickened, its weight increased, and sharp winds tossing the ice-heavy wires around added to the danger. Then one after another the power lines snapped, and as they broke, sections of the city one by one fell silent and dark. When a last telephone wire to Canyon fell, no telephones, no radio stations, and no electric lights operated in the city.

Amarillo was essentially closed off from the outside world.

Conditions in the city remained hazardous. Most people heated their homes with gas, but folks without kerosene lamps or generators or a generous supply of candles spent a night in darkness. Utility servicemen came from neighboring towns and, aided by WPA workers under A. A. Meredith, restored communication. The task was not easy. In fact, Meredith, the WPA district director, drove to Clarendon, where phone service was available, to seek additional help. After thirty hours, the workmen had restored power, but clearing the streets of tree limbs, downed telephone poles, and other debris took longer.[9]

But 1940 was not all bad either. The Veterans Administration Hospital opened that year. Located on West Ninth (Amarillo Boulevard) and built by WPA workers in a Spanish Colonial Revival style, the regional facility served a wide area that included Colorado, Kansas, New Mexico, Oklahoma, and the Texas Panhandle. A woman who had been a U.S. Army nurse was the first patient. In 1987 the three-story structure held 132 beds with plans for adding some forty more plus a "120-bed skilled nursing home." During World War II, the army built a stage on the hospital grounds for touring USO camp shows.

During the same year, 1940, the WPA also expanded Northwest Texas Hospital. Its workers completed a 75-bed addition to the community facility located between Sixth and Seventh avenues. Further additions in 1952 and 1960 increased the number of beds to 275.

The expansion of health care facilities was only part of what Amarillo could boast. A statewide safe driving campaign sponsored by Governor James Allred and led in part by *Amarillo Daily News* editor John L. McCarty had resulted in a meaningful decline in automobile accidents across the state and through the Texas Panhandle. Indeed, the drop in Amarillo was significant enough—71 percent in 1939—that the city in early 1940 ranked as the "Safest City in Texas."[10]

Chamber of Commerce advertisements reflected a positive image of Amarillo, of course. One of them, dated 1942, talked about "an invigorating 3676-foot altitude, 81% sunshine, cool nights in summer, moderate winters, and year-round golf." Another boasted of the city as a fast-developing recreation and vacation center, noting Amarillo's golf courses, the tennis courts at Ellwood Park, sailboating at Buffalo Lake, plus the opportunities for swimming, fishing, and hunting.

Amid positive developments came World War II. Indeed, for some it came earlier. On November 25, 1940, a year before the United States entered the war and while WPA personnel cleaned tree limbs and downed power poles from Amarillo's streets after the great November ice storm, Texas National Guard troops of the 142nd Infantry and 131st Field Artillery regiments mobilized. They met at the National Guard armory located on the west side of Taylor Street and between Second and Third avenues. Many of the National Guard troops served for five years, or throughout the remainder of the war.

One group, the Second Battalion of the 131st Field Artillery, suffered great indignities. Military authorities detached the battalion, commanded by Blucher S. Tharp, and sent it to Camp Bowie at Brownwood, Texas, for further training. Men of the battalion then volunteered for overseas duty and left for the South Pacific. After the deadly attack at Pearl Harbor, the men landed at Java, but shortly afterward, on March 7, 1942, Japanese troops overran the island and captured the Americans. As Price and Rathjen write, all "contact with the Second Battalion was lost . . . and at a terrible price [it] became immortalized as the Lost Battalion of Java."[11]

In the meantime, many Amarillo men and women volunteered to serve in the armed forces. On December 8, 1941, the day after the Pearl Harbor attack, for example, people jammed the local military recruiting stations. Lines formed at eight o'clock in the morning, and they remained full until late in the evening. The eager applicants, noted the *Amarillo Daily News,* "stormed" the recruiting offices, "milled in the halls of the post office," and "clamored to take the quickest route" into the armed services. Some of the people "were crippled; some were overage; some were single; some were married; some were poor and some were rich." They wanted a service that "would offer them action at the first possible moment." Many got their wish, including women, who joined auxiliary military groups. The military, under a 1940 conscription law, drafted many men, and Amarillo soldiers, sailors, marines, airmen, coastguard men, and merchant marines served all over the globe.[12]

At least one of them, Lt. John C. "Red" Morgan, received the Congressional Medal of Honor. Morgan, an airman and copilot of a B-17 bomber plane, found himself at the controls of his aircraft after German gunners killed his pilot and struck the airplane. Although the bomber was badly damaged, Morgan kept the B-17 in formation, completed the bombing run, and returned to the English air base from where he had started. With no tires and with the bomber's hydraulic system inoperable, he landed the airplane without further loss of life.

Others were not so lucky. Many suffered injuries and battle wounds, some lost limbs, and some died. Amarillo's Jay Pietzch, whose father lived on Tyler Street, became the first Texan casualty of the war. An army air corps navigator who had played football and basketball in high school and college and was the Amarillo district Golden Glove boxing champion and the state AAU boxing champion, Pietzch died at Pearl Harbor. Two days later news arrived that Durward Meadows, a twenty-year-old radio operator on an army plane, had died in the Japanese attack at Hickam Airfield in Hawaii.[13]

Back home in Amarillo the war created big changes. In the summer of 1941, Mayor Joe A. Jenkins, Gene Howe, Judge R. E. Underwood, Sam Davis, and others had gone by train to Washington, D.C., to lobby for a military base for Amarillo. With Senator Tom Connally providing support, they approached War Department officials for an airbase. As part of their campaign pitch, they inflated a helium balloon with "Amarillo" on the side. The balloon caused a stir, especially as it deflated, but their campaign worked: they got an airfield.[14]

The Amarillo Army Airfield opened in April 1942. Located on a 1,523-acre tract about eleven miles east of the city, it stood adjacent to the older English "airport." At first the army used the new airfield to train ground mechanics and technicians to maintain the B-17 bomber, one of the key airplanes the Allies used in their air offensive against Germany. While it was still under construction, the airfield received some of its first units, and its first class of trainees arrived in September. Later, the army used the field to train aircrews and technicians for the larger B-29 bombers, the airplanes that saw major service in the air offensive against Japanese positions in the Pacific.

Col. E. C. Black, commander of the air base, described the school's purpose. Speaking on April 6 at an evening meeting of the Amarillo Kiwanis Club, he told the audience that a military airplane is a "complicated machine" that requires skilled mechanics. "The army needs many thousands of those men," he said. "They are the men we are going to train here." He predicted, incorrectly as it turned out, that the base would house sixteen to seventeen thousand troops, a number that would have overrun the population of Amarillo.[15]

About the same time that it opened the airfield, April 1942, the U.S. government established the Pantex Army Ordnance Plant. Indeed, as Price and Rathjen put it, the air base and the plant were "twin-born." An acronym for "Panhandle, Texas," Pantex was a conventional ordnance operation designed to manufacture bombs and artillery shells. The plant, located on the western edge of Carson County near the hamlet of Saint Francis, soon became Amarillo's largest employer, and together with the airfield it greatly enhanced the city's economy.[16]

But not everyone benefited. The army removed seventeen farm families and two nonresident farmers from nearly sixteen thousand acres of rich soil on which the Pantex plant was located. Called to a meeting at the Saint Francis community center, Liberty Hall, the families received the army's news that the land was to be used for strategic purposes. Army officials gave the families two weeks to remove themselves and their personal property from their homes. The people protested, of course, and urged the government to find less productive land, but as it was wartime, they had little recourse. Although compensated for their material losses, the families sold their cattle at reduced prices, left their ripening wheat in the fields, abandoned their windmills and granaries in the yards, and sadly drove away.[17]

Although most of them were tenants and renters, three of the resident farmers owned their property. In April 1942 the *Amarillo Daily*

News reported on the situation. One of the more successful owners, J. J. Vance had lived with his wife on their place for thirty years. The Vance farm was the "show place" of the Saint Francis community. Their home had electricity, a sewage system, and its own butane power system with an eight-hundred-gallon underground storage tank. It had a "double hot water heating system and a water softening system." In capacity, a huge grain storage elevator on the farm rivaled commercial elevators. A "brick machine shop [held] over head cranes, complete machine equipment, and storage space." The Vance's brick garage held four vehicles, and they had built their driveways of concrete. The fences around the house and barnyard had steel posts set in concrete. Even the outhouses were of brick and concrete construction.

Vance was not resentful. He planned to store his equipment and household goods and go on a long trip. We are going to Temple, Texas, he said, so that his wife "can go through the clinic, and then perhaps we will go to Hot Springs." Afterward, he indicated, he and his wife would look for another farm, but they would live in town, for he was too old, he believed, to start over with kerosene lamps in a rural area without electrical power.

Other farmers were less sanguine. Harve Lusk and Fred Haiduk, who also owned their farms, worried about moving. They were being forced to leave even before land and property appraisals had been completed and before they knew what the nature of the government's monetary settlement would be.

R. B. Lathem, who lived in Amarillo but operated his own farm, had mixed emotions about the move. Leaving "is alright with me," he reported, but he was "aggravated." Before the end of the two-week period to get off the land, his place was "a beehive of activity" as well-digging crews moved in and tore out fences in the hog pen, thus inadvertently allowing the hogs to run loose. Lathem left behind his feed, but he collected his hogs and herded his other livestock off the property.

Still worse off, the tenant farmers had to leave at a season of the year when trying to rent or lease property was not easy. One of them, Mrs. Leo Gables, the mother of ten children, worried about finding another residence. "It is our main concern," she noted. "My husband has been out almost every day looking for another place. I hope he comes home with good news tonight." Another tenant farmer, an elderly man named J. W. Jones, said, "the place we have is all a man could ask [for, but right] now my big job is trying to find some truckers to help move my stuff."

Clearly, the move was difficult. The families had two weeks to pack up household belongings and furniture. They needed to find a new place to live—temporarily, if not permanently. They had to tow or haul their farm equipment, including tractors, plows, planting machines, and combines, off their former property. They needed to load what livestock feed they could save into wagons and trucks and get it out of the granaries. The livestock, mainly cattle, hogs, and chickens, had to be moved.

Consequently, in mid-April the few dirt and gravel roads around and south of Saint Francis were heavy with traffic. Farmers used them to move out their equipment and cattle, and the government used them to haul in surveying crews, loads of lumber, heavy machinery, and road-building equipment. The roads were also filled with pickup trucks and automobiles of the construction workers. In addition, railroad crews built tracks onto the property to connect with the Santa Fe and the Fort Worth and Denver lines.[18]

Maj. H. P. Burgard was in charge of the Pantex construction work. He too worried about the farm families being dispossessed. In occupying the land, he said, "we want to do [it] with the least possible inconvenience to the farmers, . . . [for] we realize that the farmers face many problems and we intend to give them every possible consideration."

On the other hand, Burgard understood the seriousness of his military responsibilities. "We have a tremendous job to do in limited time," he said. Thus, construction moved ahead at a rapid pace even as the farmers, such as R. B. Lathem, packed goods, loaded trucks and wagons, and left behind a wheat crop that promised "to be the best since 1924."

Pantex construction crews were close behind. They engineered roads, opened offices, drilled wells, and used the farmstead windmills that were already in place. They planned and laid out assembly buildings, storage facilities, and power plants. In addition, from Amarillo to the Pantex reservation, they widened roads, built power lines, dug sewer and water pipelines, and improved stretches of Highways 60 and 66.

By summer's end, Maj. P. S. Irvine, the commanding officer at Pantex, his staff, and Certain-teen Products Corporation, operators of the facility, had hired assembly plant personnel and set them to work. The workers received careful training, of course, and then established the initial line—many more would follow—for bomb and artillery shell production. On September 18, some five months after ground had been broken on the huge Pantex site, bomb assembly began, and before the day was out assembly line workers "poured" the first bomb at the Pantex Ordnance Plant.[19]

Just before the Pantex plant and the army airfield had opened, Amarillo, named the "City of Parades," held another one. Called the Army Day Parade, it was something of a military tribute to the entire Texas Panhandle. Held on a warm spring day, April 6, the parade attracted tens of thousands of people who, standing six to eight rows deep, lined both sides of Polk and Taylor streets for the giant, ninety-minute procession. Thousands of soldiers marched in the parade, and behind their trim marching formations rolled jeeps, howitzers, antitank and antiaircraft units, field kitchens, hospital corps, six-wheel trucks, and other mechanized equipment. Boy Scouts, 4-H Club students, a long line of mothers with sons at war, and floats formed parts of the parade.

Over three hundred horsemen participated, coming from all parts of the Panhandle. A group of thirty-four came from Dumas. Another group was the Will Rogers Range Riders. Made up of Amarillo business and professional men, the group, organized in 1938, not only rode in parades and similar celebrations but also kept busy during World War II by spending weekends helping Panhandle ranchers who needed extra hands.

More than twenty bands marched in the parade. Most were high school bands from such towns as Happy, Friona, Dumas, Plainview, Hereford, White Deer, Shamrock, and Spearman. The band from Dunbar High School, the African American high school in Lubbock, marched in the parade, as did bands from Amarillo High School and Sam Houston Junior High School. Myers Cadet Band from Emil Myers Music School in Amarillo marched, and a band from West Texas State College in Canyon participated.

The parade offered colorful reminders that World War II was a "united nations" effort against Axis powers. Gaily attired Spanish Americans in native costumes marched, for example, and a group of Chinese children paraded with a sign that read, "We'll march on Tokyo jointly." And one of the floats, sponsored by local folks of Greek heritage and decorated in Greece's colors of blue and white, held a beautiful Greek girl shackled to a post with a sign reading: "Greece will be free again," a reminder that Adolph Hitler's German armies had invaded the Mediterranean country a year earlier.[20]

After the parade, Amarillo joined the rest of the country in settling into the business of war. Because the federal government through its War Production Board halted what it called "nonessential construction," building projects in Amarillo slowed and building permits dropped. Construction of such durable goods as washing machines and automobiles slowed or even stopped. Tire and gasoline rationing began in earnest, and soon other products, especially durable household goods, joined the ration list.

Shortages developed—in both essential and nonessential goods. To compensate, people collected scrap metal for the war effort and grew food for themselves in backyard or neighborhood "victory gardens." They received government ration tickets for certain items, including tires, gasoline, sugar, and butter, and used them to trade with neighbors to help one another in what amounted to heroic efforts to get through the war years. To compensate for a developing paper shortage, the Amarillo Globe-News Corporation cut back the size of its daily newspapers.[21]

Finding jobs was no longer a problem. Government spending, as at the Pantex plant, and the pressure of wartime needs created positions that employers were unable to fill. The Amarillo newspapers switched their want ads section masthead from promotion of real estate opportunities to "Want a Better Job?" The listings in 1942 and 1943 showed plenty of positions available, and the federal government struggled to fill some of its available jobs: the Cactus Ordnance Plant at Dumas, for example, posted a front page announcement in the *Amarillo Daily News* for four hundred additional laborers.

The growing job market during World War II attracted people to Amarillo. And the booming city population coupled with War Production Board controls on lumber and nonessential building created housing shortages. Some families doubled up in single-family units. Some converted their garages into efficiency apartments or bedrooms and rented the temporary spaces to new arrivals. Likewise, attics became upstairs bedrooms or small apartments.[22]

The war created other changes. A teacher shortage developed, for one thing, and class sizes, especially in the secondary schools, increased. Amarillo College, whose enrollment stood at 350 students in the fall of 1942, established a National Defense School. College personnel designed the special classes to train men and women for war production and a skilled profession once the war ended. Among women, housewives, waitresses, sales clerks, stenographers, and beauty operators enrolled for training in sheet metal, machine shop, and airplane engine mechanics classes. They became Amarillo's version of "Rosie the Riveter," a beautiful woman dressed in overalls and working in heavy industry. Men, who had to receive draft board exemptions to do it, signed up for similar classes.[23]

About the same time, September 1942, West Texas State College opened a teaching center in Amarillo. Located in the Early Building at 2101 Harrison, the center, with Roy G. Boger as director, offered upper division and graduate course work. The branch offered more than twenty different classes, including traditional courses in English, history, geography, education, government, economics, and business. Tuition costs, low by modern standards, ranged from ten dollars for one class to twenty-five dollars for four or more courses. The Amarillo Center, ahead of its time, also provided a nursery school for married students with children two, three, and four years old.[24]

A different kind of instruction was available to personnel stationed at the Amarillo airfield's Army Technical School. The soldiers who wanted it got "old fashioned dance instruction." Sponsored by the WPA Recreation Division, the classes were held each Tuesday evening in the Blue Room of the Amarillo Hotel. At least forty soldiers signed up for the first three-hour dance class.

Dancing, in fact, was a major part of the Amarillo-based recreation available to soldiers. Sacred Heart Cathedral, the USO, Woodmen of the World (WOW), the Security Benefit Association, and the Service Men's Civic Center all sponsored weekly dances on different afternoons and evenings. Light meals and teas sometimes accompanied the dances, held at Municipal Auditorium, Sacred Heart Hall, the WOW Hall, the Amarillo Hotel, and Amarillo High School.

Other recreation included bowling, roller-skating, swimming, and barbeques. Or the soldiers, as well as citizens of Amarillo, might enjoy one of the well-manicured golf courses in the city. Several churches and Temple B'Nai Israel sponsored social hours and religious services, afternoon teas, and light suppers.[25]

Amarillo radio stations KFDA and KGNC plus the national networks, NBC, CBS, and MBS, provided music, sports, news, and variety shows. Such programs as *Charlie McCarthy, One Man's Family, The Shadow,* and *The Lone Ranger* were popular in Amarillo. KFDA offered Glenn Miller's Orchestra, Will Bradley's Orchestra, popular music, and, on Sunday mornings, part of the services at Glenwood Baptist Church. KGNC broadcasted Joe Marsala's Orchestra and Rogerio Garcia's Orchestra plus lighter music, news, and programs given over to the day's sports in review.

Downtown theaters during World War II remained popular places. They included the Paramount, of course, and the Mission, plus Capitol, Rialto, Star, Texas, State, Liberty, and Leon. In late September 1942, the Capitol showed *Sergeant York,* starring Gary Cooper, and the

Paramount advertised its movie, *The Talk of the Town,* starring Cary Grant and Jean Arthur. At the Leon, Edward G. Robinson, Marlene Dietrich, and George Raft starred in *Manpower.*

During Tri-State Fair week, Amarillo brought in the Dodson Shows, featuring "America's Largest Midway," to provide carnival rides and other amusements. The carnival set up its booths and rides along Johnson and Grant streets in east Amarillo near the fairgrounds. One of its highlights was the shooting off of a human cannon ball, an event that occurred twice each day. While playing in Amarillo during the war, the "world fair," as it called itself, catered its advertisement to government workers at Pantex and federal military personnel at the airfield's Army Technical School.

Then, suddenly, the federal government enlarged its presence in Amarillo. It determined to expand helium production and at the same time decentralize the operations. Thus, although the small plant just west of Amarillo at Soncy remained the base of operations, the government opened additional helium plants, including one in New Mexico and a very large one in the small community of Excell some thirty miles north of Amarillo. The Excell Helium Plant began operations on March 13, 1943.

Helium has multiple uses, medicine, space exploration, and oceanography among them. During World War II, the government wanted helium for blimps, some of which escorted naval convoys across the Atlantic; in blimp-guarded convoys not a single ship was lost to enemy submarines. The government also needed helium for use in the atomic bombs that it later dropped on Hiroshima and Nagasaki, Japan. Those extraordinarily deadly bombing raids, on August 6 and August 9, 1945, brought an abrupt end to World War II.[26]

Amarillo celebrated the war's end. V-E Day—victory in Europe—celebrations occurred on May 8, 1945, but President Franklin Roosevelt's death a month earlier and the desperate fighting against Japan still in progress in the Pacific tempered the celebrations.

But victory against Japan, V-J Day, was a different matter. In the early evening of August 14, President Harry S Truman announced over the radio that Japan had surrendered. For fully ten minutes afterward, Amarillo "citizens maintained a suspicious calm," claimed an *Amarillo Daily News* reporter, "before they were sure this time was real and the war was over." Then the people exploded with much the same raucous joy that characterized victory celebrations across much of the United States. Thousands of Amarillo people poured onto the streets in celebration. Downtown streets turned "into a bedlam of screaming, hilarious, shouting celebrants blocking traffic on Polk Street from Third to Ninth Avenue." Automobile horns blared and whistles and bells rang, adding "to the deafening roar of a joyous populace."[27]

Pedestrian and auto traffic was heavy and thick. A news reporter noted that it took him seventeen minutes to drive eight blocks along Polk Street. Motorcycle riders whirled across traffic lanes, soldiers and sailors with civilians of all ages walked arm in arm shouting and screaming, a large military truck filled with soldiers and girls and driven by a local businessman sped in and out of the crowded traffic, and ticker tape fell from upper story windows. Marchers carried beer and half-empty liquor bottles, waved flags, and shouted with unrestrained joy.

Various individuals found "special ways to celebrate." An older man, perhaps in his eighties, stood on the Amarillo Hotel corner and, as he watched the excited participants before him, held a small flag in the breeze and enjoyed the thundering noise. Two dancing girls and a man with a fiddle entertained celebrants on the corner of Seventh and Polk. A couple of blocks away a soldier and a civilian led an impromptu group in singing. People set off at least three fire alarms, and "a youthful prankster pulled a main switch at the State Theater," closing down all the lights and sounds for several minutes.

Then rain began falling. The first significant rain in several months, it drove the downtown merry-makers inside. By nine o'clock, drenched from the heavy rain (one and a half inches by ten o'clock), people dispersed and their celebrations became less animated. Several churches opened their doors for quiet prayers of thanksgiving that the war was over, and in the chapel at Saint Anthony's Hospital, Father Bartholomew O'Brien held special vespers.[28]

The next day, Wednesday, August 15, Amarillo took a holiday. Most stores, businesses, and banks did not open. City and county offices remained closed. The post office did not deliver mail. At 11:00 a.m., Rabbi Arthur Bluhm conducted a solemn victory service at the Temple B'nai Israel. Several Amarillo churches also conducted morning worship ceremonies, and F. A. Foster, rector at Saint Andrew's Episcopal Church, offered Holy Communion services. Churches that held regular Wednesday night prayer meetings planned thanksgiving observances for the evening. Sacred Heart Cathedral, for example, planned special masses for six, seven, eight, and nine o'clock.[29]

The great joy and relief over the war's end continued on Thursday, as most people went back to work. Mayor Joe Jenkins and Chief of Police Sid Harper asked that liquor stores and nightclubs remain closed, and they got cafés and other beer dispensers to refrain from selling beer until Friday. The federal post office did not open, and postmen did not deliver the mail, but banks, businesses, and stores resumed operations—without many of the wartime controls.[30]

Reconversion to a peacetime economy began quickly. On the national level, the government encouraged the big automobile companies to begin again to manufacture private vehicles. The Department of Agriculture indicated that meat rationing would end soon, and a government announcement noted that such sundry, but important, items as radios, nylon stockings, and durable goods for use in homes would soon be available again. The government lifted war manpower controls over employment. The Office of Defense Transportation lifted the national thirty-five-mile-per-hour speed limit—designed to conserve rubber tires—that had been a federal order since 1942. J. Monroe Johnson, who announced the speed limit change, warned motorists, however, that neither the older tires nor cars still being used could stand high speeds.

In Amarillo some stores, such as Levine's, White and Kirk, and

Gordon's Shoe Depot, advertised that shoes, once rationed, were available on a limited basis. The Sears Roebuck store offered tires, which were temporarily off the ration list, for sale. Grocery stores began for the first time in three years to sell processed foods without ration stamps being required, and service stations likewise began dispensing gasoline without asking for ration stamps.[31]

Pantex closed. Government officials made the announcement on August 15, 1945, and the people of Amarillo received the sobering news amid their joyous celebrations over the war's end. The gates closed on the seventeenth. H. F. McFarland Jr., manager of the plant, retained only those employees needed for essential operations and safety, and he stated that all other workers were "free to move about and seek new jobs without war manpower restraints." Combined with the closing of the Cactus Ordnance plant, some four thousand or more people were suddenly without work.

The Amarillo Helium Plant also stopped production. Although the plant at Excell continued its operations, the Soncy plant ceased producing helium on September 1. It remained open as a research facility and as headquarters for helium activity.

With the war over, the airfield's strategic use also decreased. As a result, army and civilian personnel at the field declined in numbers through the fall. Although it remained active for another year, the Amarillo Army Airfield closed on September 15, 1946.[32]

The closings put thousands of people out of work. Indeed, the War Manpower Commission, citing forty-seven hundred military jobs in the city as being lost, listed Amarillo as one of seven cities in Texas facing "serious unemployment." To help, government agencies issued reports about employment opportunities and encouraged local officials to find work for the people discharged from defense jobs. One of the officials, a Mr. Wells, noted that in the Texas Panhandle in general and in Amarillo in particular wholesalers, retailers, and transporters needed employees. The transportation industry, he indicated, "including motor freight and bus lines, railroads and airlines are understaffed and need truck and bus drivers, mechanics, cargo handlers and dock-men."[33]

For these reasons and others, getting back to a "normal," nonwar way of life in Amarillo represented little difficulty. Agriculture and petroleum were the keys. The two dominant Texas Panhandle industries helped the local economy grow. Amarillo, already the administrative heart for oil operations, soon became the busy center of an agribusiness industry expanding to fill opportunities associated with a boom in irrigated farming. City manufacturers needed workers to produce pumps, tubular goods, sprinklers, and other equipment connected to large-scale irrigation.

Moreover, individual savings, which had accumulated during wartime controls, provided citizens with purchasing power that had not existed since before the Great Depression. Consumer goods, particularly durable goods, were in demand, and people could afford them. Thus, as the federal government lifted controls on radios, washing machines, and other household goods, the American people went on a buying spree.

Amarillo followed the national trend. In dollar amounts retail sales in the city more than doubled in the five years before 1951, expanding from $49 million to $118.5 million. Home construction boomed, and when they became available in the city, new automobiles from the reconverted Ford, Chrysler, and General Motors plants fairly jumped off the reestablished car lots. Between 1946 and 1951, write Price and Rathjen, automobile "registrations in Randall and Potter counties . . . increased from 20,000 [to 42,473]."[34]

A dominant feature of post–World War II Amarillo was the city's remarkable prosperity. The economy soared, and living standards improved. As elsewhere in America, people in Amarillo who had lived through the Great Depression and World War II had known for fifteen years mostly deprivation and sacrifice. Now, after the war, they enjoyed a growing prosperity, a rising affluence, and an improving sense of social contentment. Life was upbeat. Families increased in size. People sought to accumulate goods.

The city's population expanded. Indeed, despite the closings of Pantex and the Amarillo Army Airfield, it increased by nearly 50 percent during the war decade, reaching in 1950 a total of 74,246 residents. Part of the increase came from Amarillo-area war veterans returning home to school, new jobs, and wives. The babies that followed helped to produce the nationwide "baby boom" generation.

In Amarillo, the postwar population surge spread the city's newer residential districts away from the downtown area toward the southwest. Although growth followed Route 66 northeast of the city, most people looked to buy homes in subdivisions that stretched away from downtown toward the southwest along Highway 87. A warehouse district, the Tri-State Fairgrounds, and the huge Amarillo Army Airfield cut off expansion east of the downtown district.

Problems appeared. Perhaps the most devastating one occurred on Sunday evening, May 15, 1949, when a huge tornado ripped through the city killing five people, injuring nearly three hundred others, and bringing major wreckage to homes and businesses. Called the "first destructive tornado in the [sixty-two-year] history of Amarillo," the storm struck hard in a residential section south of Thirty-sixth Avenue and east of Washington Street, but the whirling twister also smashed into several other areas of the city. A heavy rain accompanied the tornado, flooding "the entire city," and hail, ranging "up to the size of a baseball," added to the damage.[35]

For several days prior to the Amarillo tornado, typical spring storms had moved across the Texas Panhandle. High winds, significant rainfall, and pelting hail accompanied the storms, and on May 14 a series of five separate twisters danced through Potter and Carson counties.

The five tornadoes damaged wheat fields and farm buildings, including homes. The first one, appearing about five o'clock in the afternoon, dipped out of the clouds about ten miles northeast of Amarillo. It moved toward the northwest, apparently, before rolling eastward to "drift . . . across Carson County" and disappear in the dense rain. A period of quiet followed, but then "multiple attacks from [four] twisters turned the [evening] into a nightmare." The tornadoes struck in Carson County near Panhandle and along U.S. Highway 60, where everyone "was driving with a half-eye to the road and the rest of their attention . . . centered on the cloud." No one was injured.[36]

The next day Amarillo took its turn. The vicious, three-pronged tornado dipped to earth at 8:22 p.m., flattened a twenty-block area of residential homes in south Amarillo, and blew a train of thirty-five cars off the tracks on the Santa Fe line. It skipped around the city, striking the area near Thirty-sixth and Fillmore, the Tradewinds Airport, the Tri-State Fairgrounds, and the Amarillo Air Terminal. It destroyed seventy-six homes, damaged three hundred others, wrecked forty-five aircraft at the Tradewinds facility, leveled buildings at the fairgrounds, and smashed the Massey-Harris farm machinery company near the air terminal. Destruction amounted to nearly five million dollars.

The tornado damaged several businesses. It wrecked the Barfield Lumber Company, El Rancho Motel, Craig Implement, Munday-Cooper Lumber Company, four service stations, and a restaurant. The Santa Fe train that derailed contained eleven livestock cars, each loaded with either cattle or hogs. The animals escaped from the broken train cars and, write Ray Franks and Jay Ketelle, wandered "around in the post-storm rubble."

For many people the tornado was a catastrophe. The five people who died—George A. McPherson and his wife, Mrs. Charles Maserang, Lois Martin, and Myrtle Marrs—all lived in the south Amarillo area that suffered the severest blow. Others lost their homes, household goods, personal possessions, and automobiles. The storm scattered small pets such as cats and dogs. It knocked out utilities, some of which the city was not able to restore for several days, and power lines went down. The hospitals filled with dozens of injured people.

Mayor Gene Kline ordered the worst-stricken area closed. He called in the city police and asked county officers and highway patrolmen to secure the area. National Guardsmen moved into the region to help, and by midnight the area was under police control. The guardsmen kept would-be looters, curious sightseers, and others out of the damaged zone.

Early the next morning, people turned to cleaning up. They boarded up or repaired homes, raked up and hauled off debris, sought temporary places in which to live, tidied less-damaged homes, and in general moved to reorder their lives. To help families who had suffered various losses from the tornado, the Amarillo Globe-News Corporation created a Tornado Fund and asked citizens of the city to contribute. Within twenty-four hours some twenty-three thousand dollars had been raised, and the contributions increased afterward.[37]

Amarillo and its citizens recovered from the shocking tornado, and they recovered quickly. Indeed, the post–World War II prosperity that characterized Amarillo at the time of the tornado aided the recovery and helped launch the city into a two-decade-long period of expansion. But other events, both at home and abroad, also marked a turning point in Amarillo's history.

9

A Period of Expansion, 1950–1975

During the two decades following the 1949 tornado, Amarillo grew up. Its population doubled, and to accommodate such growth the city expanded, extending its boundaries toward the south and west. New businesses came to town, and older ones enlarged operations and often relocated them. The downtown area changed and then lost the retail heart of the city to suburbanlike shopping centers scattered near the distant residential sections. Along a colorful stretch of highway—"the Strip," people called it—in northeast Amarillo, where for about six miles Routes 60 and 66 run together, motels, restaurants, service stations, and other businesses catering to automobile traffic sprang up. During the period, the city also witnessed important changes in its social and cultural life.

The Graham Plow Company illustrates the growth and change. Its history dates to the Depression years of the early 1930s, when Fred Hoeme, a farmer in Hooker, Oklahoma, noticed that wheat in a field across where he had dragged some chisel-like scrap metal grew better and produced a higher yield than the rest of the crop. Surprised but "realizing that he had something," the innovative farmer experimented with his field equipment, trying to develop a workable plow that might exercise wheat lands in ways similar to the scrap metal.[1]

While he may not have understood soil science, Hoeme created the prototype for a remarkable piece of farm equipment. Through a series of chisel-like plowshares, the Hoeme plow reached under the topsoil and broke open the ground. The action, as B. Byron Price and Frederick W. Rathjen note, "helped the soil catch and retain rainfall while leaving the topsoil intact and covered with a stubble mulch which, in turn, served to hold moisture and to prevent the soil from blowing." The two Panhandle historians, referring to the dry, semi-arid farmlands of the region, call the Hoeme plow possibly "the most important single technological innovation in the cause of soil and water conservation."[2]

About 1938, after a few years of experimenting on his chisel plow, Hoeme sought help. He sent his son with the plow to William T. Graham of Silverton in Briscoe County, Texas, to demonstrate the machine to Graham, a highly regarded "scientific" farmer. Impressed, Graham in 1940 bought the invention, formed a partnership with Hoeme, and continued to improve the plow, obtaining some fifty-two patents in the process.

The new business, called Graham-Hoeme Plow Company for a time, opened a small shop at 407 Fillmore in Amarillo. Because the chisel plow it produced "revolutionized the farming industry," the company, with orders coming from places as far away as South Africa and Australia, soon moved to a larger manufacturing plant on West Seventh near the old Northwest Texas Hospital. It employed more than one hundred workers to build what Graham called in company advertising "the plow that saves the soil." Eventually, Graham dropped "Hoeme" from the company name, and in the late 1940s and in the 1950s his company "attracted world-wide attention" and enjoyed sales on a growing international market.[3]

Other agribusiness activities helped push Amarillo's growth. One of them, occurring across much of the Texas Panhandle, was the expansion of irrigated farming.

The dramatic increase in irrigation stemmed from at least two developments: declining rainfall and, to fuel the huge irrigation pumps needed for such work, cheap natural gas. During World War II the larger Texas Panhandle–South Plains region had received an abundant amount of moisture to support the important cotton and wheat crops. Then, in the period from about 1948 to 1951, the upper Panhandle again got sufficient rain, especially during the spring and summer growing seasons, to sustain dry-land farming operations.

But beginning in 1951, the Texas Panhandle, and in fact much of West Texas, entered a long period of drought. Rainfall amounts declined well below levels to sustain agriculture, and the return of dust clouds revived concerns of another Dust Bowl phenomenon. Amarillo, for example, recorded only 12.15 inches of rain in 1952, an amount some six inches short of average, and in 1956, the worst year in terms of the 1950s drought, the city received only 9.94 inches of moisture. San Angelo–based farm and ranch writer Elmer Kelton in his popular novel *The Time It Never Rained* described the long drought's impact on cattlemen in the Edwards Plateau country. In the Panhandle, write Price and Rathjen, the soil conservation practices learned in the 1930s perhaps prevented a "mini-Dust Bowl."[4]

Irrigation followed. Farmers drilled wells; purchased pumps, tubular goods, and related equipment; and prepared their fields for over ground irrigation. The number of wells on the Texas High Plains increased from 14,000 irrigating 1.86 million acres in 1950 to 27,500 irrigating 3.5 million acres four years later. The large Panhandle Oil and Gas Field provided cheap fuel in the form of natural gas, and the huge, deep Ogallala aquifer, which extends from Texas to the southern edge of South Dakota, provided the water.

In Amarillo, irrigation-based agribusinesses increased in number. Entrepreneurs opened shops to manufacture and sell pumps, tubular goods, and sprinklers. The city's banks provided financing, and its businesses provided fertilizers, pesticides, processing plants, and grain and cotton storage facilities. Irrigation increased such row-crop agriculture as cotton and grain sorghum production, which in turn increased the popularity of tractors and, of course, tractor-drawn equipment. Thus, farm implement and tractor dealerships opened. The result was an irrigation-inspired agricultural boom that increased Amarillo's growth in the 1950s.

The reopening of the Pantex Army Ordnance Plant also impacted Amarillo's economic and population growth. Texas Technological College since 1949 had been using the Pantex grounds as an agricultural experiment station, but as a result of the increasing post–World War II tensions between the United States and the Soviet Union—the beginning of the Cold War—and the outbreak in 1950 of the short but bitter war in Korea, the federal government needed the place. Thus, in 1950 the government's Atomic Energy Commission occupied the giant Pantex facility. It wanted to manufacture conventional bombs and similar weapons as it had produced in World War II, plus, now in the 1950s, the new, controversial, and highly explosive nuclear warheads.

Shortly afterward, the federal government contracted with Procter and Gamble to manage the plant. Pantex became a typical "go-co"—government-owned, contractor operated—ordnance plant. Its workers, about twenty-six hundred of them in 1986, became involved in the fabrication and testing of conventional high explosives and in the assembly, disassembly, modification, and repair of nuclear weapons. In 1956 Mason and Hanger-Silas Mason Company, a Kentucky-based engineering firm that had built the Lincoln Tunnel in New York City and the Grand Coulee Dam across the Columbia River, replaced Procter and Gamble.[5]

The war in Korea and the Cold War that had inspired the reopening of Pantex also caused the federal government to reactivate the old Amarillo Army Airfield. Reestablished in March 1951 as Amarillo Air Force Base, the place became a giant multipurpose facility. The Department of Defense increased the installation to 5,273 acres. Its military and civilian employees trained jet engine mechanics and guided missile technicians, and they retrained airmen. The base, which at peak times may have accommodated as many as twenty-five thousand airmen with one of the longest runways in the world, also supported units of the Strategic Air Command (SAC) with their high-flying, high-speed B-58 Hustler aircraft that in the sky created sharp contrails and sonic booms.

The air base also served as a technical training school for SAC units. In addition to the B-58 Hustler, SAC located its 461st Bombardment Wing (Heavy) at the base. The 461st included the 764th Bombardment Squadron (B-52s) and the 909th Refueling Squadron (KC-135s). SAC units practiced simulated radar bombing on theoretical targets—various Panhandle communities—and such other high-flying maneuvers as refueling while in flight.

Pantex and the Amarillo Air Force Base provided economic, social, and cultural benefits to the city. Because they made Amarillo an important part of America's national defense efforts, local citizens took some pride in having the key facilities located near their city. More importantly, however, federal money in the form of impact funds went to local school districts. The two facilities, in addition, provided regular payrolls and purchased large amounts of goods and services. Their employees and their military personnel patronized local restaurants, coffee shops, and retail establishments. Some of them purchased homes. They supported cultural activities like school concerts and stage plays. They attended performances of the Amarillo Symphony Orchestra and participated in events at the Amarillo Little Theater and the Amarillo Art Center. They visited local theaters and amusement parks.

The reactivated facilities helped change Amarillo. A building boom in 1952, for example, saw more motels open in the city than in any other year. In 1925, the city directory listed four "tourist camps." In 1952, as a result of the reactivation of Pantex and the air base coupled with the growth of cross-country automobile traffic, the directory listed sixty-eight motels, tourist courts, inns, and lodges.

Many of the new motels appeared along the Strip, that is, Northeast Eighth Avenue, or Amarillo Boulevard, where U.S. Highways 60 and 66 run together. It became "motel row," or, as some people called it, "the Main Street of America." Schuyler A. Woody, for example, in 1952 opened his twenty-unit Palo Duro Motel at 2820 Northeast Eighth.

According to Ray Franks and Jay Ketelle, he advertised "reasonable rates, free ice, newspapers and coffee bar." Also in 1952, James W. Bailey built Bailey's Motel at 2830 Northeast Eighth. And far out on the east end of the strip, at 5407 Northeast Eighth Avenue, Keith Applegate in 1955 opened his Colonial Courts. With forty units, the operation was one of the largest motel complexes in Amarillo at the time, and because it existed near the Amarillo Air Force Base, it proved to be a favorite lodging place for dependents of military personnel and visitors to the base.[6]

On the west end of Route 66, other motels and restaurants also appeared. The Skyline Motel, for example, opened in 1952 at 5711 West Ninth, across from the Veterans' Hospital. The location remained the same, but the address later changed to Amarillo Boulevard West. Ralph Cox ran the motel, and in his advertisements he featured the motel's Tumbleweed Café. Nearby, at West 66 and the Circle, Homer Jacob started the Broncho Lodge and Restaurant. Opened in 1952 and called the "Home of the Chuck Wagon Spread," the motel included in its advertisements "refrigerated air, heated swimming pool, and free television."

Restaurants, cafés, and service stations also appeared along Route 66. One of the most impressive was Rice's Dining Salon. Opened as Long Champ Dining Salon in 1945 at 705 Northeast Eighth Avenue, its name changed in 1953. Homer Rice had purchased the Long Champ in 1947 from Harry Kindig, changed the name six years later, and built, according to Wes Izzard of the *Amarillo Daily News*, the "largest restaurant sign between New York and Los Angeles." A long-time city landmark, the restaurant's five-thousand-bulb billboard also "served as a beacon for hungry people traversing Highway 66" for nearly thirty years.[7]

In 1956 Underwood's Bar-B-Q opened at 4513 Northeast Eighth Avenue. Don Rappe managed the facility, one of many such cafeterias in the Southwest, for a time. His advertisement read: "serving delicious hickory-smoked barbecued beef, chicken, ham, ribs and sausage with all the trimmings." A few years later Underwood's moved to 301 West Amarillo Boulevard.

he Great West Mill and Elevator Company facility was built in 1921 at 2400 Northeast Third venue. (Courtesy Amarillo Public Library)

hen the Potter County Free Library building was built in 1922 at a cost of twenty-five thou-nd dollars, it became the first county library in Texas to be housed in a building built specifi-lly for it. (Courtesy Amarillo Public Library)

Left to right: Cowboy Sam Dunn; W. H. Bush, owner of the Frying Pan Ranch; W. W. Wetzel, mayor of Amarillo; and Mrs. Wetzel stand before the Tacovas Springs headquarters of the Frying Pan Ranch in 1922. (Courtesy Panhandle-Plains Historical Museum)

At Tacovas Springs in 1922. Front row (left to right): W. H. Bush, Jack Hall, two unknown, Sam Dunn, and W. W. Wetzel. Back row (left to right): C. O. Wolflin, James Bush, and Tom Curry. (Courtesy Panhandle-Plains Historical Museum)

Municipal Auditorium opened in 1923. (Courtesy Panhandle-Plains Historical Museum)

Gateway to the Tri-State Exposition, 1924. (Courtesy Amarillo Public Library)

Melissa Dora Oliver-Eakle and her daughter, Oliver Rea Eakle. (Courtesy Panhandle-Plains Historical Museum)

The M. D. Oliver-Eakle Building was located at the southwest corner of Sixth and Polk streets. Melissa Dora Oliver-Eakle built the ten-story office building in 1927; it became the Barfield Building in 1947. (Courtesy Amarillo Public Library)

glish Field hangar with a biplane parked in front, 1930. (Courtesy Amarillo Public Library)

The Paramount Theater, 817 Polk Street, 1936. The theater opened in 1932 and closed in 1969. (Courtesy Amarillo Public Library)

Looking north on Polk Street in the early 1930s. (Courtesy Amarillo Public Library)

ieneral Tire Company building with employees standing in front, 1933. (Courtesy Amarillo ublic Library)

onfederate annual reunion, 1935. In the second row, the two men on the left end (l to r) are am Page and Gene Howe; on the front row are, fourth from left, Ross Rogers, and, second from ght, John Snider, known as the Amarillo Barbecue King. (Courtesy Amarillo Public Library)

The Double Dip Drive-In was located at 1323 Polk Street. It was built in 1930, and the tower was added in 1935. One of the first drive-ins in Amarillo, it was across the street from Amarillo High School, and it was very popular among students from the 1930s to the 1960s. (Courtesy Amarillo Public Library)

Children and their Easter baskets on the grounds of the Amarillo Country Club, 1937. (Courtesy Amarillo Public Library)

Iother-in-law Day Parade, 1938. The bouquet of five thousand fresh roses, weighing approxi-ately twenty-five hundred pounds, was presented to Eleanor Roosevelt. (Courtesy Amarillo ublic Library)

lk Street was the center of activity, circa 1938. Automobiles line the street as people attend the ramount Theater. (Courtesy Amarillo Public Library)

Spanish Courts tourist motel showing apartments and sign in 1939. (Courtesy Amarillo Public Library)

Gene Howe, "Mr. Hare," an unknown visitor to Amarillo, and Ross Rogers. (Courtesy Amarillo Public Library)

bert R. Young (left) and Amarillo newspaper publisher Gene Howe with Howe's dog, Princess, 17. (Courtesy Amarillo Public Library)

Lawrence Hagy. (Courtesy Panhandle-Plains Historical Museum)

Airmen march in Amarillo's Armistice Day Parade, which marked the official opening and dedication of Amarillo Air Force Base in 1951. (Courtesy Amarillo Public Library)

marillo Stadium, 1952. (Courtesy Amarillo Public Library)

uffalo Lake, located thirty-one miles southwest of Amarillo on U.S. Highway 60, served recreational and sporting needs for many years. (Courtesy Amarillo Public Library)

Snow covers Polk Street on this winter day in the late 1950s. (Courtesy Amarillo Public Library)

An aerial view of downtown Amarillo shows the Santa Fe Building at the top left. The street jus to the right (east) of the Santa Fe Building, running north-south, is Polk Street. To the east of Polk is Taylor, then Fillmore, then Pierce, and finally Buchanan Street on the right side of the photo. (Courtesy Amarillo Public Library)

Boone Pickens. (Courtesy Panhandle-Plains Historical Museum)

Sybil Harrington. (Courtesy Panhandle-Plains Historical Museum)

Route 66 was not the only part of Amarillo that experienced growth. In 1953 Charles A. Wolflin, a developer and son and nephew of the Wolflin brothers who operated George H. Wolflin Dry Goods, opened Wolflin Village at the corner of Georgia and Wolflin streets in the city's southwestern section. Amarillo's first suburban shopping center, it contained thirteen stores including a service station (Duvall's Texaco Station) and McCartt's Super Market plus the convenience of store-front parking. Three years later, the developer completed a second unit that included Barnes Jewelers, T.G.&Y., and Colbert's Department Store.

Similar shopping malls went up in other parts of the city, and over time they drained Polk Street and the downtown area of significant retail operations. Sunset Center, Amarillo's first enclosed mall, opened in 1960 with forty-eight stores, including J. C. Penney, which was the largest, F. W. Woolworth, Safeway, Western Auto, Wyatt's Cafeteria, S. H. Kress, Lerner, and others, including the Hub, one of Polk Street's most successful clothiers. M. T. Johnson Jr. developed the ultra-modern mall, which he located on land that had been the Sunset Golf Course.[8]

It was a major blow to downtown retailing when Sears, Roebuck, and Company moved. Sears, which had anchored the corner of Tenth Avenue and Polk Street for twenty-eight years, moved in 1957 to a 115,000-square-foot building on land across from what became the Sunset Center. Twenty-five years later it moved again, this time to Westgate Mall.

City expansion and population growth accompanied by national political issues brought changes to the Amarillo public schools. Prior to 1950 the Amarillo Independent School District (AISD) consisted of twelve elementary schools, three junior high schools, and two high schools: Amarillo High and North Heights, located in a predominately black neighborhood. But in response to the phenomenal increase in Amarillo's population, the school district built during the decade of the 1950s twelve additional elementary schools, four junior high schools, and three new high schools: Palo Duro, Tascosa, and George Washington Carver.

Carver, located at 1905 Northwest Avenue, opened in 1958 as a junior/senior high school to replace the aging North Heights school building. It served Amarillo's black community, which made up about 6 percent of the city's population. But in 1954 the U.S. Supreme Court in *Brown v. Board of Education of Topeka* had ruled that segregated schools were unconstitutional. Because President Dwight Eisenhower moved cautiously to enforce the ruling, however, Amarillo's white citizens were slow to desegregate their schools.

After passage of the Civil Rights Act of 1964, pressure on Amarillo to integrate mounted. And after 1966 district leaders phased out the upper grades at the eight-year-old building, and Carver became a junior high school. Black high school students enrolled in Amarillo, Palo Duro, and Tascosa high schools, but integration at all levels did not occur until 1972 in response to a federal court order demanding an end to segregation.

As part of the educational changes taking place in the 1950s, the AISD closed McKinley Elementary School, which had been constructed in the 1920s just west of downtown at Seventh Avenue and Washington Street near Old Town Amarillo. District personnel remodeled the structure and converted it into an administrative offices building for the AISD system. They opened it in 1958.

As economic growth in the 1950s and physical expansion altered the city's appearance, Amarillo's politics underwent something of a transformation. People of the city for the most part had always been conservative in political outlook, but Amarillo's politics, write Price and Rathjen, were a "pragmatic conservatism . . . articulated by such public spokesmen as Gene Howe" and expressed through "the traditional virtues of openness, trust, and personal respect upon which Panhandle people took justifiable pride." Although conservative, Amarillo had generally voted Democratic in local, state, and national elections. Such a voting pattern began to shift in the 1950s and afterward.[9]

Presidential elections reveal the trend. In the 1948 election, Harry S Truman, the Democratic candidate, carried both Amarillo and Potter County by a better than two-to-one ratio over the Republican candidate Thomas E. Dewey. In Texas during the 1952 and 1956 elections, both pitting Republican Dwight D. Eisenhower against Democrat Adlai E. Stevenson, a "Democrats for Eisenhower" movement was strong, and, in part because of the "tidelands" oil dispute, the Democratic governor of Texas, Allen Shivers, openly backed Eisenhower. Then in the 1960 presidential contest, although Democrat John F. Kennedy won on the national level, the election in Potter and Randall counties, including Amarillo, went to the Republican candidate, Richard M. Nixon, by a margin of three votes to two.[10]

But clearly more than party switching was involved. In the 1960 election, for example, religious bigotry may have been a factor, as many Texans, including some from Amarillo, voted for the Protestant candidate Nixon over the Catholic Kennedy. Of greater importance, however, was the idea that the Democratic Party had fallen into the hands of an "eastern establishment" and the perceived shift of the party toward a traditional liberal agenda that included "internationalism" and big government.

Moreover, America in the 1960s gave the impression of a country "coming apart." Civil rights demonstrations that turned violent; major rioting in some of the larger cities over several summers; the growing rift with the Soviet Union; the Vietnam War and unending protests related to it; such colorful, but sometimes disgusting, motorcycle gangs as Hell's Angels; new music trends, such as those represented by the Beatles, that some people found incomprehensible; the assassination of President John F. Kennedy; and other developments added to the tensions, confusion, and sense of chaos.

Communities across the country responded in different ways. In Amarillo and the Texas Panhandle, one form of response was to turn toward the conservative wing of the Republican political party. Most people in the area supported what has been described as "a kind of 'aristocratic' intellectual 'new conservatism'" that found voice in the *National Review,* edited by William F. Buckley Jr.—ideals not much different from the region's traditional "pragmatic conservatism."

Other people, in what Price and Rathjen call a dramatic departure from the region's political norms, turned to the more dogmatic and far-right wing John Birch Society. Founded by Robert Welch, a New England candy manufacturer, the "militant," doctrinaire, strongly anti-Communist group saw Communist conspiracies everywhere in America and accused such distinguished Americans as President Dwight Eisenhower, Secretary of State John Foster Dulles, and Chief Justice of the Supreme Court Earl Warren as harboring Communists. For a time in the 1960s and early 1970s, Amarillo claimed a large and active John Birch Society, but because its political ideals repulsed many people, the group declined in popularity and membership. Indeed, it and the ideals it espoused seem to have been little more than an "aberration."[11]

Political confusion aside, Amarillo continued its economic expansion. Highway improvement represented some of the growth, particularly south along U.S. Highway 87 toward Canyon. On December 1, 1960, the cities of Canyon and Amarillo held simultaneous dedication ceremonies at either end of the new Amarillo-Canyon Expressway. Marshall Formby of Plainview, former chairman of the Texas Highway Commission, cut a symbolic ribbon in Canyon, and Hal Woodward, an active member of the commission from Coleman performed the honors at the Amarillo end. A four-lane super highway, the expressway, called "the greatest single achievement in West Texas in highway history," carried a price tag of nine million dollars. Dedication activities included speeches and a flyover by four T-33 air force jet trainers. The Amarillo Air Force Band played, and a drill team from Laughlin Air Force Base in Abilene performed. Afterward, Stanley Blackburn of the Chamber of Commerce and Joe Pool of the Amaday committee hosted an "Amaday luncheon" at the Amarillo Country Club.[12]

Eight years later in a similar ceremony, Amarillo leaders officially opened Interstate Highway 40. The big concrete marvel, made possible by a 1956 federal highway construction law that authorized the government to accept 90 percent of the cost for building limited-access roadways, sliced through the heart of Amarillo just south of the downtown district. Running east and west, the major thoroughfare not only cut

Amarillo in half but also replaced portions of U.S. Highway 60 through the city and in effect eliminated Highway 66, the glorious old "Mother Road" of John Steinbeck's novel.

Super highways, such as Interstate 40 and the Amarillo-Canyon Expressway, added to the economy. Construction activity, materials contracts, and worker payrolls boomed auxiliary businesses, and the completed highways eased automobile traffic and increased the motor freight.

But some things were lost. On a national level, for example, the new commitment to automobile transportation came in part at the expense of the country's railroad system, already in a state of advanced decay. On a local level, Amarillo's railroads continued to lose customers, cut back operations, and lay off workers. On the other hand, as depots closed and freight offices handled smaller amounts of traffic, bus lines and motor freight companies, especially the large, cross-country firms, moved into the carrying niche, opened local offices, hired drivers and truckers, and in general assumed responsibility for transporting people and freight.

There were other losses. To make room for the new highways, for example, scores of people lost their homes through condemnation proceedings. Old businesses, such as the El Rancho Motel along U.S. Highways 60 and 87 in the thirty-five hundred block of South Fillmore, became isolated and lost their identity. Some businesses closed; some moved; and some, like El Rancho Motel, changed the nature of their operations. Along old Route 66 (Northeast Eighth Avenue), many service stations, motels, and restaurants that had served tourists moving through Amarillo, having lost their economic viability, closed or moved—some to access roads along the new Interstate 40. And, as indicated earlier, even Route 66, America's Main Street, lost its identity and eventually its designation.

Nonetheless, other construction added to Amarillo's growth. Under the leadership of Mayor F. V. Wallace, a special commission early in the 1960s designed something of a master plan for the city's enhancement, and in 1964 the people of Amarillo accepted the plan and approved the issue of $13 million in bonds for capital improvements. The plan called for the construction downtown of a new civic auditorium, convention center, and municipal office building, and in southwest Amarillo, an area of the city that was rapidly growing, the creation of a public library branch building. The downtown complex, bounded by Third and Seventh avenues and Buchanan and Fillmore streets, covered some eight square blocks.

Forty years later, the people of Amarillo remained justifiably proud of the large complex. As described by Price and Rathjen, the auditorium, equipped for dramatic and musical productions, contained seating for twenty-five hundred people. The spacious and adaptable coliseum, capable of seating seventy-four hundred people, has hosted three-ring circus performances, ice hockey games, and other large indoor events. Exhibit halls and banquet facilities cover twenty-seven thousand square feet in a design flexible enough to accommodate both large and small events of varying kinds.[13]

Meanwhile, on November 1, 1966, northeast of the city, Texas Panhandle and South Plains leaders dedicated the large Sanford Dam. Standing 228 feet high and extending more than a mile in length, it stretched across the Canadian River in Hutchinson County. Designed for many purposes, the dam created a huge reservoir, Lake Meredith, whose waters became a recreation area, controlled down river flooding, and provided a precious natural resource for some eleven cities that had joined the Canadian River Municipal Water Authority and financed the dam's construction.

The vital project was a long time aborning. As early as the mid-1920s, Amarillo leaders, including A. S. Stinnett, Alson Asa "A. A." Meredith, Gene Howe, and others, sought a dam on the Canadian River to provide for the future water needs of their city. Many people wanted some measure of flood control along the shallow, sandy river that in years of heavy spring rains caused crop and livestock damage, washed away shorelines, and threatened human lives. In the semi-arid regions of the Panhandle, some people liked the idea of using the dammed-up waters for irrigation. Everyone seemed to support the idea of recreational use of the reservoir behind the dam.[14]

In December 1936, inspired by the decade's drought and dust storms, some forty-eight men met in Amarillo to form a "conservation association." The men, who came from several different Panhandle communities, wanted to protect and conserve water resources, "the most valuable" of Panhandle assets. Within a week, they had created the Panhandle Water Conservation Association and made John L. McCarty, editor of the *Amarillo Daily News,* president of the organization. With headquarters in the Amarillo Chamber of Commerce office, the group went to work, seeking to get legislative authority for their work. They succeeded, and on May 4, 1937, Governor James V. Allred signed legislation creating the Panhandle Water Conservation Authority (PWCA).[15]

The new agency gave thirty-two counties in the Panhandle broad conservation authority. It held legal powers to control, store, preserve, and distribute waters of the Red, Canadian, and Brazos rivers and their tributaries. As a state agency, its authority extended to domestic, municipal, flood control, irrigation, hydroelectric power, recreational, irrigation, reclamation, and other useful purposes of the upper river basins. But when related federal government agencies, such as the Department of Agriculture, refused to cooperate, the PWCA floundered.

Still, it got for the Panhandle some water conservation projects. With WPA funds and workers, dams went up across several Panhandle creeks: Tierra Blanca, McClellan, and North Tule. Water impounded behind the 835-foot-long earthen dam across Tierra Blanca Creek created Buffalo Lake in western Randall County. Some fifty thousand people attended the dam's formal opening in May 1939. Besides the dam, the visitors saw that workers had erected an all-purpose pavilion and several cabins. Buffalo Lake was a major recreation area for Amarillo until 1978, when a flood led to its closing.[16]

With such success, the PWCA turned to the Canadian River. With help from the Amarillo Chamber of Commerce, it approached the U.S. Army Corps of Engineers and the federal Bureau of Reclamation for a dam across the Canadian north of Amarillo or near Sanford. Both agencies, unconvinced of the need for a dam to control flooding, delayed decisions on a dam.

Then came the great Canadian River flood. Following several days of heavy rains, the river on September 22, 1941, spilled out of its banks, flooding bordering lands along the stream from New Mexico through Texas to Oklahoma. The flood broke gas lines, downed bridges, isolated such communities as Boise City, Oklahoma, and prevented trains from reaching other towns such as Dalhart, Texas. North of Amarillo, the river rose twenty-four feet, with water surging to within inches of the U.S. Highway 87 bridge and threatening highway and railroad traffic in the area.[17]

Still no dam was built. Although the flood altered the thinking of Bureau of Reclamation personnel, the Japanese bombing of Pearl Harbor in December ended all dam projects for Amarillo and the Texas Panhandle. After the war, mainly because the Corps of Engineers worried over cost-effectiveness, delays continued. But efforts to get the dam continued. Amarillo mayor Lawrence Hagy, Lubbock mayor W. H. Rogers, and others joined John McCarty, A. A. Meredith, and the PWCA campaign. In August 1948, with the help of governors from three states, the PWCA held a meeting in Amarillo to push for a dam, and in the months that followed, dam activity, including meetings, petitions, economic impact statements, lobbying, and state and federal legislative proposals, increased. Although a powerful group of farmers from the Hereford area pushed for a dam across the river at Tascosa, most efforts centered on a dam near Sanford.[18]

The work paid off—or so it seemed. In August 1949 the U.S. House of Representatives approved a bill calling for some eighty-five million dollars in spending on the dam project, President Truman promised support, and Texans Tom Connally and Lyndon Johnson planned to sponsor the bill, called the Worley Bill for Representative Gene Worley. The bill was delayed as powerful Senator Clinton Anderson of New Mexico balked, but a few months later, after Secretary of the Interior Oscar Chapman endorsed the Worley legislation, the dam possibility looked good. Then, suddenly, the outbreak of the Korean War closed all efforts for a Canadian River dam.[19]

The need and the idea remained. As a result, leaders from Amarillo, Lubbock, Plainview, and several other Panhandle–South Plains communities, concerned about future water needs for their cities, continued to look for financial, engineering, and construction assistance. They continued to lobby with state and national political figures, and in May 1953 they got Texas governor Allen Shivers to sign legislation creating the Canadian River Municipal Water Authority (CRMWA), an agency with powers to seek government loans for a dam, award construction contracts, and oversee the wider issues of water use and distribution connected with the project.

The new agency, to which eleven cities belonged, began the slow process of securing land, settling mineral rights, obtaining funds, designing the dam and pipelines, and solving related problems. Over the next several years, leaders solved key issues one by one, but funding remained a major hurdle. Then in May 1960, voters from the eleven CRMWA member cities approved a financing and loan repayment plan with the federal government that mayors A. F. Madison of Amarillo and David C. Casey of Lubbock had devised. On January 9, 1961, representatives of the CRMWA and the federal government signed the repayment scheme, and a year later, on January 30, 1962, signed a construction contract with the large H. B. Zachry Company of San Antonio. Finally, on June 30, 1962, groundbreaking ceremonies were held.

Just over four years later, representatives of the federal government, CRMWA officials, and community leaders dedicated the Sanford Dam. At the event, held on cold and windy November 1, 1966, a crowd of 1,250 "chilled spectators" stood to hear short speeches by Secretary of the Interior Stewart Udall and Texas governor John Connally. Mayors from the eleven member cities attended the ceremony, as did U.S. representative George Mahon, Texas attorney general Waggoner Carr, and Brig. Gen. W. T. Bradley of the regional office of the U.S. Army Corps of Engineers.[20]

The lake behind the dam, named for A. A. Meredith, one of the key figures in the long struggle for the dam, was huge, capable of holding 821,300 acre feet of water. It became a multi-purpose recreation area, wildlife sanctuary, and tourist attraction. Lake Meredith recorded 277,000 visitors in the first six months after it opened, and during the last half of the 1960s, it attracted more than 1 million people per year to its waters for boating, fishing, swimming, camping, and picnicking.

The CRMWA was significant. It operated the dam, of course, and 322 miles of pipelines in its aqueduct system. The pipes varied in size from sixteen inches to ninety-six inches. Today it runs ten pumping stations, and to control the high levels of natural chlorination from the Canadian River, it manages some water treatment plants. For three decades the CRMWA provided quality water in adequate amounts, but as the twenty-first century approached, Amarillo and other member cities began seeking additional sources of the precious resource.

Meanwhile, even as they cheered the opening of Lake Meredith, Amarillo's citizens mourned the closing of the Amarillo Air Force Base. The closing announcement, which apparently caught Amarillo officials off guard, came on November 19, 1964. Secretary of Defense Robert S. McNamara delivered the news, and he indicated the air base was one of ninety-five military installations—army, navy, and air force—that would be phased out over the next few years. Although McNamara announced deactivation plans in November 1964, the federal government had determined a few years earlier to close the base. In fact, as part of a major, long-range defense department reorganization, it had since 1961 closed 574 other military installations around the country and overseas. Three years after the stunning announcement, the air base still held about 16,300 personnel, but before the end of July 1968 it was closed.[21]

The effects were severe. School records for the 1963–64 academic year showed 3,200 air base–connected students enrolled in the Amarillo schools. Of the 817 students at Highland Park School (grades one through nine), located two miles east of the north entrance to the air base along U.S. Highway 60, 80 percent were from air base families. Other schools on the east side, including Palo Duro High School, and Oak Dale and Eastridge elementary schools, enrolled air base–connected students. Obviously, student enrollments at the schools dropped. Amarillo superintendent of public schools Bob Ashworth, who called the closing announcement a "shock," indicated that the district would put off new construction plans and close all its thirty-seven portable two-room classroom units.[22]

Other city leaders were likewise shocked. F. V. Wallace, Amarillo's mayor, although he refused to be pessimistic over the closing, noted that the deactivation would "have a substantial impact on Amarillo." L. O'Brien Thompson of the city commission, who also remained hopeful, said the closing "is an economic shock to us." And Cliff Milnar, president of the Amarillo Chamber of Commerce, said, "We are quite concerned about losing the air base payroll in the next four years, but are glad it didn't come overnight and we have at least four years to adjust to a somewhat shock to the economy."[23]

The loss was in fact staggering and the city's economy buckled. Consumer businesses and the housing market suffered first and most directly. Real estate prices tumbled, homes went unsold, and mortgage loans went unpaid. Businesses, especially those catering to air base personnel, closed. Soon, as Price and Rathjen suggest, "almost every other phase of community life felt the withdrawal of Air Force families and the interest and talent they brought to activities in the city." Most churches saw their weekly attendance fall, with some churches "barely clinging to life." Youth athletic and cultural programs lost leaders and participants. Community groups and social activities that encouraged, and relied on, the participation of military personnel lost their purpose and meaning. The tax base slipped, and city and county income declined.[24]

Amarillo's population dropped. It had been increasing at a strong, steady pace during the 1960s: from 137,969 inhabitants at the beginning of the decade to a peak of some 166,000 people in 1966. Four years later, in 1970, the city's population, having plunged by nearly 40,000 persons, had dipped to 127,010 residents, and, writes Mike

Cox, seemingly with tongue in cheek, at least a few people "worried that Amarillo would become a ghost town, a modern-day Tascosa."[25]

It did not happen—it could not have happened. Although it owed much to the air base, including a monthly payroll that reached to over $2.5 million in 1965, Amarillo's economy in the late 1960s stood solidly on two legs: agriculture and petroleum. The city remained the center of a huge agricultural marketing area, and the Panhandle agribusiness industry continued strong. The oil and gas industry, while not reflecting the older boom times, still provided jobs and still pumped money into the Amarillo economy.

Moreover, city leaders, led by Mayor Wallace, fought back. They sought new industry, and they advertised and promoted Amarillo. In one of their first efforts, begun in 1965, they moved to get a branch of the Texas State Technical Institute (TSTI) established in the city, and they were successful. Led by Roy W. Dugger, who was from Waco and who headed the statewide TSTI system, they convinced the state legislature in 1969 to authorize the purchase of some of the abandoned Amarillo Air Force Base property. A year later, on June 25, 1970, the Mid-Continent Campus, or Amarillo Campus, of TSTI officially opened with ceremonies at the Civic Center Coliseum.[26]

About the same time, 1968, city leaders also secured a division of the Fort Worth–based Bell Helicopter. The airplane company took over some of the old Amarillo Air Force Base hangars and used them to maintain a major overhaul, modification, and repair unit. Because helicopters had emerged as a significant new weapon during the Vietnam War, especially with the big build-up after 1965, the Bell Company's Amarillo facility became a vital war-based operation, employing several hundred people. On June 25, 1970, just over two years after opening, its workers delivered repaired helicopter number five hundred. With Bell Helicopter and the Texas State Technical Institute occupying several buildings, the old air base, although it still contained empty hangars, was filling up.[27]

There was more. Along the old air base property on the eastern edge of Amarillo, city leaders and Governor Preston Smith on May 16, 1971, dedicated a new Amarillo Air Terminal. Opened the next day, the 4.1-million-dollar facility contained two levels and eight gates for the four airlines that serviced the city. Built on the south side of what has been called "the longest runway in the world"—the one that had been built to accommodate B-53 bombers of the Strategic Air Command and could land the space shuttle—the terminal became an American "port of entry," and officials designated it Amarillo International Airport.[28]

Other changes occurred, some of them downtown. At Sixth Avenue and Tyler Street, for example, the Texas American Bank–Southwestern Public Service Tower opened in 1970. At thirty-two stories high, it was Amarillo's tallest building. A year later, on the corner of Sixth Avenue and Taylor Street, Amarillo National Bank—the Ware family business, led by Tol Ware—completed construction of its five-million-dollar, darkly beautiful, sixteen-story Plaza I office building.

On Polk Street, Amarillo High School burned. Of undetermined origin, the fire occurred in the morning hours of March 1, 1970. As quickly as possible, and with much success, district personnel moved to get its students back in school and to set plans in motion for a replacement structure. Utilizing a few salvageable classrooms, converting the gyms and the cafeteria into classrooms, and using Sunday school rooms and sanctuaries of churches across the streets, students and faculty members managed to complete the school year. For two more years, while another building was under construction, they occupied the facilities at the Polk Street location, but in the fall of 1973 the new Amarillo High School, relocated to 4225 Danbury in the city's southwest section, opened.

Shortly afterward, in 1972, Amarillo citizens approved revenue bonds for a variety of civic improvements, including a new, downtown central library. For fifteen years, 1940 to 1955, the main library had existed in a wing of the Municipal Auditorium. It moved in 1955 to the beautiful Mary E. Bivins home at Tenth Avenue and Polk Street, but even with timely additions to it, the large house could not keep pace with Amarillo's growth and the library's acquisitions. Consequently, the 11.25-million-dollar bond issue called for, among other things, a modern, stand-alone building, and in 1976 the library opened in a large, airy facility located west across the street from the new Civic Center.

A year earlier, American Smelting and Refining Company (ASARCO), which had operated in Amarillo for more than fifty years, closed its zinc smelting plant. The plant, which stretched across five blocks, was obsolete, and the cost of installing expensive pollution control systems was prohibitive. Although the closing meant the loss of some five hundred jobs, ASARCO opened a copper refining plant along Route 136, the Fritch Highway. Designed to be pollution free, the plant employed several hundred workers, used natural gas from the nearby fields for power, and took advantage of the city's rail connections for transportation.

By 1975 Amarillo had recovered from the air base closing. Indeed, the city prospered again. Buildings permits increased in number; new businesses, especially chain stores and restaurants, appeared; growth once again moved toward the south and west; and the Amarillo-Canyon corridor began to develop with such trendy housing subdivisions as South Georgia and Brook Place. Nearby, the upscale Briarcroft subdivision, located just west of Western Street on Fifty-third Avenue, offered new homes starting at $37,000. And in northeast Amarillo, the Eastgate division opened along the Fritch Highway with new homes starting at $21,200.[29]

There were plenty of bright spots. Owens-Corning Fiberglas placed a major plant in the city. Amarillo College expanded and participated with city art leaders in creating the Amarillo Art Center, including a music building and concert hall and an art center gallery. The Amarillo Little Theater, which had been founded in 1928, hired a full-time director in 1969 and expanded the number of plays and performances it offered each season, including musicals, comedies, an occasional modern farce, and powerful dramas.

The large Amarillo Medical Center continued to expand. Situated on 417 acres on the city's northwestern outskirts adjacent to Amarillo Boulevard West, the center in the early 1970s held several facilities, including the 240-bed High Plains Baptist Hospital, the 156-bed

Veterans Administration Hospital, the 100-bed Psychiatric Pavilion of Northwest Texas Hospital, an office building, an outpatient clinic, and the Bivins Memorial Nursing Home. At the site, the City of Amarillo operated Medical Center Park, fifty-four acres of improved grounds with two lakes and walking paths, and the Amarillo Council of Garden Clubs operated the Amarillo Garden Club with its offices, meeting rooms, greenhouses, general purpose building, and colorful gardens.

In January 1976 the Don Harrington Discovery Center opened on the grounds of the Amarillo Medical Center. A planetarium and "hands-on" museum, the discovery center quickly attracted the attention of area schools, and soon teachers and their aides were bringing annually to the planetarium some thirty thousand students ranging from kindergarten through high school to view the stars and explore outer space.

The Amarillo public school system, in response to a growing population, expanded in the 1970s. The city's largest employer in 1971, the system held thirty-three elementary schools, nine junior high schools, and four senior high schools: Amarillo, Caprock, Palo Duro, and Tascosa. In the early 1970s the annual budget exceeded $20 million, and its funds supported programs for exceptional and handicapped students, vocational shop and part-time work courses, and comprehensive educational programs that included college preparatory programs in addition to salaries, building maintenance, equipment, and other expenses.

Then, in a related move, citizens on Amarillo's northern edge, in the River Road Independent School District, in 1975 approved a bond issue that included provisions for a new high school. In the fall, although temporarily located in River Road Junior High, it began with grades nine and ten, and in 1977 River Road High School opened with students in all four high school classes. Eleven years later, in 1988, on the city's southern edge the Canyon Independent School District opened Randall High School.[30]

Clearly, during the quarter century after 1950 Amarillo experienced a period of remarkable expansion. The economic growth, fueled by agribusiness innovations, oil and gas production, and air base improvements, led some optimistic urban planners to predict that in 1980 the city's population would reach 350,000 or more people. Such wild growth did not occur, in part because the air base closing in 1968 cut short the booming economy. But thanks to the diligent work of its leaders, Amarillo and its citizens recovered from the hard blow and in the late 1970s faced the new decade with growing confidence.

10

Amarillo in 1980

In 1980 Amarillo's population stood at 149,230, but its metropolitan area numbered 173,699 people. The city's boundaries reached south into Randall County, and its extraterritorial limits extended for many miles east and west along Interstate Highway 40. The expanding city had engulfed the smaller communities of Soncy, established in 1908, Fulton, and Pullman, and threatened such villages as Cliffside, established in 1915, and Saint Francis. Amarillo's downtown area continued to change as the city spread with housing and shopping districts far from its former heart along lower Polk and Tyler streets. Amarillo had become a small but modern American city. A service, retail, and distribution center, it was also the home to more than two hundred manufacturing firms making products from clothing and farm tools to helicopters and oil field equipment.

Agribusiness and oil dominated the Amarillo economy. Statewide only about 2 percent of the population engaged in farming or ranching in 1980, and another 20 percent worked in agricultural service industries. Still, Texas agribusiness added some thirty-three billion dollars to the economy. A significant portion of the industry centered on the

Texas High Plains, including the Panhandle where changes had been occurring.

One change was in the cultivation of grain sorghum. As explained by B. Byron Price and Frederick W. Rathjen, a combination of factors brought various sorghums to West Texas, including the growth of mechanized agriculture, the increase in irrigation, the limitations on cotton and wheat acreages that were part of farm programs associated with the federal government's 1930s New Deal initiatives, and the development of hybrid grain sorghums that worked on the arid High Plains.

J. Roy Quinby, an employee of the Texas A&M University Experiment Station at Chillicothe, helped develop modern sorghum varieties. His experiments produced hybrids from feterita, kaffir, and milo sorghums, and during the 1960s and 1970s the growing popularity of cattle feeding in the Panhandle provided a steady market for the modern hybrids. In response, farmers in the southern Panhandle counties of Deaf Smith, Randall, Parmer, Castro, and Swisher, where an active irrigation belt existed, produced a lot of the grain sorghum, but after the mid-1970s they began to replace sorghum crops with corn or soybeans.[1]

A related change was the growth of cattle feeding. Although the practice had existed for many years in Texas, cattle feeding in the Panhandle gained popularity in the 1960s. Two events stimulated the growth. First, in 1961 Paul Engler, a Nebraska cattle buyer, recognizing the region's strengths for such a business, opened Hereford Feed Yard. Apparently, he had determined that the Panhandle with its great open space, favorable climate, abundant cattle, and feed-producing potential was an ideal place for "finishing out" cattle for market. Second, in 1962 and 1963 some four hundred Panhandle–South Plains farmers, ranchers, and businessmen sponsored by the West Texas Chamber of Commerce and led by W. L. Stangel, a retired agriculture professor from Texas Technological College, visited feedlots in Arizona and California. As explained by Richard Mason, they "saw West Texas cattle finished out on West Texas grain" in lots far from West Texas.[2] Their discovery led them to encourage cattle feeding locally in West Texas.

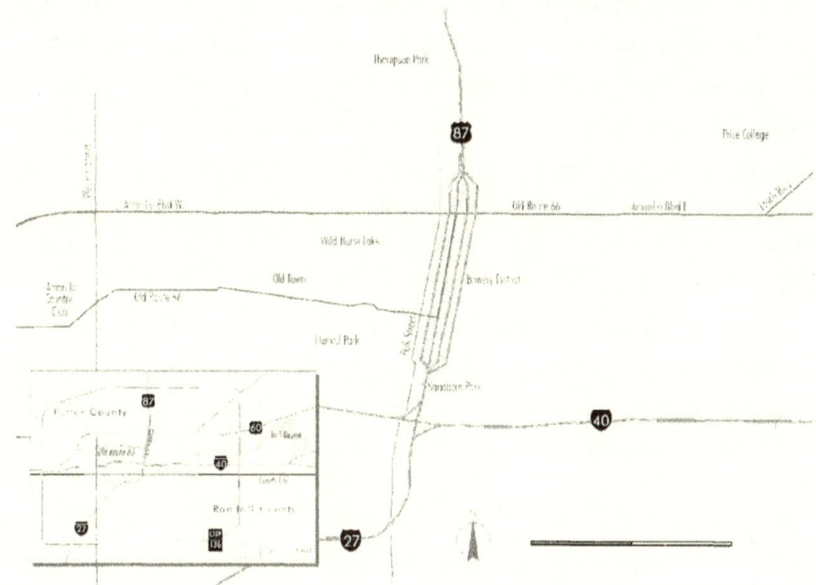

The City of Amarillo

Cattle feeding boomed. Across the Panhandle, the number of fed cattle increased from 221,000 head in 1966 to 1,686,000 in 1974. By the mid-1970s Texas, dominated by Panhandle–South Plains operators, had become the country's leading producer of fed cattle. Speculators and corporate enterprises otherwise unrelated to agriculture invested in feedlots and cattle feeding, and meat packing companies established plants in Amarillo, Lubbock, Plainview, and elsewhere.[3]

Unfortunately, the fed cattle business soured in 1974, causing financial losses and economic hardship. Within a couple of years, however, the boom and bust business recovered and began a second, even more spectacular period of growth. In 1980 producers on the High Plains of West Texas fed some 4,891,000 cattle, and in the mid 1980s, according to two local historians, "feedlots in the Amarillo trade area . . . moved as many as seven million head through their gates annually."[4]

Amarillo benefited from the fed cattle operations. Bankers offered loans, nutritionists and veterinarians provided essential expertise, and workers gained employment. Feed yards appeared in or near the city, and older ones, such as Western Stockyards, expanded for a time before city growth forced consolidation and retraction. In 1980 Western Stockyards, which dates to 1905 and which in 1940 associated with the Amarillo Livestock Auction Company, continued to operate at 100 South Manhattan Street. Local historians called the Amarillo Livestock Auction "the world's largest cattle auction"; in 1980 it sold 624,409 head of livestock valued at over $236 million.[5]

Other feedlots appeared, including C and S Cattle Company, Caviness Cattle Company, Eslabon Cattle Company, and Tejas Feeders. Southwest of the city, Randall County Feedyards opened. At one time the largest feedlot in the world, the Randall County firm could handle up to one hundred thousand head of cattle, but in the mid 1980s it cut back its operations.

Meat packing businesses also increased. Cattle feeding operators and local business leaders sought meat processors to handle the huge amount of beef the region produced. Older processing firms in the city, such as the Pinkney Packing Company, which had been founded by Ray Pinkney in 1930, expanded for a time before consolidation or other developments, including city growth, eliminated them. Pinkney Packing, located near Western Stockyards in east Amarillo, closed in 1970.

But other meat packers arrived. In 1975, for example, Iowa Beef Processors moved to Amarillo. Located on the city's north side along Farm to Market Road 1912, IBP served in the 1980s as one of the city's largest and most visible industrial operations with over thirty-six hundred employees. In 2003 the company became Tyson Fresh Meats.

In a related development, trucking companies organized or reorganized to haul processed beef. Baldwin Distribution Services, for example, which Charles Baldwin had started in Amarillo as a sand and gravel hauling operation in 1964, gradually shifted its trucking responsibilities to the oil and gas industry. When the oil and gas business slumped in the early 1980s, Baldwin moved into the beef industry, hauling processed meat for such companies as IBP, Ben E. Keith, and Affiliated

Foods. In 2003 the Amarillo-based company operated 100 trucks and 185 refrigerated trailers in forty-eight states.[6]

In 1980 the average yearly income from agriculture in Potter County stood at twelve million dollars. Eighty percent came from beef cattle and hogs, and wheat, sorghums, and corn represented the chief crops. Farmers in the county irrigated 14,700 acres. Clearly, agribusiness activities remained an important foundation of the city's economy.[7]

Oil and gas production also provided an economic foundation—and in terms of total value in dollars, one greater than agribusiness. The Texas Panhandle Oil Field, which stretched across several counties, remained a large producer of oil and gas, and Amarillo citizens, accordingly, worked in the fields and on the wells, in petroleum refining, in carbon black operations, on pipelines, as fuel oil dealers, as gasoline service station attendants, as truckers, in corporate offices, and in other aspects of the industry.

Potter County in 1980 produced 432,308 barrels of oil, and its wells averaged a bit over 1,181 barrels per day. As of December 31, 1980, county wells, since they first went on line in 1925, had produced 3,190,985 barrels of crude oil. In 1980, with several companies still maintaining offices in Amarillo, the value of oil-related activities in Potter County reached $16,203,783.

In 1980 T. Boone Pickens Jr. was Amarillo's leading oilman. Born in Oklahoma, Pickens came to Amarillo as a youth when Phillips Petroleum Company transferred his father to the Texas Panhandle. A star athlete, he played basketball in high school and later at Oklahoma State University before forming Mesa Petroleum, a tightly run exploration and production company that operated drilling rigs around the globe. In 1981 the company drilled 85 exploratory wells, of which 42 were productive, and 385 development wells, of which 248 were productive.[8]

Lawrence R. Hagy, eighty years old in 1980, was another influential oilman. In 1927 Hagy and Don D. Harrington had formed an exploration company, and a short time later Stanley Marsh joined them. The company drilled gas wells, acquired oil and gas leases plus some fifty-thousand acres of rangeland, and in 1933 built Cargray Gas Processing Plant to extract gasoline from petroleum. The partners in the late 1940s established the Panoma Corporation. Hagy, who also turned to ranching, was a civic leader, and in 1949 he won election as mayor of Amarillo.

Like Hagy, other Amarillo oilmen turned to ranching as something of a sideline. Harold Dunn, T. Boone Pickens Jr., Jay Taylor, Don D. Harrington, and others all invested oil and gas earnings in land and cattle operations. In fact, Pickens's Mesa Petroleum Company at one time owned Randall County Feedyards, once the largest feedlot in the world. Other oil and gas operators, such as the Whittenburg, Masterson, and Bivins families, were cattlemen first before turning to oil and gas production.

Gas production, including natural gas and helium, remained important to Amarillo, which, as noted earlier, was once called the "helium capital of the world." Through 1980 gas operators in Texas had removed since the first wells went down some 334 trillion cubic feet of conventionally recoverable natural gas in the state. In 1980 statewide production stood at about 7.04 trillion cubic feet, down about 17 percent from the peak year in 1972. The Panhandle—Amarillo's trade area—in 1980 produced much of the nation's natural gas and helium.[9]

The availability of gas and oil encouraged some manufacturers to set up operations in Amarillo. One such company was Crouse-Hinds, a division of Cooper Industries and a builder of electrical construction materials. In part because of the proximity of oil and gas resources and in part because of what it saw as low utility costs, the company built its Amarillo plant in 1978, and within a few years the facility, located on West Farmers Avenue, employed 150 people. The workers operated electric furnaces to melt scrap metal for castings that they machined, plated, painted, assembled, and shipped to distribution centers.[10]

The Owens Corning Plant opened in Amarillo about the same time—1979. Called "one of the largest glass fiber manufacturing facilities in the world," the company's five-hundred-thousand-square-foot operation in the seventeen hundred block of Hollywood Road employed 740 people. The workers produced glass fibers for automotive, construction, and recreational applications.

The location of the Owens Corning Plant on the northern edge of Randall County highlighted a nagging concern for Amarillo: city boundaries extending across two counties. Consequently, in 1980 three government units—the City of Amarillo, Randall County, and Potter County—held the key to Amarillo's future as a metropolitan city, and in another decade the City of Canyon added to the political mix. As it grew, Amarillo faced the challenges of providing services to rural, unincorporated areas, a squeeze on the city's central core, a loss of its tax base to suburban areas, and maintaining without duplicating water and sewer connections. There existed, in other words, a mutuality of problems, but the three governments did not always cooperate in attempting to solve them.

The collection and disposal of garbage, for example, was a highly publicized problem the three governments faced in the 1980s. Amarillo's city commissioners, according to Carroll Wilson, for years "attempted to close down . . . their sanitary landfill operation in North Amarillo and begin dumping city garbage in a landfill more removed from the city." But residents in both Randall and Potter counties backed by their county governments and supported by state agencies concerned with environmental issues blocked city attempts to open a new site.

Fire protection was another challenge. Amarillo charged the counties a fee each time its city firemen and equipment fought rural fires. When, writes Wilson, the city "announced an upward adjustment in fees"—to $845 per fire call—officials of Potter and Randall counties "blanched at the figure and began looking for alternate ways to handle their own fire problems." By 1980 Potter County had created a series of volunteer fire departments and Randall County had secured cooperative agreements with several local fire departments to handle rural fires.[11]

In 1980 the central business district of Amarillo was changing. Businessmen, investors, and others removed some buildings, remodeled others, and created small downtown parks or plazas and parking garages. Mesa Petroleum Company, for example, dynamited the old Amarillo Hotel to create a park. Just west of the ten-story Vaughn Building, which it had acquired in 1976, it built a block-long parking garage and an exercise gym called the Mesa Physical Fitness Center. "Mesa Square," with its remodeled buildings and grassy park with shade trees, had become, according to Thomas Thompson, "one of the most eye-appealing layouts anywhere around."[12]

Merchandising activities changed too. A few traditional, old-line commercial stores, such as Blackburns, Hollywood, Colbert's Harry Holland, and the Hub, had opened branch stores in suburban shopping malls. Some four hundred or more businesses remained in the downtown area and perhaps ten thousand people worked there, but major shopping had moved to such malls as Wolflin Village, Sunset Center, Western Square, Los Tiendas Shopping Center, Wellington Square, Westgate Mall, Puckett Plaza, Western Plaza, and Coronado. For the most part downtown shoppers were clerical, managerial, and professional employees who worked in the area.[13]

In 1980 only the State movie theater remained downtown. Once nine theaters clustered close together in the area of lower Polk and Taylor streets, but only El Teatro State, as owner Gregorio "George" Pauda called his Spanish-language theater, had not closed or moved to a shopping mall. Located in the five hundred block of Polk Street since 1921 when it was Fair Theater, it became State Theater in 1937, and in 1976 El Teatro State. Pauda showed, he said, "the most up-to-date Spanish movies." Most were Mexican-made films that, technically, were "of no less quality in picture and sound than Hollywood-made movies." El Teatro State opened only on Saturdays and Sundays.[14]

Even at the edge of downtown changes came. In July 1980, for example, construction workers demolished the old Double Dip Drive-In. Once a teenage hangout that featured gourmet hamburgers, the Amarillo landmark located in the thirteen hundred block of Polk Street gave way to a parking lot for Polk Street United Methodist Church.

Causes for the change were many. City growth and expansion toward the south and southwest accounted for part of it. The Amarillo-

Canyon Expressway eased access to the south, and a growing number of Amarillo businesses moved to sites along U.S. Highways 60 and 87, which shared the corridor stretching to Canyon.

Commercial development along Interstate Highway 40 also drew businesses, including both fast food and high-end restaurants, away from downtown. One of the most colorful restaurants was the Big Texan Steak Ranch. Opened in 1962 on Amarillo Boulevard East in an old Underwood Bar-B-Q building, the popular place moved eight years later to East I-40. A fire temporarily closed the restaurant in 1976, but owner Bob Lee reopened and continued to feature his famous seventy-two-ounce steak: an effective advertising gimmick that offered the large steak free if one could eat it and the shrimp cocktail, baked potato, salad, and roll that came with it in an hour. In 1980 the cost of the big meal, that is if one failed to eat it all, was $31.48. In 2005 the same Big Texan meal cost $51.14.

The Country Barn Steakhouse at East I-40 and Lakeside, even as it catered to Amarillo and Panhandle residents, attracted tourists from the busy highway. Built in 1964 by John Marrs along Amarillo Boulevard East (Route 66) to resemble, well, a country barn, the place boasted such celebrity diners as Ronald Reagan, Chill Wills, Kenny Rogers, George Peppard, and Edgar Buchanan. Dale Robertson, another Hollywood actor, walked into the restaurant's kitchen, or so the story goes, and showed the chefs and cooks how to make "hoecakes," a southern cornbread dish. In 1974 Marrs had relocated the facility with its rustic charm, high ceilings, and checkered tablecloths to I-40. Twenty years later, the Country Barn, retaining its popular décor, moved along I-40 to Soncy Street on the western edge of Amarillo.

Another Amarillo tourist attraction was the American Quarter Horse Heritage Center and Museum. In 1946, when Amarillo horse breeder Raymond Hollingsworth became executive director, the American Quarter Horse Association moved its offices and registry from Fort Worth to Amarillo. It operated in an office downtown first but then moved to Plains Boulevard, just west of Georgia Street, where it remained for thirty years. In 1984 the association opened a new office and registry along East I-40, and next door, the magnificent Heritage Center and Museum attracts each year thousands of visitors. The museum features equine artwork, interactive exhibits, and demonstrations of various kinds, including proper handling of horses and horseshoeing. Visitors can view exhibits that show the evolution of the horse from prehistoric times to the development of the American quarter horse.[15]

On the city's west side, along Interstate Highway 40, sits Cadillac Ranch. Created in 1974 by a small group of California artists calling themselves the Ant Farm and sponsored by Stanley Marsh 3, Amarillo's favorite purveyor of unusual fun and serious good cheer, the "ranch" featured ten Cadillac automobiles "planted" in a wheat field. Buried nose down at forty-five degree angles—the same angle as the pyramids of Egypt—with their tops facing west and representing selected model years between 1949 and 1963, the Cadillacs display various changes in tail fin design. Visitors could walk a short distance through the field to the automobiles, scribble a message on the vehicles, and ponder perhaps what it is about Cadillac Ranch that attracted national attention to the site.

On the twentieth anniversary of Cadillac Ranch, Marsh hosted a giant cocktail party in the wheat field. It was a gala event. More than a thousand people attended, many of them dressed in tuxedos or evening gowns and cocktail dresses. Marsh served sparkling wine and beer with tables piled high with tasty hors d'oeuvres. Having ordered the Cadillacs painted white for the occasion, he passed out large felt-tip pens and encouraged everyone present to draw, write, and sign on the automobiles. In 2003 Marsh moved the automobiles a couple of miles west, wryly suggesting that "the girls"—his Cadillacs—worried about a growing problem of pollution from Amarillo.

For Amarillo, Palo Duro Canyon State Park remained a major tourist destination. Located southeast of the city in what Frederick W. Rathjen calls "the geological and ecological wonder that is Palo Duro Canyon," the park with its wide vistas and deep gulf represents one of the most scenic and pleasant surprises of the region. It attracted thousands of visitors for hiking, camping, and picnicking. People toured

Palo Duro State Park to marvel at the rock formations, to ride the two-mile-long Sad Monkey Railroad, and to photograph such spectacular canyon landmarks as Spanish Skirts, the Lighthouse, Catrino Cave, and Mesa Mecca. Each summer the musical drama *Texas,* written by Paul Green, brought additional thousands of tourists to Palo Duro, and more recently a new information and visitor center includes a small museum, gift shop, and observation deck.[16]

In 1980, Lake Meredith, the reservoir behind Sanford Dam on the Canadian River, was an attractive tourist destination. Some forty-five miles northeast of Amarillo, the long, wide lake, called "a virtual inland sea," provided water-based recreational opportunities, including fishing, swimming, camping, picnicking, and boating, for many people. After entrepreneurs built a big marina on the lake, Panhandle citizens, including many from Amarillo, bought large boats and larger cabin cruisers and placed them on Lake Meredith, which had replaced Buffalo Lake as the city's favorite water retreat.

Meanwhile, in Amarillo entertainment opportunities were abundant. The Don Harrington Discovery Center remained open to the public on a daily basis. In November 1980 its weekend planetarium showings featured a program called "Visions Beyond Time."

Live theater was available. The Country Squire Dinner Theatre, for example, offered Broadway-style productions, buffet dining, and preshow musical entertainment. At the Hilton Inn on Interstate Highway 40, the Frenchy McCormick Dinner Theater also provided buffet dinners, preshow music, and Broadway plays, including musicals, with a professional acting cast. In July 1980 the cast at Frenchy McCormick's performed *An Almost Perfect Person,* and in November it put on the Neil Simon comedy *Chapter Two.* At the same time the Amarillo Theatre Center offered several performances of *Music Man,* and just down the road in Canyon, West Texas State University students played in a musical at the university's Branding Iron Theatre.

A brief review of cultural and popular amusements available in November 1980 is revealing. In addition to those already mentioned, the Amarillo movie theaters were busy, and West Texas State University sponsored an operatic performance at its Mary Moody Northern Recital Hall. The Amarillo College Drama Department presented its fall show in its Concert Hall Theatre. At the same place, Jerry Davice of San Francisco presented a public lecture on art and Amarillo's boot print designer Jack Boyton. Men's and women's basketball games were played at the high schools, at Amarillo College, and at West Texas State. The Amarillo Public Library hosted "Children's Book Week," and a public showing and open discussion of the film *Self-Fulfilling Prophecy.* At the Amarillo Civic Center, the local rodeo association sponsored the Superkicker Rodeo, and on the Tri-State Fairgrounds others held the Old Time Ropers National Finals. The Amarillo Civic Center Exhibit Hall hosted the annual "Christmas Roundup" and the popular Chamber of Commerce "Arts in Action" events.

Art galleries were plentiful. Since the days of Georgia O'Keeffe just before World War I, Amarillo has attracted artists whose most common themes focused on western and southwestern traditions, including especially cowboys, cattle, American Indians, and regional landscapes. One of them was Dord Fitz, an Oklahoma-based artist, instructor, and gallery owner, who in 1953 had opened the Dord Fitz Gallery in Amarillo. Fitz taught painting, encouraged artists, and hung the work of local painters at his downtown gallery.

Another gallery operator was John L. McCarty, a former newspaperman, editor, historian, and for a time perhaps the Texas Panhandle's most famous promoter. In 1960 McCarty, who had written *Maverick Town: The Story of Old Tascosa* (1956) and as editor of the *Amarillo Daily News* had produced in 1938 the 280-page golden anniversary history of Amarillo in a special edition of the paper, opened his High Plains Art Gallery on the Amarillo-Canyon Expressway. At the gallery, writes Sean J. Flynn, he "exhibited and sold local art works devoted to 'the depiction of the West in America.'" And, "using his ties to regional newspapers and journals," he "published numerous stories on local artists and their works."[17]

McCarty not only displayed and sold works of art but also he encouraged local artists, including Jim Thomas, D. Crow, Ted Bell, and others. Thomas "Tommy" Thompson, a longtime reporter and editor for the *Amarillo Globe-News* and one of McCarty's harshest critics, conceded that such local painters and sculptors "as Kenneth Wyatt of Tulia and Carl Smith of Canyon can be forever grateful to [McCarty, who] promoted their talents and helped make them into financially successful artists."[18]

In 1980 several art galleries promoted local artists. The Red Door Gallery at Thirty-fourth and Bell, for example, featured fine antiques, paintings, and handicrafts. It sold local art on a consignment basis. The Glass Gallery at 103 South Travis offered original works in stained and painted glass, beveled glass, and hand-beveled windows. The Thomas Gallery on Boys Ranch Road sold paintings and sculptures, including some in bronze. Perhaps the largest gallery was the James M. Harvey Gallery. In October, it displayed the works of twelve artists who painted and drew abstract, floral, landscape, still life designs in watercolor, oil, pencil, and ink. It showed the work of four sculptors who worked in wood, ceramic, and bronze, and it hung prints, rugs, and handwoven Navajo rugs. The Amarillo Art Center, Designs in Glass, and A H Arts Unlimited also sold local art.

A different kind of art appeared on the edge of town. Stanley Marsh 3, who in 1974 had sponsored the Ant Farm's Cadillac Ranch, now supported the efforts of Andrew Leicester, a Minneapolis-based artist, in building *Floating Mesa,* an outdoor art project on a hill along Tascosa Road about twelve miles northwest of the city. During the summer of 1980, one of the hottest on record, Leicester erected a shiny steel curtain—a mirror, in effect—near the top of the elevation, hoping to create with the curtain an illusion of a floating mesa. In late September, after the artist had completed phase 1 of the project, Marsh hosted a party in the field below the 384-foot project. According to editors at *Accent West,* an upscale monthly devoted to Amarillo, some "seven hundred invited guests enjoyed Marsh's ranch-style hospitality."[19]

Despite cultural successes, life in Amarillo was not all rosy. A serious national gasoline shortage in 1979 had raised gas prices, contributed to record levels of inflation, and destabilized the economy.

Amarillo was adversely affected, of course, and the city's economy stumbled a bit more when in 1980 the local housing market slumped—partly because interest rates on real estate loans had soared. In the mid 1970s some observers had adopted the term "stagflation" to describe the nation's struggle with a fiscal situation that combined inflation and recession: high unemployment and inflationary prices went hand in hand. During one month in 1980 inflation measured at an annual rate of no less than 18 percent.

President Jimmy Carter complained about a national malaise. Having inherited from Presidents Gerald Ford and Richard Nixon a struggling economy when he took office in 1977, Carter tried to affect a federal "cure" by cutting taxes and increasing public spending. It did not work, and by 1979 he had reversed himself: delaying tax cuts and vetoing government spending on programs he had advocated a year earlier. Conditions worsened. In 1980 national unemployment neared 7.5 percent, home mortgage rates averaged 15 percent, general interest rates reached an all-time high of 20 percent, and inflation averaged between 12 and 13 percent.[20]

The national economy floundered. And, coupled with such unwelcome international events as the Soviet Union's 1979 invasion of Afghanistan and the yearlong Iranian crisis in which a frenzied mob in 1980 stormed the American embassy to take fifty-three hostages, it ended Carter's presidency. In the November 1980 presidential election, Ronald Reagan, a man who, many have pointed out, seldom attended church and was not particularly pious, defeated Jimmy Carter, a self-professed born-again Christian, in part because, somewhat ironically, the politically active and moralistic "religious right" supported Reagan. Moreover, many Democrats, especially inner-city Democrats, did not vote.

In Amarillo, voters followed national trends. In both Potter and Randall counties, the Ronald Reagan–George H. W. Bush ticket swamped the Jimmy Carter–Walter Mondale team. Indeed, the Republicans captured nearly 60 percent of the popular vote in Potter and Randall counties, enjoying winning margins of 6,694 votes in

Potter County and 6,113 votes in Randall County. Although the Thirteenth Federal Congressional District race and the various state contests were closer, the Republicans were cutting deep into former Democratic Party strongholds, including Amarillo and the Texas Panhandle.[21]

The mayor of Amarillo in 1980 was Jerry Hodge. A pharmacist who had become a city commissioner in the early 1970s, he moved into the mayor's office in April 1977 after defeating John "Bulldog" Drummond, the conservative incumbent. Hodge left in 1981, suggesting that the pressures of office "were just too much to handle." Although a popular mayor, Hodge's term for several reasons was a controversial one. For one thing, he was young—in his mid-thirties—a situation that grated on older, more experienced politicos. For another thing, with fellow pharmacists Jerry Ammerman and Houston "Dee" Deford on the city commission, Hodge's "Rx connection," as it was called, dominated local politics. In addition, he fought a bitter but losing battle with Southwestern Public Service Company over a proposed rate hike.[22]

For Hodge, there was other controversy. An independent in politics, which in Texas in 1980 meant that he was a Democrat, Hodge wanted to play a key role, at least in the Texas Panhandle, in Attorney General John Hill's 1978 campaign for the governorship. (Hill was a Democrat running against Republican William Clements.) When the Panhandle's leading Democrat operatives, including former state representative Ben Bynum and advertising executive Joe Batson, cut him out of the campaign picture, Hodge went over to the Republican side. He set up a "Texas Mayors for Clements" organization, sandbagged Democratic campaign efforts in the Panhandle, arranged a statewide televised political debate in Amarillo—called by downstate newspapers "the Amarillo Hour"—between Hill and Clements, and worked tirelessly on Clements's behalf.

The election on November 7 was close—very close. It was not decided until about 4:00 a.m. on the eighth. Across the state less than 17,000 votes out of over 2,350,000 ballots cast separated the candidates.

In Potter County, Clements received 7,491 votes to Hill's 7,188, and in Randall County Clements defeated Hill by 3,600 votes. When, the *Amarillo Daily News,* which backed Hill, ran an early edition with a headline reading "Hill Edges Clements," Hodge carried the paper to Austin and in front of a large number of newspaper reporters and television cameramen showed it to Clements. Because the paper was embarrassed and a bit angry over Hodge's antics, the incident, according to Patrick Casey of *Accent West,* "triggered bad blood between the newspaper and Hodge for the remainder of his tenure as mayor." Hodge saw the Austin event as his finest political moment.[23]

Another problem was city taxes: they went up. One former Hodge supporter noted that his taxes had been raised nearly 200 percent, and in 1980 he complained. A more vocal and irritating tax critic was Tom Gilley, former basketball coach at Palo Duro High School. Gilley, who was a hamburger cook in 1980, began attending city commission meetings, and during the "open mike" period at the close of each formal session he took to insulting the mayor. Hodge, who had inaugurated the popular open mike practice to allow Amarillo citizens to address the commission, accepted the verbal attacks for several weeks, but in March he erupted. The "quick tempered mayor," as Patrick Casey has characterized Hodge, said, "I've had enough of your lies, Mr. Gilley. . . . [You] have gone just too far this time." People in the commission chambers audience, including the media, "sat stunned as Hodge" asked "police officers [to] remove Gilley."[24]

Amarillo's African American community also complained. As Casey describes it, in December 1979 a fatal automobile accident "in the heart of the North Heights section of Amarillo," a neighborhood predominately composed of black residents, "brought several police officers to the scene." Amid the emergency rescue efforts and the police investigation of the accident, tempers flared and "an angry mob" began throwing "bottles and other objects at the officers." After the police officers had left the scene, black citizens, led by Joe Jiles, filed repeated complaints against the Amarillo police and Chief Lee Spradlin. Wanting Spradlin removed from office, they marched on City Hall and police headquarters, getting substantial media coverage "but little sympathy from [Hodge and other] city leaders." Throughout 1980 they pressed their demands for the chief's removal.[25]

Tragedy in the form of two murders aided the black community's cause. Late in the evening on October 26, 1979, an intruder had savagely murdered Sarah Donn Lawrence, a thirty-year-old southwest Amarillo housewife and mother of three children, ages four, five, and nine. When he arrived home from work at the ASARCO plant about 11:30, David Lawrence found his wife's body, which had been stabbed several times, on the living room floor of their home in the five thousand block of Shawnee across from Western Plateau School. His arrival, suggested Detective Darrell Garner, "may have frightened off the killer."[26]

Panic spread across the city, apparently, and soon afterward sales figures for handguns reached an "all time high." A police department spokesman, Marvin Richardson, said, "Never in all my years on the force have I seen one murder cause such a stir among the people of the city and the news media," and Mayor Hodge and Chief of Police Spradlin at a joint news conference seemed to call for the cancellation of many Halloween festivities. The police made no arrests, and people complained about inadequate police work. As the weeks passed, the complaints mounted, but Hodge nonetheless indicated that he was satisfied with the ways in which Spradlin and his detectives were handling the case.[27]

About six months later, in April 1980, an attacker killed Sherry Lynn Welch, an employee of a Wolflin Village furniture store. Welch was twenty-six years old and married when the murderer struck as she closed the business for the evening. Again, the police made no arrests.

Months passed. Complaints against the police and Chief Spradlin increased. Hodge backed the police, and as he continued to do so, he became the object of mounting criticism, especially from the *Amarillo Daily News*.

Then, late in September, the Amarillo police arrested eighteen-year-old Jay Kelly Pinkerton. They charged him with the murder of Sarah

Lawrence, and on live television Randall County Justice of the Peace Phil Woodall read Pinkerton his rights.[28]

New investigations revealed that the police had suspected Pinkerton of the Lawrence murder from the very night the killing took place. The investigations also showed that Pinkerton was the prime suspect in the Welch murder. Hodge, now certain that "the failure to arrest Pinkerton in connection with the Lawrence case had . . . led to the needless death of . . . Sherry Lynn Welch," lost his respect for Spradlin and the Amarillo Police Department. The bungled murder investigations had been filled with mistakes and errors and, coupled with other events such as the police handling of the North Heights automobile accident, caused Hodge to backpedal in his support for the chief of police.[29]

Then on October 2, 1980, an *Amarillo Daily News* article exposed a long string of police department problems. The copyrighted article produced an uproar. After it, according to Casey, "Randall County District Attorney Randall Sherrod indicated that a grand jury meeting in Canyon would be looking into the alleged mistakes of Amarillo police officials."[30]

Now, Hodge took action. He called the city commission together to discuss the police situation, and for several hours Hodge and the commission members met with Chief Spradlin. The discussions centered on whether or not the chief of police ought to remain in his position. After several hours, the group emerged in open session to vote on Spradlin's retention. Beginning with Hodge, each member spoke briefly about his position and then voted. This time Hodge could not hold his important Rx connection together. Houston Deford broke with Hodge and Jerry Ammerman to vote with Curtis Crofford and Dean Christy in support of Spradlin.[31]

When accusations continued, however, Spradlin quit. He resigned on December 2, 1980, with his resignation to take effect in thirty days. Thus, on January 2, 1981, Lee Spradlin left a position he had held since 1975.[32]

Collectively, Amarillo in 1980 seemed a bit disordered. Downtown workers shopped in suburban malls, for example, and although the city expanded and gas prices increased, its citizens refused to support the Amarillo Transit System, which daily operated a fleet of twenty-six air-conditioned buses over eleven routes covering 2,381 miles. Parks increased in number, but the city's landscape designers, according to biologist Dick Powell, were "short-sighted in an effort to be far-sighted" in their tree-planting schemes at the new Southwest Park.[33]

Powell wanted city leaders to plant Siberian elms. First brought to the Great Plains from Canada by way of immigrants from the steppes of Russia—the same way Russian thistles (tumbleweeds) reached the region—the elms, as distinct from Chinese and American elms, had spread relentlessly across the open, semi-arid environment. Although one of the most vilified plants in the Texas Panhandle, the trees take little care, grow quickly, provide abundant shade, and in Amarillo generally thrive.

At least they did until 1980. Then, elm leaf beetles, which for some thirty years in other parts of the country had been destroying the grand and large-leaf American elms, were making their way through Amarillo's Siberian elm population. Tiny yellow and black bugs, the beetles, which had first appeared about twelve years before, each summer, notes Carroll Wilson, attacked elm trees, "skeletonizing their leaves, turning them prematurely brown and causing them to drop as if victims of an early fall." They defoliated the trees, and over a period of four or five years their continued presence killed the large plants.[34]

Many people were not concerned, for Siberian elms, they believed, were nuisance trees with little value. Forgetting that the elms served as windbreaks and shade trees, they preferred to plant maples, pines, and more popular trees that took greater effort and care in raising and grew slower. The elms declined in number, but they did not disappear; they remain abundant in Thompson Park and in many Amarillo yards.

Amarillo's disordered routine, if such it were, revealed itself in Buck Ramsey's article in *Accent West.* In July 1980, Ramsey, a popular country-western singer-songwriter-storyteller, suggested—with tongue firmly in cheek—that the Panhandle secede from Texas. Like him, most people of Amarillo believed the state government in Austin ignored far-northwest Texas, spent too little in state funds in the region, and treated residents of the area "like second-rate Texans." Ramsey offered few specifics, but he pointed out that Amarillo was closer in geography and sociopolitical character to capitals in New Mexico, Oklahoma, Colorado, and Kansas than to the capital in Austin. Most of the article outlined what his proposed new state of Cheyenne would be like rather than describing Amarillo's alleged difficulties in 1980 with the state government in Austin.[35]

Relatively, the city and the region were not in economic or other straits difficult enough to warrant even talk of secession. But Ramsey reflected, perhaps, the 1980 tone of morning discussions over coffee at favorite cafés and Happy Hour complaints at popular taprooms. Although the economy in Amarillo was no worse than elsewhere in the state or nation, the local oil and gas and construction industries and the housing market were flat. The city, for example, issued 2,516 building permits in 1980, down a bit from the previous year, and the following year, 1981, the city issued only 1,169 such permits, a number that reflected the construction slump. Unemployment in Amarillo, while high, was both lower than the national average and manageable.[36]

Amarillo's metropolitan population of 173,700 people was ethnically diverse by 1980. It was approximately 69 percent Anglo. The Hispanic population, which was growing rapidly, reached 21 percent of the total, and African American population figures stood at 6 percent. Asians, especially Southeast Asians, American Indians, and people of a Middle Eastern background represented most of the remaining portions of the population. Although people of various racial and ethnic groups scattered throughout the city and its suburbs, the North Heights neighborhood was predominately black, and east Amarillo included a large Hispanic population.

In 1980 several high schools served Amarillo. The Amarillo Independent School District contained four: Amarillo, Palo Duro, Caprock, and Tascosa. The Highland Park Independent School District, within the city limits of Amarillo, operated a high school on Farm to Market Road 1912. River Road Independent School District's

River Road High School overlooked Highways 87 and 287 on the north edge of Amarillo. The Canyon Independent School District administered Randall High School on the southeast side. Private high schools included San Jacinto Christian Academy, Holy Cross Catholic Academy (formerly Alamo Catholic), and others. Teachers at Palo Duro High School, located at 1400 North Grant, educated many of Amarillo's black students, and a large number of Hispanic students attended Caprock High School, located in the three thousand block of East Thirty-fourth Avenue. There were thirty-three public elementary schools in Amarillo and many private, usually church-sponsored, ones, including some with a Montessori-based curriculum.

Amarillo at this time counted more than two hundred Christian churches representing thirty-six denominations. As elsewhere in Texas and the South, Baptists, with nearly a third of the total, led in numbers of churches and parishioners, but Methodist, Catholic and Presbyterian churches were not far behind. The Mormon Church was growing in adherents and numbers of churches, and several Pentecostal churches existed. In Amarillo, as elsewhere in the country, nondenominational Protestant Christian churches saw their popularity increase. An Eastern Orthodox building, Saint John Greek Orthodox Church, stood at 1101 Bell Street. The Roman Catholic and Episcopal churches maintained diocesan headquarters in Amarillo. Temple B'Nai Israel remained the sole Jewish synagogue in the city.

In 1980 Amarillo contained several media outlets. City entrepreneurs owned four television stations—KFDA, KAMR, KVII, and KBUY-FM—and eleven radio stations, four of which were FM stations. The daily newspapers included the morning *Amarillo Daily News* and the evening *Amarillo Globe-Times,* and on Sunday the combined *Amarillo Sunday News-Globe.* Paid circulation totaled approximately 72,860 subscribers.[37]

The Board of City Development and the Chamber of Commerce in 1980 could point to several other positive statistics: tourist facilities, for example, included sixty-five motels with more than thirty-seven hundred units. Three major railroads served Amarillo on transcontinental routes, including the Santa Fe, which housed its Western Lines headquarters in the city, and Burlington Northern, which maintained division offices in Amarillo. Five airlines—Southwest, Braniff, Frontier, Texas International, and TWA—provided passenger, cargo, express, and mail services. Permian Airways provided commuter service. Fifty women's clubs were associated with the Amarillo Federation of Women's Clubs, whose elaborate clubhouse stood at 2001 Civic Circle, and other women's groups existed outside the larger organization.

The Chamber of Commerce moved to the old Lee and Mary E. Bivins home at Tenth Avenue and Polk Street in 1980. The large building, one of Amarillo's most famous landmarks, had housed the Mary E. Bivins Memorial Library—the city/county library—from 1955 to 1976, when Amarillo's central library opened across from the Civic Center. Twenty-five years later, the Chamber continued to operate in the stately mansion.

Amarillo claimed nine banks in 1980. Total deposits stood at 1.258 billion dollars. Don Powell's First National Bank (Boatman's in the 1990s and now Bank of America), with 42 percent of the city's bank deposits and bank loans, was the largest. Amarillo National Bank, the Ware family's beautiful institution, was perhaps the largest privately owned bank in America. Texas American Bank (now Bank One) owned the tallest building in Amarillo. Built in 1970 when the financial institution was American National Bank and Frank A. Paul Jr. was president, the new structure changed the city's skyline. The strikingly beautiful, thirty-two story skyscraper, often known in 1980 as the Southwestern Public Service, or SPS, Tower, contained eight high-speed, computer-controlled elevators and housed about one thousand employees.

On the top floor of the SPS Tower sat the posh Amarillo Club, the city's elite private dining establishment. It provided gourmet eating and fine music amid luxurious décor. Through its large windows one might admire the grand, sweeping panorama of the Southern High Plains where one could see distant Bushland many miles to the west, Canyon about fifteen miles south, and the colorful breaks of the Canadian

River to the north. At night the magnificent view of the city belied the troubled economy that characterized Amarillo in 1980.

The city during this time needed to move away from its overdependence on agriculture and petroleum. Both are extractive industries that drained raw materials from the region. To sustain its population and its growth, Amarillo also needed to rely less on the military-industrial complex as represented by Pantex and Bell Helicopter. A similar reliance on the Amarillo Air Force Base and the Strategic Air Command nearly knocked the city to its knees in the mid 1960s.

The longterm economic good health of Amarillo and the Texas Panhandle depended upon diversification, which, one should hasten to add, was occurring in 1980 and afterward.

11

Agribusiness, Oil, and Nuclear Bombs

In the twenty years that followed 1980, Amarillo experienced significant changes. Its economy shifted a bit as tourism came to play a greater role in the city's financial picture. Always the business hub of the Texas Panhandle, Amarillo enlarged its regional health care facilities and its reputation as a regional health care provider, added hospitals, and contracted with the Texas Tech University Health Sciences Center to establish a teaching institution. As the city's vigorous expansion to the south and southwest continued, commercial activities along the Amarillo-Canyon corridor pushed deep into Randall County, and Canyon, with its important West Texas A&M University, became part of the greater Amarillo metropolitan area. Amarillo College grew to over seventy-five hundred students, the public school system changed and expanded, and private schools increased in number and importance. In politics, as older "Yellow Dog Democrats" passed from the scene, the city and the region continued their drift toward the right and to the Republican Party.

In the early 1980s, Amarillo's major sociopolitical issue became—again—the Pantex Ordnance Plant. The issue first surfaced in Amarillo in October 1978 when the U.S. Defense Department announced that it was considering seven sites for a proposed $250 million MX mobile land-based missile weapons facility. One of the sites under consideration reached from Fort Sumner and Clovis, New Mexico, northeasterly into and across western portions of the Texas High Plains from Bailey to Dallam counties.[1]

Because the western Panhandle site was not the government's first choice for the new weapons system, only mild protests occurred in Amarillo. Panhandle citizens, including those in Dallam County, apparently let the matter drop. It did not disappear, however, for in other parts of the country farmers, ranchers, and others protested whenever government officials held public hearings near one of the proposed sites. As early as July 1978, for example, hearings in Colorado, Nebraska, and Kansas "brought protests from hundreds of farmers and agri-businessmen."[2]

Nationwide controversy over the MX (missile experimental) system began a year later. President Jimmy Carter in June 1979 signed with the Soviet Union a new Strategic Arms Limitation Treaty (SALT II). Because they thought the treaty gave the Soviets an advantage in the number and destructive power of land-based intercontinental ballistic missiles, many Americans opposed SALT II. To counter his critics, reassure Americans, and bolster the treaty's ratification chances in the U.S. Senate, Carter with support from the U.S. Air Force suggested placing the new MX system in the Great Basin states of Nevada and Utah.[3]

The MX weapons system, designed in part to replace the obsolete Minuteman missile, was huge and complex. The "incredible proposal," as it has been called, envisioned a system of "underground tunnels through which rails would carry a fleet of nuclear missiles" in such a way that the Soviet Union "could never be sure where the launchers would be at any specific moment." In 1979 the system would cost, according to Michael P. Malone and Richard W. Etulain, "a mind-numbing $100 billion." Over a wide area, it would displace existing property owners, bring in new inhabitants, and threaten not only the scarce groundwater supplies but also other elements of a fragile desert ecosystem.[4]

For many Great Basin residents, the MX missile system was unacceptable. An environmental impact study that had accompanied the earlier 1978 announcement indicated that the planned system "would have considerable impact on the agricultural economy of the . . . region." Moreover, plans for the new program called "for an 'area security' option that would result in sealing off a 6,500-square-mile radius around [the] MX missile site and removing all residents and domestic animals from the area for up to 30 years."[5]

When people in Nevada and Utah, including the politically influential Mormon Church, objected, Carter and the air force backed off. But they did not give up. They turned to other, secondary, sites for the MX system in Montana, Wyoming, and North Dakota, where minuteman missiles had existed since the 1960s, and in the Texas Panhandle, where few people had complained about Amarillo's Pantex Ordnance Plant. Since the 1950s, workers at the Pantex plant, in addition to building and testing conventional high explosives, had been assembling, disassembling, modifying, and repairing nuclear weapons, including large bombs. The western Panhandle, dominated by Amarillo, seemed a good choice.[6]

It wasn't. Panhandle citizens, including many people from Amarillo, for at least two years had been objecting to plans for a nuclear waste disposal facility in a subterranean geological formation called the Palo Duro Basin, a region that stretched from Motley County west and northwest through portions of Floyd, Hale, Lamb, Briscoe, Swisher, Castro, and Deaf Smith counties. Although studies, including the deep-drilling of two test sites, occurred in the basin, officials, led by E. G. Wermund of the Texas Bureau of Economic Geology, in late 1978 thought the possibility of developing a nuclear waste disposal installation there was small. Nonetheless, Panhandle citizens organized to stop the drilling and to prevent the establishment of a nuclear waste dump in the area.[7]

Thus, in December 1980, when the Air Force announced eastern New Mexico, near Clovis, and the Texas Panhandle, especially the area near Dalhart in Dallam County, as alternate sites for the MX system, many Amarillo citizens were set to protest. Sister Mary Regina Foppe, a missionary catechist and a social justice advocate, and Bishop Leroy T. Matthiesen, who in the late 1940s had come to Amarillo as a parish priest, took the lead. Foppe urged the new bishop—he had been ordained bishop of the Amarillo diocese on May 30, 1980—to oppose the MX system and to do it through a public statement.[8]

Matthiesen moved cautiously. In a Christmas sermon at Saint Laurence Cathedral on North Spring Street, he writes, "I included an appeal for an end to the arms race." The response, he notes, was "ho-hum." Nonetheless, it caught the attention of Ladon Sheats, a former IBM employee from Lubbock who had a record of opposing nuclear weapons through civil disobedience. A month later, in early 1981, Sheats invited the new bishop to be part of a nonviolent protest at Pantex. Because he was scheduled to be away from Amarillo on the appointed day, February 6, Matthiesen could not be present.

But Matthiesen did become involved. At the protest, which unfolded as scheduled, a half-dozen people led by Sheats and calling themselves "the Pantex Six" climbed a security fence, and within thirty minutes guards arrested them. Another of the six protestors was Father Larry Rosebaugh, a social justice advocate and Catholic priest who had recently returned to the United States from Brazil. Matthiesen visited Rosebaugh in the Potter County Detention Center, talked to him, and called his home station in Minneapolis to report the jailed priest's whereabouts. Later, in federal court in Amarillo, the government convicted all six of the protesters of criminal trespass. Sheats served several months in prison, including three months in Amarillo. The court, ostensibly because he was a first-time offender, paroled Rosebaugh.[9]

Matthiesen became less hesitant. Claiming that the new defense system "would take [149,000] acres of farms and ranches out of production and displace up to [fourteen hundred] families" in the western

Panhandle, he now opposed not only the international arms race but also, upon Mary Regina Foppe's continued urgings, the federal government's large and expensive MX weapons program.

When the Department of Defense organized a public hearing on the system and scheduled the meeting in Amarillo for April 20, Matthiesen took part. At the gathering, where many farmers and ranchers protested but many businessmen supported the system's Panhandle location, Matthiesen not only objected to placing the system in the Texas Panhandle but also argued against the whole idea of additional intercontinental ballistic missiles and nuclear arms. "I do not ask you to move the MX Missile System elsewhere," he said to assembled government officials. "I ask you to forget it entirely." In his concluding remarks, he told them "that the present atomic armament race is madness."[10]

A short time later the Pantex Ordnance Plant and the larger issue of nuclear weapons grabbed Matthiesen by the throat. Across his desk, he writes, came a publication from Pax Christi, U.S.A., titled "A Catholic Call to Conscience." The little document urged the Catholic Church and its leaders to actively oppose "modern war and weaponry" on a large scale. More specifically, it called upon Catholics "not to give or obey orders to use nuclear weapons," not to engage in the manufacture of such weapons, and not to seek employment in occupations that "contribute to the immorality of modern war."[11]

Bishop Matthiesen was troubled. Many Amarillo-area Catholics worked at the Pantex plant, where they were engaged in the assembly of nuclear and other weapons of mass destruction. Matthiesen told one of them, Robert Gutierrez, a deacon in the church and an assembly operator at Pantex, that he should quit his weapons job just as soon as he could find other employment.[12]

Shortly afterward, Matthiesen moved boldly. Concern about newly elected President Ronald Reagan's defense policy initiatives that called for a major buildup of both conventional and nuclear weapons, he reacted when Reagan in August announced that, in Matthiesen's words, "the United States would go ahead with the assembling of the enhanced radiation warhead, the so-called neutron bomb." Although the neutron bomb had been developed during President Jimmy Carter's years in office, the government in response to SALT II negotiations had delayed its production. It was a major new weapon, and the bishop believed it would accelerate the international arms race. In addition, the immorality of destroying human and other life "while leaving machines, buildings, and other material things intact" was especially reprehensible to him. And, moreover, he knew that workers at the Pantex Ordnance Plant in Amarillo would assemble the sophisticated warhead.

As a result of these concerns, Bishop Matthiesen on August 23, 1981, published in the *West Texas Catholic,* the weekly newspaper of his Amarillo diocese, a short but sharp and direct statement about the arms race and the Pantex connection with nuclear weapons. In it, he urged the Reagan administration to halt the arms race, and he asked American military leaders to "use common sense and moderation" in defense plans. But most startling of all, he called upon "individuals involved in the production and stockpiling of nuclear bombs to consider what they [were] doing, to resign from such activities, and to seek employment in peaceful pursuits."[13]

Reaction was swift—much of it hostile. Amarillo residents, especially Pantex employees and their friends and relatives, sent notes, letters, and cards to Matthiesen. Most of them complained about his strong stand against the assembly plant work. The bishop received angry and often anonymous phone calls, with some people inviting Matthiesen "to take a one-way trip to the Soviet Union."[14]

Matthiesen got some support from Amarillo residents, but most of it came quietly and privately. West Texas State University in Canyon, however, openly invited him to speak about Pantex and about his position on the MX missile hearings, radioactive waste, and the arms race in general. He did, and his well-publicized appearance attracted a large crowd of students and faculty who were receptive to his ideas about the need to abolish nuclear weapons.[15]

Not long afterward Matthiesen spoke in New York City. This time he delivered his anti-Pantex and anti–nuclear weapons talk at a major disarmament conference, one that filled Riverside Church with people who, like Matthiesen, supported an easing of the arms race. The bishop entitled his speech "I Didn't Know the Gun Was Loaded," and during the next few months he made the same basic presentation over and over again.

As a result, Amarillo and its Pantex Ordnance Plant attracted national—and international—notice. Matthiesen writes that the "*New York Times* sent Kenneth Briggs to Amarillo and carried his report on its front page." National television networks, particularly ABC, CBS, and NBC, sent film crews to the city, and similar crews came to Amarillo from England, Germany, Italy, Japan, and elsewhere. Reporters and photographers, writes Matthiesen, came from such national and international publications as *Time, Newsweek, Life,* and the *New Yorker. Pravda,* the Soviet Union's influential newspaper, sent reporters, as did the homegrown, liberal *Texas Observer.* Moreover, Matthiesen appeared on the national television news shows *60 Minutes, Nightline,* and *Good Morning, America.* Clearly, Matthiesen's jeremiad and his subsequent public appearances drew to Amarillo and the Pantex plant an enormous amount of attention.[16]

The attention, in turn, brought outside protestors to Amarillo. People concerned over the international arms race and opposed to nuclear weapons converged on the city. They set up protest vigils at the Pantex plant, monitored the so-called white trains that carried nuclear warheads from the plant to other parts of the country, and encouraged Pantex assembly plant workers to quit their jobs.

Citizens in Amarillo generally disliked the negative publicity and the protesters. Consequently, few called for the plant's closing, and at Pantex itself, resignations in protest were rare. If, however, A. G. Mojtabai, who has written in detail about the Pantex-Amarillo relationship, is correct, many people in the city for the first time began to talk seriously about Pantex's role in assembling nuclear weapons, in the international arms race, and in making Amarillo a prime target for missile strikes from the Soviet Union. They also began to consider, or reconsider, their own intellectual, philosophical, and moral positions on nuclear warheads and neutron bombs.[17]

Still, most people wanted to keep Pantex open. It employed about twenty-three hundred people in 1981, and independent contractors and subcontractors who handled construction and repair activities employed many more. In 1982 the plant's operating budget reached ninety-seven million dollars, and in the next few years both the number of employees and the operating budget increased. Mayor Rick Klein backed the plant. "Pantex," he said, "is good for the business community. It's good for Amarillo. We've never had any trouble with Pantex."[18]

Some religious leaders also backed the plant and its employees. J. Alan Ford, the fundamentalist pastor of Southwest Baptist Church, held a "Pantex Appreciation Sunday," and he appeared with Matthiesen on a national television show to counter the bishop's ideas. W. Winfred Moore, pastor of the First Baptist Church, which was the largest church in Amarillo, also opposed Matthiesen's position, and on April 8, 1983, at Amarillo College he and Matthiesen appeared in what was publicized as a debate over the nuclear arms race. The meeting, which was described as more "successive monologue" than "dialogue," caused few people to change their positions, but in some ways it represented an endpoint—a denouement, if you will—for the larger issue of the morality of assembling nuclear warheads at Amarillo's now world-famous Pantex Ordnance Plant.[19]

The issue did not go away, but other events diverted some of the attention away from the Pantex plant, its right to an existence, and its place in Amarillo society and the city's economy. For one thing, even as Matthiesen broke open the Pandora's box that was Pantex, other issues, such as prayer in Amarillo's public schools, grabbed a large share of the local public's scrutiny. For another, as the number and value of building permits and bank deposits increased through 1981, Amarillo's two-year-long economic slump, while still significant, seemed to be on the mend. And, third, Johnny Frank Garrett's brutal murder of seventy-six-year-old Sister Tadea Benz in late 1981 and the subsequent arrest and trial of the suspect for a time deflected public interest.[20]

The murder of Sister Tadea Benz occurred on October 31—Halloween—in Saint Francis Convent at Forty-third Street and Northeast Eighteenth Avenue. Only seventeen years old but deep into drug use, Garrett, who had failed at school and previously had committed a series of minor crimes, broke into the convent. High on drugs and alcohol, he then raped and murdered Sister Tadea, "a much-loved, elderly member" of the Franciscan Sisters of Immaculate Conception. Many people in Amarillo admired Sister Tadea, who had been born in Switzerland and had served as a missionary in South America before coming to Amarillo, for her expert needlework and for her contributions to the Catholic Church and to the Amarillo community.[21]

A week after the murder, Amarillo police arrested Garrett. Because an abundance of evidence connected Garrett to the crime, the Potter County district attorney got an indictment, and at the subsequent trial he won a first-degree murder conviction. Later, despite a controversial appeals process led by Bishop Matthiesen and others connected with the Catholic diocese of Amarillo, the State of Texas executed Garrett.[22]

As local and national attention shifted away from Pantex and MX missile systems, Amarillo residents sought for their city a more comfortable, attractive image than the one provided by nuclear weapons assembly. Jack Speer, for example, writing in *Accent West* in January 1983 called for "a self-image that is tied to the hitching post of its western past." Noting that "Amarillo's roots go deep into what became popular western lore," Speer, an operations manager for the Amarillo Chamber of Commerce, hoped that the city might more aggressively promote a slogan that the Board of Convention and Visitors Activities (later the Amarillo Convention and Visitor Council), which had been created in 1973, had developed: "Amarillo, where the West lingers on."[23]

While the slogan did not stick, the image of Amarillo as a western town—albeit a modern West—did. Through the 1980s agribusiness, for example, remained a vital part of Amarillo's economy, and at the turn of the twenty-first century, writes Mike Cox, "nearly thirty percent of the jobs in the Amarillo area were related to agriculture." In 1987, as another example, Cactus Feeders, Inc., founded in 1975 by Paul F. Engler and Thomas H. Dittmer, was the largest custom cattle feeding company in the world. According to Orville Howard, it funneled "more than $1 billion into the Texas Panhandle economy," and annually "finished out more than 800,000 head of cattle." In 1991 feed yards in the Amarillo area held about 1,450,000 cattle, and the Amarillo Livestock Auction sold over 200,000 head of cattle, producing receipts that totaled over ninety-six million dollars. In 1997 feedlot operators in the Amarillo area handled about 85 percent of all fed cattle in the state. With cattle feeding still a very large business in 1997, the city could claim its place as a "major cowtown."[24]

Farming was also important, and wheat production in the 1980s continued to contribute to the city's economy. Cargill's grain elevators at 620 North Marrs, for instance, once called the "world's largest grain elevators," in 1987 held a capacity of 3.6 million bushels of wheat or other small grain. Moreover, Panhandle farmers grew about half of the state's wheat and corn crops and 20 percent of the grain sorghum. In 1991 farm products, including wheat, corn, sorghum, hay, oats, barley, sunflowers, and sugar beets, in Potter and Randall counties generated over sixty million dollars in revenue. In 1997 agribusiness remained the city's number one industry.[25]

Likewise, oil and gas production contributed to Amarillo's economic good health. In the 1980s the Panhandle Oil Field, one of the great petroleum reserves of Texas, continued to produce huge amounts of oil, natural gas, and helium. Between 1973 and 1994, workers pumped from the field over eight trillion cubic feet of gas, and in 1994, some 4,499 gas wells remained in operation. Helium extraction, which occurred at Soncy, on the west edge of Amarillo, and Excell, north of the city, came from gas fields near Cliffside that were the largest in the United States. The annual production of oil in 1994 reached to over five million barrels. In Potter County, including Amarillo, the oil and gas industry in 1997 employed hundreds of people and generated income that impacted a wide sector of the economy. In fact, at the turn of the twenty-first century, it remained Amarillo's second largest industry.[26]

Tourism became Amarillo's third largest private industry. And—consciously or not—much of the tourism centered on Jack Speer's call for respecting the city's western past. Palo Duro Canyon and its summertime play *Texas,* with its western motifs, dominated the local tourist industry; fully 50 percent of all tourists who stopped in Amarillo in the mid-1980s planned a visit to Palo Duro Canyon. Business leaders, especially the Chamber of Commerce, promoted the eye-catching lapel pin featuring Amarillo's name dominated by the western-style boots that represent the two Ls. Indeed, as part of Amarillo's name, the boots serve as something of an unofficial symbol for the city, and visitors who travel on Interstate Highway 27 notice images of the large boots that serve as decorations on Interstate 40.[27]

Tourism, important to the city since the completion of Route 66, was part of the new economy of Amarillo. Palo Duro Canyon State Park may have dominated the interests of most tourists, but other activities brought people through Amarillo. In the 1980s, as noted earlier, the Lake Meredith Recreation Area attracted boaters and swimmers plus people who wanted to fish, camp, or picnic at the large lake. The Alibates Flint Quarries National Monument, established in 1965 to preserve the archaeologically important site, became a popular tourist spot. The American Quarter Horse Heritage Center and Museum, the Don Harrington Discovery Center, the Kwahadi-Kiva Indian Museum and Performance Center, and the Cadillac Ranch also continued to attract visitors.

In the early 1990s, West Sixth Avenue, the original path of Route 66 through the city, became a favorite tourist stop. The charming stretch of road, located in the San Jacinto Heights neighborhood just west of downtown, centered about the old Natatorium, which is still standing. In 1994, when the government listed the area on the National Register of Historic Places, a mile-long section on Sixth between Georgia and Western streets contained restaurants, tap rooms, art galleries, and antique shops that flourished—until higher taxes ruined many of the businesses.

In nearby Canyon, people in increasing numbers visited the Panhandle Plains Historical Museum, the largest such museum in the state. In 1986 the museum, under the leadership of Bill Griggs, Byron Price, and others opened the superbly designed Don D. Harrington Petroleum Wing, which provided visitors a dramatic visual and interactive history of the Panhandle Oil and Gas Field.

To promote tourism, the Amarillo Convention and Visitor Council encouraged a wide variety of organizations to hold annual meetings and other activities in the city. The group, which worked closely with the local Chamber of Commerce, was successful, for not only did it point to area attractions but also it offered spacious, modern facilities. The Amarillo Civic Center, for example, contained a 2,324-seat auditorium, the 6,670-seat Cal Farley Coliseum, and, when including the corridors, some ninety thousand square feet of exhibit space. The Tri-State Fairgrounds was the site of a coliseum that seated ten thousand people and held fifty-seven hundred feet of exhibit space. In addition, Amarillo in 2005 counted fifty-eight hotels and motels with a total of 4,668 rooms.

Moreover, Amarillo, as it had been in the past, remained a crossroads. Several U.S. highways—U.S. 60, 87, and 287—converged in the city, and Interstate Highways 27 and 40, the latter of which included U.S. 66, intersected near the downtown area. Amarillo sat at midway point in transcontinental traffic along Interstate 40, and both business and tourist travelers, especially truckers, saw the city as a key stopping point along the main road between Oklahoma City and Albuquerque. Amarillo also represented a major stop for rail or highway traffic moving between Dallas and Denver, and the Burlington Northern–Santa Fe Railroad maintained operations in and through the city.

One of Amarillo's most significant events of the late 1980s was the city's centennial celebration in 1987. A nearly yearlong affair in which many local organizations and clubs participated, the centennial's major activities kicked off in April and continued through December. The Amarillo Centennial Committee, co-chaired by Pattilou Dawkins, who for years was active in civic organizations, and the Panhandle Heritage Society coordinated most of the celebrations and festivities, but the Women's Forum, the Amarillo Council of Garden Clubs, local churches, neighborhood groups, the Amarillo Public Schools, the Amarillo Fine Arts Association, the Amarillo Art Center, the Catholic Historical Society, the Don Harrington Discovery Center, the Palo Duro Bow Hunters, and more than a dozen other groups sponsored events.

Churches were particularly active. Polk Street United Methodist Church, First Presbyterian Church, and First Baptist Church were each celebrating along with the city their own centennials and each produced a history of their dynamic institutions. Many churches, including First Church of the Nazarene, Central Church of the Nazarene, Christian Heritage Church, Blessed Sacrament Catholic Church, and others, sponsored "Frontier Sunday," an event that was sponsored by a different church nearly every week through the year.

Events associated with the Amarillo centennial were eclectic. In April, for example, the Potter County Home Economics Advisory Committee sponsored a history of ethnic groups in the Panhandle. A week later the Panhandle Barbed Wire Collectors Association sponsored an exhibition of antiques that played a role in Amarillo's beginnings. The High Plains Poetry Society of Texas sponsored a poetry contest. Near the end of the month the Amarillo Art Center sponsored a presentation, "The Mexican Influence on Texas," by Yolanda Romero of Texas Tech University, and Amarillo College sponsored presentations by Jacinto Alderete and Coco Medina titled "The Hispanic History of Amarillo."

Several histories of the city appeared. The Amarillo Globe-News Corporation published a large, newspaper-style retrospective of the city's past. The popular work, which contained numerous short pieces on a wide range of topics written by Amarillo citizens, ran to over one hundred pages in a newsprint format. The year previous, B. Byron Price and Frederick W. Rathjen produced their highly readable, narrative history *The Golden Spread: An Illustrated History of Amarillo and the Texas Panhandle,* and Ray Franks and Jay Ketelle printed in 1986 and 1987, respectively, their two colorful volumes of picture postcards.

But the big celebration peaked during the last week of August. Called "Amarillo Centennial Week," the citywide party featured activities "all day, every day." Bob Hope, perhaps America's most famous comedian, spoke at the Civic Center on August 29, and on August 30, to commemorate the 1887 vote that gave birth to the city of Amarillo, the Women's Forum sponsored "Amarillo's Birthday Party."[28]

Unfortunately, near the end of the city's yearlong centennial celebration a fire gutted the Amarillo Independent School District (AISD) offices at Seventh Avenue and Washington Street. The fire on December 9–10 not only ruined the office building but also destroyed AISD records, including personnel, student, academic accomplishment, athletic achievement, and other files, such as transcripts, legal documents, and award certificates. In effect, the school district by losing its archives also lost much of its one-hundred-year history.[29]

Elsewhere there were gains. In the 1980s women in Amarillo were making substantial economic and political advances. Betty Bivins and Sybil Harrington, both highly active in business, civic affairs, and philanthropy, were familiar to the people of Amarillo. Their enormously beneficial work and accomplishments were legion. Indeed, editors of *Accent West* suggested that to list the women's "achievements would be to write a volume of many pages."[30]

Bivins and Harrington were not alone among successful women. Mariwyn Dye in 1981 started an advertising agency with three clients. Six years later she had built the business to thirty accounts and had collected a wallful of advertising awards. Anndel Hodges, president of Opinions Unlimited, Inc., headed up an Amarillo research firm that provided opinions and information to a series of national clients. With thirty employees and billings reaching to "half a million dollars" in 1987, Hodges dominated a remarkable enterprise. Janis Alexander Cross was a corporate attorney who kept busy with work, her family, and community activities. Pamela Oglesby, a graduate of Texas Tech

University law school, worked for the Potter County attorney's office before she opened a private practice. In 1986 she became a judge in the Amarillo Municipal Court.

Gwendolyn "Wendy" Marsh, although she usually stayed in the background, was a Panhandle power broker for some three decades. For a time in the 1980s she owned Sylvan Learning Center, but this remarkable woman with a law degree from the University of Texas is better known for her philanthropy and her civic work. Among her many roles, she was chairman of the Amarillo College Board of Regents, a member of the Texas Higher Education Coordinating Board, and chairman of the Amarillo Heart Association.

More recently, Jane Gripp, Barbara Miller, and Hazel Kelley Wilson represented Amarillo women in prominent positions. Gripp, president of Plains Transportation, Inc., oversaw an interstate trucking firm that in 2005 employed about thirty people in its Amarillo headquarters and about two hundred truckers scattered across the country. From their office and shop at 6699 South Washington Street, Gripp and her staff directed truckers who mainly hauled groceries and refrigerated cargo through much of the continental United States.

Barbara Miller, who worked for a local paper company for several years, in 1995 established Miller Paper Company, which just a few years later maintained a product line of fifteen hundred items from janitorial supplies to quality gift wrap. In 2000 the U.S. Small Business Administration recognized her as the Texas Small Business Person of the Year.

Hazel Kelley Wilson was a driving force in the operations of Jack B. Kelley, Inc., a major transporter of helium. She became one of Amarillo's important philanthropists, particularly to area cultural groups, the First Baptist Church, and West Texas A&M University.

Janie Rivas and Debra McCartt assumed educational and political leadership. Rivas was the first woman to head the Amarillo Independent School District (AISD) board of trustees. Her leadership was a key factor in getting the district's largest bond issue, one that called for $108 million dollars worth of building and remodeling projects, approved in 2003. In 2004 the Amarillo Hispanic Chamber of Commerce selected Rivas as Citizen of the Year, and Texas Plains Girl Scout Council named her one of its Women of Distinction.

In 2005 Rivas and her fellow school trustees presided over a school system that employed 3,689 people, most of them teachers. Some 29,348 students with an ethnic distribution that was 48.7 percent Anglo, 37.9 percent Hispanic, 10.6 percent African American, 2.5 percent Asian, and 0.3 percent American Indian attended AISD schools. The class of 2004 counted 2,863 graduates. The system's annual budget approached two hundred million dollars, and the district included over fifty campuses—four high schools, nine middle schools, thirty-four elementary schools, and five specialty schools—plus a maintenance plant and the administrative offices, the latter of which were located in a former bank building in the seventy-two hundred block of West Interstate Highway 40.[31]

Debra McCartt became Amarillo's mayor in 2005. The first woman elected to the post, McCartt, a former school teacher and businesswoman who was active in community affairs, on May 7, 2005, defeated millionaire Jerry Hodge, who some twenty-five years earlier had served as mayor, in what most political observers saw as an upset victory. But McCartt, who spent far less money than Hodge in seeking the position, proved to be a lively and tireless campaigner who projected a dynamic image of confidence and sophistication. Knowledgeable and articulate, she displayed a remarkable ability to connect with people. She represented the future of Amarillo: bright, youthful, positive, and full of hope.

In the meantime, Amarillo citizens in the 1990s saw leaders of several manufacturing businesses establish plants in the city. One of the largest of the new companies was Bell Helicopter Textron, which opened its huge facility in 1999. Bell Helicopter used its plant to produce such tiltrotor aircraft as the V-22 Osprey and the Bell 609 Tiltrotor. In 2005 the plant counted 650 workers, making it one of the twenty major employers in Amarillo.

Instrumental in convincing Bell Helicopter and other companies to move to the city was the Amarillo Economic Development Corporation (AEDC). Founded in the early 1990s with the approval of city voters who authorized a small sales tax increase to finance development operations, AEDC was successful in most instances in attracting and assisting businesses in their relocation to Amarillo. AEDC provided such incentives as cash grants, tax abatements, and interest-free loans to companies that could provide new jobs in Amarillo.

At the same time, Amarillo's medical facilities expanded. Texas Tech University Health Science Center, for example, established a School of Medicine in Amarillo in 1972, and its first full-time class began in 1978. Then, in the 1990s, the Texas Tech Medical Center at Amarillo—Tech-Amarillo, as people called it—opened a School of Allied Health (in 1994) and a School of Pharmacy (in 1996). The Allied Health program, which began by training physical therapists, shared a building with the School of Medicine, but Amarillo and Panhandle residents generated thirteen million dollars for a separate building for the School of Pharmacy. When finished in 1996, the building contained a pharmacy museum, a drug information center, a clinical research unit, a wellness center, a large lecture hall, a video conferencing center, classrooms, labs, offices, and other features. Its first class graduated in 2000.

Additional expansion included the Northwest Texas Healthcare System, which was the primary teaching hospital for Tech-Amarillo. It was the Harrington Regional Medical Center, the 410-acre campus in the northwest corner of Amarillo that also housed the Veterans Administration Medical Center, the Don and Sybil Harrington Cancer Center, Tech-Amarillo, and the Baptist Hospital. In addition, the Baptist Hospital and Saint Anthony's Hospital merged, but retained separate campuses, as Baptist–Saint Anthony's Health System (BSA). *U.S. News and World Report* ranked it three years running—2002–4—as one of the 175 best hospitals in America.

Clearly, Amarillo in 2005 had much about which its citizens could boast. In addition to its abundant health care facilities, the city embraced professional, if minor league, hockey, arena football, and baseball teams. It was home to eight golf clubs, including three country clubs; a zoo; Wonderland Park, the largest amusement park between Dallas and Denver; a large downtown library with four branches scattered through the city; four movie theaters, including Tascosa Drive-In, with nearly thirty screens; eight local television stations; sixty-six parks and recreation areas totaling 2,392 acres; and an abundance of restaurants, shopping malls, and radio stations.

The city might boast too of its natives or residents who gained some measure of national fame. Tula Finklea, for example, made the "big time" as Cyd Charisse, a dancer who starred in such megamovies as *Singing in the Rain* and *Ziegfeld Follies.* Roger Miller, a country singer/songwriter who became known for "King of the Road," worked for KZIP radio station and as an Amarillo fireman. Ben Johnson was a Hollywood character actor who played in various John Wayne movies. Ben Sargent, a cartoonist, won the Pulitzer Prize for editorial cartoons in the *Austin American-Statesman.* Carolyn (Baker) Jones was the actress who played "Morticia" in the television series *The Addams Family.* There were plenty more, including Jimmy Gilmer, Carol Sobieski, Buddy Knox, Mary Jane Johnson, J. D. Souther, Randy Carver, Joe Anderson, Charlie Phillips, and others.[32]

The city's public schools produced two graduates who became astronauts. Rick Husband, an Amarillo High School alumnus, was commander of *Columbia STS-107* on February 1, 2003, when the space craft disintegrated over the southern United States and with his crew he died. In his honor the city renamed its airport the Rick Husband Amarillo International Airport. Paul Lockhart, a Tascosa High School alumnus, flew two space shuttle flights in 2002 and four years later remains in the program.

The list, as partial as it is, suggests that Amarillo's cultural life in the early twenty-first century had flare. Indeed it did. In June 2005 the city dedicated the Globe-News Center for the Performing Arts. Located downtown near the Civic Center, the large, ultramodern and strikingly handsome building with seating for 1,279 provided additional public performing space for such groups as the Amarillo Symphony, the Lone Star Ballet, and the Amarillo Opera, which Mila Gibson had founded in 1988. Planners also hoped to use the building in providing an arts education to some eighty-thousand children in the Texas Panhandle.

Amarillo College and West Texas A&M University in Canyon also added to the cultural flare. In addition, Wayland Baptist University opened a temporary branch campus in Amarillo before moving in 2002 to permanent quarters on Canyon Drive. Over the years, professors and students at the schools have contributed to Amarillo's cultural life. In the 1920s and 1930s, Hattie M. Anderson and L. F. Sheffy, historians at the West Texas college in Canyon, for example, were the driving forces behind the Panhandle Plains Historical Society. J. Evetts Haley, a superbly gifted storyteller and feisty conservative historian and politician, became the first editor of the society's journal, the *Panhandle-Plains Historical Review.* When Haley left, Sheffy took over the editor's duties, and then, in the depths of the Great Depression in the 1930s, he directed efforts to raise funds for the Panhandle Plains Historical Museum, whose original Pioneer Hall opened on April 14, 1933.

Others continued the Anderson and Sheffy intellectual leadership. For Amarillo and the Texas Panhandle, perhaps most notably among them was Frederick W. Rathjen, a professor of history at what was West Texas State University when he arrived there in the 1960s. With a PhD from the University of Texas, Rathjen published in 1973 *The Texas Panhandle Frontier,* a sophisticated and engaging book that traces the region's pioneer past. A second, revised edition appeared in 1998. Rathjen, who also edited *The Panhandle-Plains Historical Review,* was one of only two people—Garry L. Nall of Amarillo the other—who has served as president of both the Panhandle-Plains Historical Society and the West Texas Historical Association.

Rathjen has been described as a regionalist—a writer who deals with that elusive idea of "place," that is, nature and history and environment considered, as Rathjen himself writes, "in the sense of shared experience and concern for the past." Other regionalists include Ima C. Barlow, Floyd V. Studer, and Garry L. Nall of West Texas A&M

University, and Joe F. Taylor of Amarillo College. Each has written about the area's history and archaeology. Laura V. Hamner, John L. McCarty, Ernest R. Archambeau, A. G. Mojtabai, and Thomas Thompson have also contributed significantly to Amarillo and Panhandle writing.

Some exceptional fiction writers have come from the Amarillo region. Carol Sobieski, a screenplay writer, penned such works as *Christmas Sunshine,* a movie produced for television; *Neon Ceiling; Sylvester;* and *Annie.* John R. Erickson, who has written serious ranching history about the Texas Panhandle—*The Modern Cowboy,* for example—produced the highly popular Hank the Cowdog series of children's books. Loula Grace Erdman, who taught in the Amarillo public schools for fifteen years, wrote the prize-winning novel *Years of the Locust* plus such works as *Separate Star* and *Fair Is the Morning.* Kimberly Willis Holt received the Boston Globe Horn Book Award for *My Louisiana Sky* in 1997 and the National Book Award for Young People's Literature in 1998 for *When Zachary Beaver Comes to Town.* Exceptional cowboy poets included Buck Ramsey and Red Stegall, called the "Cowboy Poet of Texas."

Few Panhandle writers, however, have surpassed the literary accomplishments of Al Dewlen, an Amarillo newspaperman turned novelist. His *Twilight of Honor* won the McGraw-Hill Fiction Award, was an international best seller, and became the basis of a popular Hollywood film starring Richard Chamberlain. He wrote several other novels, including *The Night of the Tiger,* which was his first novel; *Servants of Corruption;* and *Next of Kin.* But people of Amarillo and the Texas Panhandle remember Dewlen best for *The Bone Pickers,* a story, writes one critic, "of human needs, hidden dreams, and battered aspirations." Set in Amarillo in the late 1950s, it is a tragicomic tale of the slow descent of the wealthy and powerful Munger clan, a tale many people in the city understood to be based on an important Amarillo family. But, as A. C. Greene and W. U. McCoy suggest, the Mungers are universal, and the story could be set in any part of Texas.[33]

In many ways, the arts dominated Amarillo's cultural life at the turn of the twenty-first century. Art galleries remained abundant, for example, and in the twenty-two hundred block of South Van Buren Street the Amarillo Museum of Art, founded in 1967, held a variety of exhibits. Some of the on-loan displays featured shows of American and European master works, twentieth-century modernists, Asian collections, and contemporary art. The museum provided educational programs, lectures, gallery talks, video shows, and symposia. The Amarillo Opera, as another example, staged annually two productions and across much of the Panhandle offered various outreach programs and educational services. And the celebrated Amarillo Little Theatre, active since its founding in 1927, continues to present yearly a diverse collection of stage plays.

At the time of the writing of this book, Amarillo is economically healthy, socially and culturally vibrant, ethnically mixed, and poised for growth. Building permits are up in both number and value. The general outlook of its citizens is encouraging—and it should be. The city's bonded indebtedness is relatively minor; its cost of living, including housing, utilities, grocery items, and miscellaneous goods and services, is comparatively low; and its unemployment rate is only 3.1 percent.

Not everything is "rosy," of course. As Amarillo enters the twenty-first century, the region's economic reliance on the raw material–based industries of petroleum and agribusiness remains a concern. While economic diversity has been a keynote of the Chamber of Commerce and the Amarillo Development Corporation since the closing of Amarillo Air Force Base in the late 1960s, heavy reliance on extractive businesses—oil and gas and agriculture—to drive the economy tends to promote something of a colonial economy, one in which leaders can control neither the price of raw materials leaving the region nor the cost of goods coming into Amarillo.

Local business leaders and others worry about a trend in mergers or acquisitions that has been taking several major corporations and their headquarters out of Amarillo. The electric energy firm known as Southwestern Public Service Company, for example, merged with Public Service Company of Colorado and then later joined with

Northern States Power to become Xcel Energy with headquarters in Minneapolis. Pioneer Natural Gas Company, which had first supplied fuel for Amarillo residents in the 1920s, changed its name to Energas and is part of the Atmos Corporation of Dallas. Shamrock Oil and Gas Company became Diamond Shamrock upon joining with a group in Cleveland, Ohio, and is part of Valero Energy headquartered in San Antonio.

Another concern, one shared by most people in the modern West, is the future availability of water. Lake Meredith water is not sufficient enough in either quantity or quality to service adequately the eleven members of the Canadian River Municipal Water Authority, including Amarillo; and the finite, below ground resources in the Ogallala formation, under growing pressure from farmers, municipalities, and businesses, seems to decline each year. In addition, environmental degradation across the fragile, semi-arid Texas Panhandle is relentless.

These concerns aside, Amarillo is still the crossroads it has been since humans first entered the region nearly twelve thousand years ago. Despite its apparent isolation in the expansive, seemingly empty range country of the Southern Great Plains, Amarillo is at the center of a vast web of connections with military and industrial operations throughout the nation: Interstate Highways 40 and 27; U.S. Highways 60, 66, 87, and 287; and transcontinental rail and air connections make it so. In addition, as indicated in the opening chapter of this book, Amarillo remains in many ways midwestern in outlook and orientation. It is the hub of a huge market place that looks more often northeastward toward the Midwest than south or southeastward toward Austin. Its citizens may vacation in the high Rocky Mountains, but its business leaders look to the Midwest and the East for economic guidance.

Nonetheless, in major ways Amarillo remains a western town. Many of its citizens, at least, enjoy projecting the Old West image, and why not? The western ranching legacy continues to be strong and dynamic, and other manifestations of a western heritage, including the colorful Chamber of Commerce logo with the tall boots, the touristy cowboy breakfasts, the cowboy steak houses, and the ever-present cowboy paraphernalia of boots and pickup trucks all remain as outward and visible signs of Amarillo's western traditions. Amarillo, the local Chamber of Commerce boasts, is a place where one might "Step into the Real Texas," where its western past is important, and where "Texas of lore, from horses and cowboys to big skies and big land, still exists."

Outsiders also view Amarillo as a western town. *True West Magazine,* for instance, as part of its fiftieth anniversary celebration in 2003, named Amarillo one of the fifty most western towns in the United States. Amarillo, both the Queen City of the Texas Panhandle and the great hub of the Golden Spread, is indeed a western town where, some of its citizens might argue, western life remains wonderfully mainstream and remarkably prominent.

Notes

1 The Golden Spread

1. See, for example, Bill Crane, "The Three Faces of Texas," *San Antonio Express-News,* March 16, 1975, 1-H.

2. See *Texas Almanac, 2004–2005,* 256.

3. Fagan, *Ancient North America,* 96, 98–101; Holliday, *Paleoindian Geoarchaeology,* 76–89, 211–15.

4. Hughes, "Lake Creek", 65–84; Rathjen, *Texas Panhandle Frontier,* 33–34.

5. Rathjen, *Texas Panhandle Frontier,* 35. See also Fagan, *Ancient North America,* 135–56.

6. Brooks, "From Stone Slab Architecture," 331–44; Rathjen, *Texas Panhandle Frontier,* 35–38; Studer, "Archeology of the Texas Panhandle," 331–44; Krieger, *Culture Complexes and Chronology,* 17, 41–49; Hughes, "Prehistoric Cultural Development," 30–33; Fagan, *Ancient North America,* 135–56.

7. La Vere, *Texas Indians,* 30–31; Huebner, "Late Prehistoric Bison Populations," 343–58.

8. Wallace and Hoebel, *Comanches,* 12–14, 304, 310; Kavanagh, *Comanche Political History,* 1–19.

9. The Comanche-Spanish parallel stories are familiar ones. Historians, such as Frederick W. Rathjen and John Miller Morris for the Panhandle and Donald Chipman and David La Vere for the larger Texas experience, and anthropologists, such as Thomas W. Kavanagh and William C. Meadows for Comanche political life, have described in various degrees of detail Spanish and Comanche activity in Texas during the eighteenth and early nineteenth centuries.

10. La Vere, *Texas Indians,* 134–39.

11. McClure, "Battle of Adobe Walls," 18–65; Lavender, *Bent's Fort,* 246–47, 308–10; Rathjen, *Texas Panhandle Frontier,* 74–75, 77–80. See also Price and Rathjen, *Golden Spread,* 39–42.

12. Archambeau, "Fort Smith–Santa Fe Trail," 1–26.

13. Rathjen, *Texas Panhandle Frontier,* 105–13.

14. See Connor, "Early Ranching Operations," 45–69; Carlson, "Panhandle Pastores," 1–15; Rathjen, *Texas Panhandle Frontier,* 181–93; Carlson, *Empire Builder,* 18–23, 28–30, 32–35; and Price and Rathjen, *Golden Spread,* 51–61.

2 The Founding of Amarillo

1. Price and Rathjen, *Golden Spread,* 68.

2. Gober and Price, *Cowboy Justice,* 85, 86.

3. Ibid., 68–69. See also *Tascosa Pioneer,* May 28, 1887; Overton, *Gulf to Rockies,* 167–69, 171–72; Boaz, "History of Amarillo, Texas," 112; Carlson, *Empire Builder,* 37–39.

4. Carlson, *Empire Builder,* 36–37, 39; Price and Rathjen, *Golden Spread,* 69.

5. Gober and Price, *Cowboy Justice,* 65–86; *Tascosa Pioneer,* July 16 and August 13, 1887; Price and Rathjen, *Golden Spread,* 68–69; Key, *In the Cattle Country,* 40–41.

6. Gober and Price, *Cowboy Justice,* 95–98.

7. Price and Rathjen, *Golden Spread,* 69. See also Morris, *Private in the Texas Rangers,* 143–45.

8. *Tascosa Pioneer,* August 13 and August 20, 1887.

9. *Tascosa Pioneer,* September 3, 1887. See also Key, *In the Cattle Country,* 42; Gober and Price, *Cowboy Justice,* 102; and Crudgington, "Old Town Amarillo," 86.

10. Overton, *Gulf to Rockies,* 171–72.

11.Ibid.; McCarty, *Maverick Town,* 216, 218–20, 223–24; Haley, *XIT Ranch of Texas,* 208.

12. Overton, *Gulf to Rockies,* 173–74; McCarty, *Maverick Town,* 224–26.

13. Henry B. Sanborn to P. L. Moen, president, Washburn and Moen Co., December 30, 1886, in Hamner, *Light 'n Hitch,* 335–37.

14. Overton, *Gulf to Rockies,* 170–71; McCarty, *Maverick Town,* 212–15; Price and Rathjen, *Golden Spread,* 67.

15. Key, *In the Cattle Country,* 43–44.

16. Pate, *Livestock Legacy,* xv–xvi; Carlson, *Empire Builder,* 41–42.

17. *Amarillo Champion,* May 17, 1888; Key, *In the Cattle Country,* 50; Boaz, "History of Amarillo, Texas," 47–50; Holden, *Spur Ranch,* 132–33.

18. *Amarillo Champion,* May 17, 1888; Key, *In the Cattle Country,* 50; Price and Rathjen, *Golden Spread,* 69; J. Cox, *Historical and Biographical Record,* 697.

19. Mrs. Albert Bivins and Cora Green, interview by Mrs. L. E. Moyer, accompanied by C. Boone McClure, January 20, 1958, transcript in Wendy and Stanley Marsh 3, Records, Toad Hall, Amarillo; Duncan Kersey, "Going Back to the Wild and Woolly Days in Amarillo with City's First Native," *Amarillo Sunday News and Globe,* November 27, 1927; Key, *In the Cattle Country,* 50; Carlson, *Empire Builder,* 42–43.

20. Key, *In the Cattle Country,* 50. See also "Judge Turner Tells Realtors of Days When City Had Only One Hotel," *Amarillo Daily News,* November 28, 1926; Carlson, *Empire Builder,* 43–44.

21. Price and Rathjen, *Golden Spread,* 69; Crudgington, "Old Town Amarillo," 87.

22. Key, *In the Cattle Country,* 45, 47; Crudgington, "Old Town Amarillo," 87.

23. Key, *In the Cattle Country,* 48.

24. *American Breeder Magazine,* June 1889, as cited in ibid., 81.

25. *Amarillo Champion,* May 18, 1888. See also Price and Rathjen, *Golden Spread,* 70.

26. *Tascosa Pioneer,* September 8, 1888; Price and Rathjen, *Golden Spread,* 69–70; Carlson, *Empire Builder,* 44; Key, *In the Cattle Country,* 77–79. Berry had seven investment partners, each with a one-eighth interest in Amarillo: William Plemons, Warren Wetzel, John Hollicott, Thomas Wallace, J. J. Medaries, William Martin, and W. A. George.

27. *Tascosa Pioneer,* September 8, 1888; Key, *In the Cattle Country,* 77, 79; Price and Rathjen, *Golden Spread,* 69.

28. Key, *In the Cattle Country,* 78; Price and Rathjen, *Golden Spread,* 70–71; "Hotel Amarillo," *Amarillo Daily News,* October 6, 1915.

29. Price and Rathjen, *Golden Spread,* 70.

30. Key, *In the Cattle Country,* 77–78.

31. *Amarillo Champion,* May 18, 1888; "Judge Turner Tells Realtors of Days When City Had Only One Hotel," *Amarillo Daily News,* November 28, 1926; Crudgington, "Old Town Amarillo," 106; Price and Rathjen, *Golden Spread,* 70; Carlson, *Empire Builder,* 45, 49.

32. Price and Rathjen, *Golden Spread,* 70.

33. Bivens and Green, interview. See also Key, *In the Cattle Country,* 80, 81.

34. Daisey Currie, "The Story of Her Life as Told to Me by Her: The Life Story of Mrs. W. W. Wetsel, I," transcript in Interview Files, Archives, Panhandle-Plains Historical Museum; Hamner, *Short Grass and Longhorns,* 211.

3 Amarillo in 1900

1. See, for example, *Amarillo News,* February 9, March 2, April 6, and May 4, 1895. See also Gober and Price, *Cowboy Justice,* 111–12, 121–23, 145, 154; Crudgington, "Old Town Amarillo," 108; Price and Rathjen, *Golden Spread,* 74–76; Haley and Holden, *Flamboyant Judge,* 4–6, 10, 13–14, 22, 24–25.

2. Gober and Price, *Cowboy Justice,* 120; Carlson, *Empire Builder,* 49, 56–57, 90–91, 94–95; Crudgington, "Old Town Amarillo," 108; Loving, "H. B. Sanborn," 3, 25, 31, 33, 38–41, 60.

3. Haley and Holden, *Flamboyant Judge,* 14.

4. Ibid., 14–15.

5. Ibid. See also Price and Rathjen, *Golden Spread,* 73; Loving, "H. B. Sanborn," 28.

6. Haley and Holden, *Flamboyant Judge,* 13–14; Carlson, *Empire Builder,* 28; Key, *In the Cattle Country,* 108–9; Price and Rathjen, *Golden Spread,* 74; Parker, "Incipient Trade," 141–43.

7. Key, *In the Cattle Country,* 108–18; Price and Rathjen, *Golden Spread,* 74. See also Timmons et al., *Centennial Book,* 1–10; *Grand March,* 1–10.

8. Haley and Holden, *Flamboyant Judge,* 11, 24.

9. Currie, "Story of Her Life," 2–3.

10. Key, *In the Cattle Country,* 133.

11. *Amarillo Daily Northwest,* December 25, 1889, as cited in Key, *In the Cattle Country,* 130–31.

12. Currie, "Story of Her Life," 4. See also Carlson, *Empire Builder,* 27–28.

13. Price and Rathjen, *Golden Spread,* 74; Key, *In the Cattle Country,* 92, 133, 135.

14. Price and Rathjen, *Golden Spread,* 73; Key, *In the Cattle Country,* 120–21.

15. See Fred Post, "A Major Change in Government of City," *Amarillo Sunday News and Globe,* Golden Anniversary Edition, August 14, 1938, B-15;

16. Ibid.; Carlson, *Empire Builder,* 85–86; Price and Rathjen, *Golden Spread,* 74; Key, *In the Cattle Country,* 85–89; Haley and Holden, *Flamboyant Judge,* 18, 19n18.

17. See Key, *In the Cattle Country,* 85–89; Haley and Holden, *Flamboyant Judge,* 47; Carlson, *Empire Builder,* 85–86.

18. *Dallas Morning News,* May 6 and June 20, 1892, and July 18, 1893; Dunn, "Drouth in West Texas," 129–30. For rainfall amounts in Amarillo, see Sheffy, "Experimental Stage of Settlement," 81.

19. J. Cox, *Historical and Biographical Record,* 697; *Amarillo News,* May 4, 1895; Key, *In the Cattle Country,* 103; Price and Rathjen, *Golden Spread,* 74.

20. William Henry Bush to Carnes and Dunton (attorneys), Sycamore, Illinois, April 8, 1895, in Bush Letters, William H. Bush Collection, Amarillo Public Library; *Amarillo News,* May 4, 1895; Duncan Kersey, "Going Back to the Wild and Woolly Days in Amarillo with City's First Native," *Amarillo Sunday News and Globe,* November 27, 1927, sec. 2, pp. 1, 5; Price and Rathjen, *Golden Spread,* 74–75; Key, *In the Cattle Country,* 161–62.

21. Price and Rathjen, *Golden Spread,* 75; Carlson, *Empire Builder,* 86–87.

22. Price and Rathjen, *Golden Spread,* 75–76. See also Haley and Holden, *Flamboyant Judge,* 127, 201–2; and Key, *In the Cattle Country,* 81, 83.

23. Price and Rathjen, *Golden Spread,* 75–76. See also Haley and Holden, *Flamboyant Judge,* 127, 201–2; and Key, *In the Cattle Country,* 81, 83.

24. Haley and Holden, *Flamboyant Judge,* 47–48, 52–54. For a less flattering, contradictory portrait of Temple Houston, see Jennings, *Through the Shadows,* 28–40; but also see Wellman, *Dynasty of Western Outlaws,* 253–54.

25. Haley and Holden, *Flamboyant Judge,* 57.

26. Carlson, *Empire Builder,* 88.

27. *Amarillo Weekly News,* August 26, 1899; *Amarillo Evening News,* June 23 and August 21, 1899; "Angle of Mercy," *Amarillo Sunday News and Globe,* Golden Anniversary Edition, August 14, 1938, sec. G-3, p. 6; Herbert Timmons and Carolyn Timmons, "Plains Catholics," *Amarillo Sunday News and Globe,* Golden Anniversary Edition, August 14, 1938, sec. G-3, p. 2; Carlson, *Empire Builder,* 88–89; Haley and Holden, *Flamboyant Judge,* 57, 126–27.

28. Haley and Holden, *Flamboyant Judge,* 103. See also Crimm, "Mathew 'Bones' Hooks"; *Amarillo News,* February 4, 1951; Saunder, "Empty Saddle," 139–42; Key, *In the Cattle Country,* 293–94.

29. Haley and Holden, *Flamboyant Judge,* 6–10.

4 A City of Modern Pioneers

1. From a postcard as cited in Franks and Ketelle, *Amarillo, Texas, 1887–1987*, no. 2.

2. Sanborn to Moen, December 30, 1886, in Hamner, *Light 'n Hitch*, 335–37; Haley, "Grass Lease Fight," 1–27; *State v Goodnight*, Supreme Court of Texas, July 1, 1888, 11 *Southwestern Reporter*, 119–21.

3. *Amarillo Evening News*, March 2, April 6, and May 4, 1895; *General Laws of the State of Texas*, 793–807; Gammel, *Laws of Texas*, 10:63–77; Murrah, *C. C. Slaughter*, 84; Haley, *Charles Goodnight*, 401; Carlson, *Empire Builder*, 105.

4. *Amarillo Evening News*, March 2, 1895; Murrah, *C. C. Slaughter*, 84. Some cattlemen, including the Texas Panhandle's Charles Goodnight, apparently favored the Four Section Act. See Haley and Holden, *Flamboyant Judge*, 12n10.

5. Murrah, *C. C. Slaughter*, 104–5; Carlson, *Empire Builder*, 105.

6. Key, *In the Cattle Country*, 164; Price and Rathjen, *Golden Spread*, 76.

7. Carlson, *Empire Builder*, 95–97; Haley and Holden, *Flamboyant Judge*, 12n10.

8. Price and Rathjen, *Golden Spread*, 63; Carlson, *Empire Builder*, 105–6.

9. *Amarillo Weekly News*, June 28, 1901; *Evening News*, June 4, 1901.

10. Haley and Holden, *Flamboyant Judge*, 8–9.

11. *Amarillo Star*, September 11, 1903.

12. *Amarillo Daily News*, November 15, 1911; Key, *In the Cattle Country*, 176–77.

13. *Amarillo Star*, September 11, 1903; *Daily Panhandle*, August 27, 1907.

14. *Evening News*, May 23, 1901; *Amarillo Daily News*, July 13, 1911.

15. Key, *In the Cattle Country*, 211–13.

16. Quote in ibid., 170.

17. Ibid., 169–70; Price and Rathjen, *Golden Spread*, 76–77; Franks and Ketelle, *Amarillo, Texas, II*, no. 22; *Amarillo Daily News*, August 12, 1911.

18. Price and Rathjen, *Golden Spread*, 76–77.

19. Ibid.; Key, *In the Cattle Country*, 170.

20. *Amarillo Daily News*, August 12, 1911.

21. The University Interscholastic League did not sponsor a state championship playoff tournament until 1920. See Ratliff, *Autumn's Mightiest Legions*, 8–9.

22. Key, *In the Cattle Country*, 223–25; *Amarillo Daily News*, January 13, 1911.

23. "Present Institution Formed Six Years Ago," *Amarillo Daily News*, September 8, 1929; "Bush Likes Dairy Farming," *Amarillo Daily News*, September 29, 1914; "All-Panhandle Fair Meeting," *Amarillo Daily News*, December 27, 1911. See also Carlson, *Empire Builder*, 110–11.

24. *Amarillo Daily News*, January 5, 1910.

25. Ibid., January 13, 1911; Key, *In the Cattle Country*, 230–31; Carlson, *Empire Builder*, 92; Marsh, "Bush Memorial Collection," 299–300.

26. See the *Amarillo Daily News*, January 5, 1910, and December 24, 1911.

27. *Daily Panhandle*, August 27, 1907.

28. Quote in Plagens, "Georgia on Our Minds," 65. See also Hogrefe, *O'Keeffe*, 46–49; Goodrich and Bry, *Georgia O'Keeffe*, 8–9.

29. Messinger, *Georgia O'Keeffe*, 7, 13, 19, 24; Hogrefe, *O'Keeffe*, 69–72, 77–82.

30. Price and Rathjen, *Golden Spread,* 83; Steele, "Phebe Warner," 45–50.

31. *Evening News,* May 23, 1901.

32. Key, *In the Cattle Country,* 191–92.

5 Economic Development, 1910–1930

1. Quote in Sheffy, "Experimental Stage of Settlement," 92.

2. Nall, "Panhandle Farming," 85; *Amarillo News,* February 2, 1895; Carlson, "Campbell Ranch," 27–34.

3. Quote in "Syndicate to Buy Land Near Hereford," *Amarillo Daily News,* May 14, 1912. See also Nall, "Panhandle Farming," 85; Carlson, *Empire Builder,* 108–9; Price and Rathjen, *Golden Spread,* 89.

4. Nall, "Specialization and Expansion," 47.

5. Worster, *Under Western Skies,* 99. See also Nall, "Specialization and Expansion," 47; "Wheat Acreage Shows Increase," *Amarillo Daily News,* December 1, 1914; Price and Rathjen, *Golden Spread,* 89; Carlson, *Empire Builder,* 108–9.

6. "Wheat Acreage Shows Increase," *Amarillo Daily News,* December 1, 1914. See also "Bush Likes Dairy Cows," *Amarillo Daily News,* September 29, 1914; *Amarillo Daily News,* April 29 and October 17, 1919; Carlson, *Empire Builder,* 108–9.

7. Quote in Carlson, *Empire Builder,* 109. See also Nall, "Specialization and Expansion," 47, 56–57; "A Prosperous County," *Amarillo Daily News,* April 29, 1919; Sheffy, "Experimental Stage of Settlement," 92n25; "The Panhandle of Texas," *Amarillo Daily News,* May 9, 1919.

8. Haley and Holden, *Flamboyant Judge,* 83.

9. Price and Rathjen, *Golden Spread,* 87–88; Clark, *Three Stars for the Colonel,* 193–94.

10. William Henry Bush to William S. Rule, August 24, 1914, in Henry B. Sanborn Collection, Archives, Panhandle-Plains Historical Museum, Canyon, Texas; Price and Rathjen, *Golden Spread,* 87; Haley and Holden, *Flamboyant Judge,* 81, 82n10.

11. Price and Rathjen, *Golden Spread,* 87; Carlson, *Empire Builder,* 119–20; Bartlett, "Discovery of the Panhandle Oil and Gas Fields," 48–54; "William Henry Bush Here on Short Visit," *Amarillo Daily News,* February, 18, 1919; "The Panhandle of Texas," *Amarillo Daily News,* May 9, 1919.

12. Key, *In the Cattle Country,* 254.

13. "Work of Red Cross Is Organized Here," *Amarillo Daily News,* June 12, 1917.

14. "New Preventive for Influenza Discovered," *Amarillo Daily News,* November 12, 1918; "Influenza Epidemic Fast Waning Here Is Belief of Officials," *Amarillo Daily News,* November 15, 1918.

15. "Amarillo People Celebrate Great Victory of Allies," *Amarillo Daily News,* November 12, 1918; Key, *In the Cattle Country,* 255.

16. "American Legion Post Formed Here," *Amarillo Daily News,* July 1, 1919; "Dr. Hanson's Body Reaches America," *Amarillo Daily News,* September 13, 1921; Key, *In the Cattle Country,* 255; Clark, *Three Stars for the Colonel,* 44, 51, 79.

17. "Celebration on the Fourth to Be Greatest in History of the Entire Panhandle,"

Amarillo Daily News, July 2, 1919; "Chairman Thompson Issues Order for Victory Parade on 4th of July," *Amarillo Daily News,* July 1, 1919; "Independence Day Fittingly Observed Here," *Amarillo Daily News,* July 5, 1919.

18. "Lower Prices for Wheat Are Quoted," *Amarillo Daily News,* May 5, 1921; "Wheat Declines 33–4 Cents Net," *Amarillo Daily News,* September 11, 1921; "Drop in Wheat Is Still Unchecked," *Amarillo Daily News,* September 18, 1921.

19. See Price and Rathjen, *Golden Spread,* 87–89; Key, *In the Cattle Country,* 256–58, 263; Carlson, *Empire Builder,* 119, 123–24. See also "Many New Test Wells Will Be Drilled," *Amarillo Daily News,* May 8, 1921; and "A. J. Day's Oil Tips," *Amarillo Daily News,* May 12, 1921.

20. Key, *In the Cattle Country,* 259; Price and Rathjen, *Golden Spread,* 88–89.

21. U.S. Department of the Interior, Bureau of Mines, "Helium Capital of the World," 157–59. See also Carlson, *Empire Builder,* 129–30.

22. Roddy, "Texas Helium for War or Peace"; "New Helium Field in Amarillo Shifts Scene of U.S. Operations," *Amarillo Daily News,* August 28, 1928; Andrew Stewart, "About Helium," pp. 31–32, U.S. Department of the Interior, Bureau of the Mines, mimeographed report (IC6745), 1933, copy in John L. McCarty Collection, Amarillo Public Library; Seibel, "Development of Helium Production"; Anderson, "Helium from a Scientific Curiosity."

23. Price and Rathjen, *Golden Spread,* 88; Key, *In the Cattle Country,* 264.

24. Price and Rathjen, *Golden Spread,* 88.

25. Key, *In the Cattle Country,* 259.

26. Ibid.; "Air Mail Here Is Predicted at Early Date," *Amarillo Sunday News and Globe,* February 13, 1927; "From Canuck to Luxury Liner Is Amarillo's Flying History," *Amarillo Sunday News and Globe,* Golden Anniversary Edition, August 14, 1938, sec. G-3, p. 28; Foreman, "Birth of English Field."

27. Wallis, *Route 66,* 6, 9, 11. See also Snyder, *Route 66 Traveler's Guide,* 58–59.

28. "Many New Developments to Be Announced," *Amarillo Daily News,* June 10, 1927; "U.S. 66 Highway Convention Opens Monday," *Amarillo Sunday News and Globe,* June 19, 1927; "Five Hundred Expected Today for Highway Meet," *Amarillo Daily News,* June 20, 1927.

29. Wallis, *Route 66,* 131, 133; Key, *In the Cattle Country,* 259–60; Kelly, *Route 66,* 24.

30. Quote in Kelly, *Route 66,* 29.

31. Snyder, *Route 66 Traveler's Guide,* 59; Franks and Ketelle, *Amarillo, Texas, II,* 207; "Dance at the Nat," *Amarillo Daily News,* June 4, 1927.

32. Burt, *The Novel 100,* 239; Snyder, *Route 66 Traveler's Guide,* ix–x; Wallis, Marsh qtd. in *Route 66,* page 23, see also page 131.

33. "Record Wheat Crop Predicted," *Amarillo Daily News,* February 3, 1927; "The Panhandle of Texas," *Amarillo Daily News,* May 9, 1919.

34. Price and Rathjen, *Golden Spread,* 90.

35. Key, *In the Cattle Country,* 266.

36. "Street Car System Bumped Along," *Amarillo Sunday News and Globe,* Golden Anniversary Edition, August 14, 1938, A-24; "Building Bus Lines," *Amarillo Sunday*

News and Globe, Golden Anniversary Edition, C-21. See also Key, *In the Cattle Country,* 216–18.

6 The Jazz Age in Amarillo

1. Leuchtenburg, *The Perils of Prosperity,* 7. See also Mowry, *The Twenties,* 1–2.

2. "W. H. Bush, Known as Benefactor of City," *Amarillo Daily News,* April 10, 1931.

3. Key, *In the Cattle Country,* 245–46.

4. Ibid., 260.

5. Ibid.; "Tourist Camp Site Question Is Reopened," *Amarillo Daily News,* April 2, 1924; "Camping Grounds Question to Be Answered Today," *Amarillo Daily News,* April 6, 1924; "Site Selected for Permanent Camping Ground," *Amarillo Daily News,* April 9, 1924.

6. Chalmers, *Hooded Americanism,* 2–5, 39–48.

7. Ibid., 39–40, 45; M. Harrison, "Gentlemen from Indiana," 149; Ku Klux Klan (Amarillo, Texas) Records, 1921–25, membership roster, A158.4E, Southwest Collection, Texas Tech University.

8. *Stanford v. State* (no. 8457), Court of Criminal Appeals of Texas, January 21, 1925, 268 *Southwestern Reporter,* 161–62; *Dallas Morning News,* April 15, 1923; Alexander, *Ku Klux Klan in the Southwest,* 81.

9. "Democrats Are to 'Blame' for Klan," *Amarillo Daily News,* April 12, 1922; "Floydada Plans Action to Halt Ku Klux Parade," *Amarillo Daily News,* April 1, 1924; "Klan Must Reform or Die," *Amarillo Daily News,* April 4, 1924; "Are Rangers Ku Kluxers?" *Amarillo Daily News,* April 29, 1924.

10. "Ku Klux Klan Is Praised by Robert L. Henry," *Amarillo Daily News,* April 26, 1922.

11. Ku Klux Klan (Amarillo, Texas) membership roster.

12. Ibid.

13. Haley and Holden, *Flamboyant Judge,* 127–28, 201–3; Nail, *One Short Sleep Past,* 52.

14. "Officers Seize $8,000 in Booze, Make 4 Arrests," *Amarillo Daily News,* April 13, 1922.

15. "Two Amarillo Men Convicted," *Amarillo Daily News,* April 17, 1924.

16. "Man and Wife Arrested on Booze Charge," *Amarillo Daily News,* April 6, 1924.

17. Raymond Swindell, interview with David L. Nail, January 18, 1971, as cited in Nail, *One Short Sleep Past,* 53–54.

18. Haley and Holden, *Flamboyant Judge,* 202–3.

19. "Nat Pool," *Amarillo Daily News,* April 28, 1924; "Single Piece Bathing Suits to Be Tabooed," *Amarillo Daily News,* April 30, 1924.

20. Cited in Franks and Ketelle, *Amarillo, Texas, II,* 140.

21. "Public School History," *Amarillo Sunday News and Globe,* Golden Anniversary Edition, August 14, 1938, B-22.

22. Key, *In the Cattle Country,* 228; "Early School," *Amarillo Sunday News and Globe,* Golden Anniversary Edition, August 14, 1938, B-10; "St. Mary's in 1913," *Amarillo Sunday News and Globe,* Golden Anniversary Edition, August 14, 1938, B-25.

23. See "Public School History," *Amarillo Sunday News and Globe,* Golden Anniversary Edition, August 14, 1938, B-22; "African Church," *Amarillo Sunday News and Globe,* Golden Anniversary Edition, August 14, 1938, B-15. See also "Schools," *Amarillo Sunday News and Globe,* Bicentennial Edition, January 18, 1976, 4-H.

24. "Plans for $500,000 College Here," *Amarillo Daily News,* April 16, 1924; "University of Amarillo Recently Authorized," *Amarillo Daily News,* June 19, 1927; "Lee Bivins, Giant," *Amarillo Sunday News and Globe,* Golden Anniversary Edition, August 14, 1938, E-7; Key, *In the Cattle Country,* 228.

25. "Amarillo College," *Amarillo Sunday News and Globe,* Golden Anniversary Edition, August 14, 1938, B-12; "Amarillo College," in Hammond, *Amarillo,* 186–88.

26. "Polk Street Methodist," *Amarillo Sunday News and Globe,* Golden Anniversary Edition, August 14, 1938, C-12; "First Baptist Church in 1889," *Amarillo Sunday News and Globe,* Golden Anniversary Edition, August 14, 1938, C-14.

27. "Sunday School Reports," *Amarillo Daily News,* April 1 and April 8, 1924; "St. Mary's in 1913," *Amarillo Sunday News and Globe,* Golden Anniversary Edition, August 14, 1938, B-25; "The Buchanan Methodists," ibid., A-16; "Tabernacle Baptists," ibid., A-25; "Organization of East Amarillo Methodists," ibid., F-24; "Glenwood Baptists," ibid., F-22; "Seventh Day Adventists Church," ibid., F-25.

28. "Mexican Mission Launched in 1927," *Amarillo Sunday News and Globe,* Golden Anniversary Edition, August 14, 1938, A-30.

29. "Colored Churches Have Great Mass Meeting at Olympic," *Amarillo Daily News,* May 12, 1919.

30. "Temple B'nai Israel," *Amarillo Sunday News and Globe,* Golden Anniversary Edition, August 14, 1938, A-30. In the 1920s, the congregation sponsored Troop 24 of Boy Scouts: "Scouts Served at Ozark Trail Opening," *Amarillo Sunday News and Globe,* Bicentennial Edition, January 18, 1976, 30.

31. Cited in Franks and Ketelle, *Amarillo, Texas, 1887–1987,* 84.

32. Ibid.; "Music Festival Ticket Sales on Increase," *Amarillo Daily News,* April 18, 1924; Hammond, *Amarillo,* 123–24; Key, *In the Cattle Country,* 238, 260–61; Price and Rathjen, *Golden Spread,* 95; "City's Music Master," *Amarillo Sunday News and Globe,* Golden Anniversary Edition, August 14, 1938, D-32; "Amarillo's Auditorium Covers Entire Block," *Amarillo Daily News,* April 6, 1924; "Old Municipal Auditorium Built in 1923," *Amarillo Sunday News and Globe,* Bicentennial Edition, January 18, 1976, 28-H.

33. "Symphony History," *Amarillo Sunday News and Globe,* Bicentennial Edition, January 18, 1976, 32-H; Key, *In the Cattle Country,* 238; "Little Theater Is Acclaimed by Critics," *Amarillo Sunday News and Globe,* Golden Anniversary Edition, August 14, 1938, sec. G-3, p. 20.

34. "Many Radio Fans Enjoying Orchestra," *Amarillo Daily News,* April 2, 1924; "Station WDAG Will Broadcast Easter Program," *Amarillo Daily News,* April 13, 1924.

35. "Highlight of Summer: Harley Sadler Show," *Amarillo Sunday News and Globe,* Bicentennial Edition, January 18, 1976, 32-H.

36. Allen, *Only Yesterday,* 155–87.

37. "Sandies Have Great Record," *Amarillo Sunday News and Globe,* Golden

Anniversary Edition, August 14, 1938, sec. 1, p 12; "Looking Back on Sports," ibid., sec. 1, p 13.

38. "Cal Farley and Billy Landos Will Meet," *Amarillo Daily News,* April 8, 1924; "Looking Back on Sports," *Amarillo Sunday News and Globe,* Golden Anniversary Edition, August 14, 1938, sec. 1, p 13; Hammond, *Amarillo,* 124–25.

7 Amarillo and the Great Depression

1. Nail, *One Short Sleep Past,* 38.

2. Key, *In the Cattle Country,* 252.

3. Snyder, *Route 66 Traveler's Guide,* 59.

4. "Pig Hip King," *Amarillo Sunday News and Globe,* Golden Anniversary Edition, August 14, 1938, E-26; "Pig Hip Sandwich Shop," ibid., D-16.

5. Quotes in Clark, *Three Stars for the Colonel,* 61. See also Key, *In the Cattle Country,* 201–2.

6. Clark, *Three Stars for the Colonel,* 62.

7. Ibid. See also "City Parks Flourish After Start in 1903," *Amarillo Sunday News and Globe,* Golden Anniversary Edition, August 14, 1938, C-16; Key, *In the Cattle Country,* 201–2.

8. "Seven Parks," *Amarillo Sunday News and Globe,* Golden Anniversary Edition, August 14, 1938, D-7.

9. "Improvements to Greet Tri State Fair Visitors," *Amarillo Sunday News and Globe,* July 9, 1933; "Visitors Invited to Llano Cemetery Park Side," *Amarillo Sunday News and Globe,* August 13, 1933; Nail, *One Short Sleep Past,* 46–47.

10. Nail, *One Short Sleep Past,* 59–61, 70.

11. Tindall and Shi, *America,* 1161.

12. "Forestry Army of 600 Moves into Palo Duro Next Week," *Amarillo Daily News,* July 5, 1933; "Canyon Drive Work to Start," *Amarillo Daily News,* July 10, 1933; "Army of Conservation Soldiers Arrive Today," *Amarillo Daily News,* July 11, 1933; Price and Rathjen, *Golden Spread,* 94; Nail, *One Short Sleep Past,* 81–83; Toney, "Texas State Parks System," 20, 36, 45, 51, 53–56; Petersen, "Park for the Panhandle."

13. Kreidler, "To Anchor the Wind," 46.

14. Price and Rathjen, *Golden Spread,* 95; Nail, *One Short Sleep Past,* 93. See also articles in *Amarillo Sunday News and Globe,* September 17, 1933, and *Amarillo Daily News,* September 18 and September 19, 1933.

15. Quote in Nail, *One Short Sleep Past,* 93. For a more thorough discussion of CWA work in Amarillo, see Nail, *One Short Sleep Past,* 92–96. See also "Ultimate Expenditure to Be $7,500,000," *Amarillo Sunday News and Globe,* September 10, 1933; "Road Work Is Begun," *Amarillo Daily News,* September 12, 1933.

16. Price and Rathjen, *Golden Spread,* 95.

17. See, for example, "Amarillo Builders Organize to Plan Code for Industry," *Amarillo Daily News,* July 19, 1933; "Café Men to Outline Code," *Amarillo Daily News,* July 20, 1933.

18. "Various Industries in Amarillo Quickly Give NRA Support," *Amarillo Daily*

News, July 27, 1933; "Businessmen of Amarillo Are Mobilized," *Amarillo Daily News,* July 29, 1933; "N.R.A. Code Plan Adopted by Amarillo Firms," *Amarillo Sunday News and Globe,* July 30, 1933; "Recovery Blue Eagle to Be Shown Today," *Amarillo Daily News,* August 1, 1933; "NRA Promises Buyers' Drive," *Amarillo Daily News,* August 3, 1933; Price and Rathjen, *Golden Spread,* 95; Nail, *One Short Sleep Past,* 84–91.

19. Nall, "Dust Bowl Days," 43.

20. Price and Rathjen, *Golden Spread,* 97; Parfit, "Dust Bowl"; Carlson, "Black Sunday," 5.

21. Nall, "Dust Bowl Days," 43; Neugebauer, *Plains Farmer,* 161, 163; Worster, *Dust Bowl,* 15. See also Hurt, *Dust Bowl,* 33–47; and Bonnifield, *Dust Bowl,* 61–86.

22. Arch Lamb, interview with Paul H. Carlson, October 30, 1990, as cited in Carlson, "Black Sunday," 7.

23. "July 4 Picnic, 3000 attended at Jack Hall Ranch," *Amarillo Daily News,* July 5, 1933.

24. Quote in Franks and Ketelle, *Amarillo, Texas, II,* 19; "Prep Football," *Lubbock Avalanche-Journal,* December 19 and December 20, 2004.

25. "At Amarillo Churches," *Amarillo Sunday News and Globe,* August 13 and August 20, 1933; "Temple B'nai Israel," *Amarillo Sunday News and Globe,* Golden Anniversary Edition, August 14, 1938, D-6.

26. "Tactless Texan," *Amarillo Globe,* January 23, 1933.

27. *Amarillo Globe,* March 5, 1934. See also Nail, *One Short Sleep Past,* 79–81.

28. Nail, *One Short Sleep Past,* 144–47.

29. "Marine Band Performs to Large Crowd," *Amarillo Daily News,* September 8, 1935; Nail, *One Short Sleep Past,* 143–44; Price and Rathjen, *Golden Spread,* 100–101; Key, *In the Cattle Country,* 269–73.

30. Price and Rathjen, *Golden Spread,* 99; Nall, "Dust Bowl Days," 42, 52–54, 59–60.

8 World War II and Afterward

1. "After 23 Years," *Amarillo Daily News,* December 9, 1941. See also Flynn, "Living History," 145–46.

2. Matthiesen, *Wise and Otherwise,* 192–93, 199–200.

3. *Texas Almanac and State Industrial Guide,* 98–99, 108, 299, 447.

4. Price and Rathjen, *Golden Spread,* 101, 103.

5. Franks and Ketelle, *Amarillo, Texas, 1887–1987,* 18, 21.

6. Ibid., 21, 64, 65, 70.

7. Franks and Ketelle, *Amarillo, Texas, II,* 62.

8. Franks and Ketelle, *Amarillo, Texas, 1887–1987,* 28, 71, 94.

9. Franks and Ketelle, *Amarillo, Texas, II,* 49; Price and Rathjen, *Golden Spread,* 105.

10. "Amarillo Receives Traffic Honor," *Amarillo Daily News,* January 4, 1940; Flynn, "Living History," 136.

11. Price and Rathjen, *Golden Spread,* 105. See also "Old Troop 'B' Called into Action," *Amarillo Daily News,* April 5, 1942.

12. "Plainsmen, Ready for Action, Jam-Pack Recruiting Stations," *Amarillo Daily News,* December 9, 1941.

13. "Jay Pietzch of Amarillo First Known Casualty," *Amarillo Daily News,* December 9, 1941; "Amarilloan Was First Texan Killed in America's War with Japanese," *Amarillo Daily News,* December 10, 1941; "Second Amarillo Boy Is Killed in Action," *Amarillo Daily News,* December 11, 1941.

14. "Sam Davis, ALT's Down to Earth Angel," 15–17; Matthiesen, *Wise and Otherwise,* 126.

15. "In Nation's Aviation Program," *Amarillo Daily News,* April 7, 1942.

16. Ibid.; Price and Rathjen, *Golden Spread,* 106; Mojtabai, *Blessed Assurance,* 33–34.

17. "Defense Plant, Air School in Panhandle," *Amarillo Daily News,* April 6, 1942; "Giant Industry Rises in Wheat Field," *Amarillo Daily News,* April 18, 1942; Matthiesen, *Wise and Otherwise,* 126–27.

18. "Giant Industry Rises in Wheat Fields," *Amarillo Daily News,* April 18, 1942.

19. "First of Virile Eggs Designed for Lap of Hirohito," *Amarillo Daily News,* September 18, 1924.

20. "Giant Panhandle Army Day Parade Tomorrow," *Amarillo Sunday News and Globe,* April 5, 1942; "Tribute of Entire Panhandle," *Amarillo Daily News,* April 6, 1942; "Gigantic Parade Here Instills New Confidence," *Amarillo Daily News,* April 7, 1942.

21. "Defense Building Exempt by WPB," *Amarillo Daily News,* April 9, 1942.

22. "Construction of Non-Essential Houses, Roads and Buildings Banned," *Amarillo Daily News,* April 9, 1942; "Want a Better Job?" *Amarillo Daily News,* September 25, 1942; "Lack of Houses Key to Amarillo Rent Problems," *Amarillo Daily News,* September 25, 1942.

23. "College Defense Classes Filling," *Amarillo Daily News,* September 12, 1942; "Amarillo College Enrollment is 350," *Amarillo Daily News,* September 17, 1942.

24. "Amarillo Center Registration Opens Monday," *Amarillo Sunday News and Globe,* September 13, 1942; "Amarillo Center Is Latest Project of Pioneer Plains College," *Amarillo Sunday News and Globe,* September 20, 1942.

25. "Service Men's Social Calendar Is Crammed with Recreation," *Amarillo Daily News,* September 25, 1942.

26. "Artist Hunts Submarines in a Blimp," *Amarillo Daily News,* April 9, 1942; Price and Rathjen, *Golden Spread,* 107.

27. "Bedlam Greets Peace as Crowds Choke Amarillo's Polk Street," *Amarillo Daily News,* August 15, 1945.

28. Ibid.

29. "Joyful Amarillo Takes Holiday," *Amarillo Daily News,* August 15, 1942.

30. "Amarillo Goes Back to Work Today," *Amarillo Daily News,* August 16, 1945; "Legal Holiday Order an Error," *Amarillo Daily News,* August 16, 1945.

31. "Meat Rationing Due to Be Relaxed Soon." *Amarillo Daily News,* August 17, 1945; "Speed Ceiling Lifted," *Amarillo Sunday News and Globe,* August 19, 1945;

"Reconversion Front Busy," *Amarillo Daily News,* August 22, 1945.

32. "Amarillo Field Hopes Are High," *Amarillo Daily News,* August 15, 1945; "Workers Laid Off at Pantex," *Amarillo Daily News,* August 16, 1945; Price and Rathjen, *Golden Spread,* 110.

33. "Panhandle War Workers, Jobs in Area," *Amarillo Daily News,* August 16, 1945; "Amarillo One of 7 Cities in Texas Now Facing 'Serious Unemployment,'" *Amarillo Daily News,* August 17, 1945; "Amarillo Listed among Areas Facing 'Serious Unemployment,'" *Amarillo Daily News,* August 23, 1945.

34. Price and Rathjen, *Golden Spread,* 108.

35. Ibid., 108–9; "Tornado Toll at 4," *Amarillo Daily News,* May 16, 1949; "Death Claims Fifth Victim," *Amarillo Daily News,* May 18, 1949.

36. "5 Tornadoes Cause Damage, Hurt None," *Amarillo Daily News,* May 15, 1949.

37. "Tornado Toll at 4," *Amarillo Daily News,* May 16, 1949; "City Digging Out," *Amarillo Daily News,* May 17, 1949; "Fund Passes $23,000," *Amarillo Daily News,* May 18, 1949; Price and Rathjen, *Golden Spread,* 108–9; Franks and Ketelle, *Amarillo, Texas, II,* 4–9 ; L. O'Brien Thompson, interview with Monte L. Monroe and Paul H. Carlson, March 11, 2005, tape in Southwest Collection, Texas Tech University; Tol Ware, interview with Monte L. Monroe and Paul H. Carlson, May 27, 2005, tape in Southwest Collection, Texas Tech University.

9 A Period of Expansion, 1950–1975

1. Price and Rathjen, *Golden Spread,* 109. Quote in Franks and Ketelle, *Amarillo, Texas, II,* 14, 15.

2. Price and Rathjen, *Golden Spread,* 109.

3. Ibid.; Franks and Ketelle, *Amarillo, Texas, II,* 14, 15.

4. Price and Rathjen, *Golden Spread,* 109.

5. Mojtabai, *Blessed Assurance,* 47.

6. Franks and Ketelle, *Amarillo, Texas, 1887–1987,* 172, 173, 176, 179.

7. Ibid., 76, 77.

8. Franks and Ketelle, *Amarillo, Texas, II,* 166.

9. Price and Rathjen, *Golden Spread,* 112, 123.

10. "Potter Backs Ike, Workmen's Compensation, Re-Allocation" and "High Plains Record Vote Goes to Ike," *Amarillo Daily News,* November 5, 1952; "Potter, Randall Voters Mark Ballots for GOP," *Amarillo Daily News,* November 9, 1960.

11. Price and Rathjen, *Golden Spread,* 112, 123.

12. "Amarillo Rolling toward Bright Highway Future" and "Amaday Salutes Citizens," *Amarillo Daily News,* December 1, 1960; "Dedicated Amarillo Celebrates Amaday," *Amarillo Daily News,* December 2, 1960; Franks and Ketelle, *Amarillo, Texas, II,* 150, 162.

13. Price and Rathjen, *Golden Spread,* 112.

14. "Water Conservationists Map Organization Plans," *Amarillo Daily News,* December 9, 1936; Flynn, "Living History," 158.

15. Flynn, "Living History," 161.

16. "Buffalo Lake," *Amarillo Sunday News and Globe,* October 26, 1941; "Panhandle Lakes Program Stimulates Business"; Flynn, "Living History," 171; Price and Rathjen, *Golden Spread,* 120.

17. "New Survey of Canadian Flood Damage Ordered," *Amarillo Daily News,* August 13, 1941; "20 Feared Drowned as Flood Swamps Sections of Carlsbad," *Amarillo Daily News,* September 22, 1941; "Menace of Onrushing Flood Water Mounting at Roswell," *Amarillo Daily News,* September 23, 1941; "New Mexico Flood Peril Abates; Canadian Dam Drive Renewed," *Amarillo Daily News,* September 24, 1941.

18. "Tascosa Dam Site Is Urged," *Amarillo Daily News,* May 11, 1949.

19. Flynn, "Living History," 180; Price and Rathjen, *Golden Spread,* 121.

20. "Udall, Connally Top Area Visitors Today," *Amarillo Daily News,* November 1, 1966; "Lake Meredith, Dam Dedicated," *Amarillo Daily News,* November 2, 1966; Finger, "Sanford Dam and Reservoir," 99–107.

21. "Bases Get Ax Today," *Amarillo Daily News,* November 19, 1964; "Order AAFB Phased Out," *Amarillo Daily News,* November 20, 1964.

22. "School Planning Softens the Shock," *Amarillo Daily News,* November 20, 1964.

23. "Order AAFB Phased Out," *Amarillo Daily News,* November 20, 1964.

24. Price and Rathjen, *Golden Spread,* 111, 121.

25. "Amarillo Population 137,969," *Amarillo Daily News,* December 1, 1960; M. Cox, *Historic Amarillo,* 75; *Amarillo City Directory, 1991,* xi.

26. "TSTI Deed Papers Issued by Clerk," *Amarillo Daily News,* June 17, 1970; "Ceremonies Slated Today," *Amarillo Daily News,* June 25, 1970; "TSTI Gets Warm Send-off," *Amarillo Daily News,* June 26, 1970; "Texas State Technical Institute Mid-Continent Campus, Amarillo," 188–89.

27. "Blaze Hits Bell Hangar," *Amarillo Daily News,* June 25, 1970.

28. "Dignitaries Due Today for Air Terminal Dedication," "Sheer Size Impressive in Tour of New Air Terminal," and "'Doers' Get Credit for New Terminal," all in *Amarillo Sunday News and Globe,* May 16, 1971; "New Air Terminal Thrills Thousands" and "Air Terminal Dedication Big Success," *Amarillo Daily News,* May 17, 1971; Price and Rathjen, *Golden Spread,* 112, 123; "Amarillo International," 17–19; M. Cox, *Historic Amarillo,* 75.

29. "Amarillo Housing," 9.

30. "A New School for Amarillo," 20–22; Ashworth, "Amarillo Public Schools," 190; Lamar Lively, letter to author, June 8, 2005.

10 Amarillo in 1980

1. Price and Rathjen, *Golden Spread,* 123; Quinby, "Hybrid Sorghum," 95.

2. Price and Rathjen, *Golden Spread,* 124; Mason, "Cotton Kingdom," 15; Nall, "Cattle Feeding Industry,"105–15.

3. See Nall, "Cattle Feeding Industry," 113–15.

4. Mason, "Cotton Kingdom," 17. Quote in Franks and Ketelle, *Amarillo, Texas, 1887–1987,* 148.

5. Franks and Ketelle, *Amarillo, Texas, 1887–1987,* 208; *Amarillo City Directory, 1983,* xxii.

6. M. Cox, *Historic Amarillo,* 124–25.

7. *Texas Almanac, 1982–1983,* 324.

8. Thompson, *North of Palo Duro,* 303, 306, 310.

9. *Texas Almanac, 1982–1983,* 372, 388.

10. M. Cox, *Historic Amarillo,* 166–67.

11. Wilson, "Peeking over the Hedge."

12. Thompson, *North of Palo Duro,* 306.

13. "Downtown Revisited," 20–21; Franks and Ketelle, *Amarillo, Texas, II,* 77, 78, 166; Franks and Ketelle, *Amarillo, Texas, 1887–1987,* 7, 17, 18, 20.

14. "Spanish Film Latest Attraction at Historic Downtown Theater," *Amarillo Daily News,* October 25, 1979.

15. "Amarillo: National Head Quarters of AQHA," *Amarillo Daily News,* October 28, 1979.

16. Rathjen, "New Introduction," vi.

17. Flynn, "Living History," 246; McCarty, "Kenneth Wyatt," 2–6; Thompson, *North of Palo Duro,* 291.

18. Thompson, *North of Palo Duro,* 291.

19. "Marsh's Manifest Mesa," 31.

20. For an example of a Carter policy shift that directly impacted Amarillo, see "Neutron Bomb 'Decision' Shows Carter Indecisive," *Amarillo Sunday News and Globe,* October 22, 1978.

21. "Reagan Wins by Landslide" and "Area Presidential, State & District Races," *Amarillo Daily News,* November 5, 1980.

22. Casey, "Prescription Politics"; "City May Retreat on SPS Hike," *Amarillo Sunday News and Globe,* October 8, 1978; "City Faces 2nd Utility Rate Increase in Month," *Amarillo Daily News,* November 8, 1980; "136% Gas Rate Hike Effective Today," *Amarillo Daily News,* November 12, 1980.

23. Casey, "Prescription Politics," 31–32; "Hills Edges Clements," "Potter County," and "Randall County," all in *Amarillo Daily News,* November 8, 1978. See also "We Recommend Hill as Governor of Texas," *Amarillo Sunday News and Globe,* November 5, 1978. For a somewhat different view, see Cantrell, "What Makes Jerry Run?"

24. Casey, "Prescription Politics," 34–35.

25. Quotes in ibid., 34. For previous Spradlin difficulties, see "Once-Angry Police Now Support Chief," *Amarillo Daily News,* November 3, 1978.

26. "Off-duty Officers Search for Killer," *Amarillo Daily News,* October 29, 1979. See also "City Man Discovers Wife Stabbed to Death," *Amarillo Daily News,* October 27, 1979.

27. Casey, "Prescription Politics," 35. See also "Police Have No Leads in Slaying of Woman," *Amarillo Sunday News and Globe,* October 28, 1979; "Leads Sought in Fatal Stabbing," *Amarillo Daily News,* October 30, 1979; "AC Gun Safety Course Grows Due to Lawrence Murder," *Amarillo Daily News,* October 31, 1979.

28. Casey, "Prescription Politics"; "Judge Moves Pinkerton Trial Ahead to November Docket," *Amarillo Daily News*, October 6, 1980.

29. Casey, "Prescription Politics," 54–55.

30. Ibid. See articles in the *Amarillo Daily News*, October 2, 1980, 1; "Randall Jury Probe Resumes Tomorrow," *Amarillo Sunday News and Globe*, November 9, 1980; "Grand Jury Hears Officers Today, *Amarillo Daily News*, November 12, 1980; "Spradlin Confirms Squabbles," *Amarillo Daily News*, November 13, 1980; "Spradlin's Term Full of Controversy," *Amarillo Daily News*, December 3, 1980; "More Mishandled Evidence Revealed," *Amarillo Daily News*, December 3, 1980; "After 3 Delays, Pinkerton Arraigned in Welch Killing," *Amarillo Daily News*, September 3, 1981.

31. "814 Sign Petitions Seeking Chief's Ouster," *Amarillo Daily News*, November 12, 1980.

32. "Search Begins for Spradlin Replacement," "More Mishandled Evidence Revealed," and "Spradlin's Tenure Full of Controversy," all in *Amarillo Daily News*, December 3, 1980; Casey, "Prescription Politics," 54–55. See also "Spradlin Speaks Out," 26–27, 34.

33. Wilson, "Mysterious Case of the Vanishing Elm," 59; *Amarillo City Directory, 1981*, xiv.

34. Wilson, "Mysterious Case of the Vanishing Elm," 59.

35. Ramsey, "Should the Panhandle Secede?"

36. *Amarillo City Directory, 1983*, xii.

37. *Amarillo City Directory, 1981*, xix.

11 Agribusiness, Oil, and Nuclear Bombs

1. "Proposed Missile Base Sites Threatening to Area Agriculture?" *Amarillo Daily News*, October 10, 1978.

2. Ibid. Other regional sites included, first, land in the upper Rio Grande Valley in Texas and New Mexico stretching east of Alamogorado, New Mexico, and south into Texas, and, second, the White Sands Missile Range in New Mexico.

3. Stumpf, *Titan II*, 152; Glass, *Citizens against the MX*, xv–xvi, 3–6; Levi et al., *Future of Land-Based Strategic Missiles*, 8, 21.

4. Malone and Etulain, *American West*, 288. See also Glass, *Citizens against the MX*, 12–15, 17–20, 46–51, 64–72, 80; "Proposed Missile Base Sites Threatening to Area Agriculture?" *Amarillo Daily News*, October 10, 1978; Wilson, "M-X Shell Game."

5. "Proposed Missile Base Sites Threatening to Area Agriculture?" *Amarillo Daily News*, October 10, 1978.

6. See the U.S. Air Force Ballistic Missile Office reports "Alternative Potential Deployment Areas," 1–3, and "Socioeconomic Impact Estimates for Texas/New Mexico Deployment Region," 1–97; "MX Plans Proceeding for Clovis Area" and "Curry County Farmers, Ranchers Warned of MX Impact," *Amarillo Daily News*, November 14, 1980. See also Levi et al., *Future of Land-Based Strategic Missiles*, 7–12; "Neutron Bomb 'Decision' Shows Carter Indecisive," *Amarillo Sunday News and Globe*, October 22, 1978.

7. "Nuclear Garbage Still a Hot Potato" and "Studies Conducted in Area,"

Amarillo Sunday News and Globe, October 28, 1979; Wilson, "Wermund Report."

8. Matthiesen, *Wise and Otherwise,* 132. See also U.S. Air Force Ballistic Missile Office, "Alternative Potential Deployment Areas," 1–3; Dougherty and Hatfield, "Should the United States Build the MX Missile?"

9. "Six Arrested at Pantex Plant," *Amarillo Globe-News,* February 6, 1981; Matthiesen, *Wise and Otherwise,* 132, 134–35.

10. Matthiesen, *Wise and Otherwise,* 132–33.

11. Cited in ibid., 135–36.

12. Ibid., 136–37. See also Mojtabai, *Blessed Assurance,* 54–55.

13. Bishop L. T. Matthiesen, "Statement on the Production and Stockpiling of the Neutron Bomb," *West Texas Catholic,* August 23, 1981. See also Mojtabai, *Blessed Assurance,* 46–47; Matthiesen, *Wise and Otherwise,* 139–41; Bergman, "Caution."

14. Matthiesen, *Wise and Otherwise,* 142; Mojtabai, *Blessed Assurance,* 55, 110–14; "Bishop Matthiesen: 'Wise' or 'Otherwise'?" *West Texas Catholic,* September 13, 1981. See also letters to the editor section, *Amarillo Sunday News and Globe,* August 30, 1981.

15. "Reader Defends Bishop for Criticism of Bomb," *Amarillo Sunday News and Globe,* September 6, 1981. See also "Bishop Receives Peace Award," *West Texas Catholic,* February 14, 1982.

16. Matthiesen, *Wise and Otherwise,* 143; "Wise and Otherwise," *West Texas Catholic,* December 6, 1981.

17. See Mojtabai, *Blessed Assurance,* 55–59, 110–14. See also Terri Goodman, "The Conscience of a Pantex Worker," *West Texas Catholic,* May 9, 1982.

18. Figures in Mojtabai, *Blessed Assurance,* 66–67. Quote in Mojtabai, *Blessed Assurance,* 55, and in Matthiesen, *Wise and Otherwise,* 144.

19. Matthiesen, *Wise and Otherwise,* 143–44; Mojtabai, *Blessed Assurance,* 114–18.

20. Glass, *Citizens against the MX,* 80; Matthiesen, *Wise and Otherwise,* 179–81; Mojtabai, *Blessed Assurance,* 96–108; *Amarillo City Directory, 1991,* xi.

21. "Catholic Nun Raped and Slain at N.E. Amarillo Convent," *Amarillo Sunday News and Globe,* November 1, 1981; "Funeral Mass Today for Slain Nun," *Amarillo Daily News,* November 2, 1981; "Coroner Believes, 'I Should Have Been Called,'" *Amarillo Daily News,* November 3, 1981; "Nun's Killer Struck Twice within Hours?" *Amarillo Daily News,* November 4, 1981; "Amarillo Youth, 17, Arrested," *Amarillo Daily News,* November 10, 1981.

22. Matthiesen, *Wise and Otherwise,* 179–81; "Profile of Killer: Person in Turmoil," *Amarillo Daily News,* November 4, 1981.

23. Speer, "Amarillo."

24. M. Cox, *Historic Amarillo,* 81; Howard, "Billion Dollar Question," 71; *Amarillo City Directory, 1991,* xix.

25. Franks and Ketelle, *Amarillo, Texas, 1887–1987,* 134; M. Cox, *Historic Amarillo,* 81; *Amarillo City Directory, 1991,* xix. For more dramatic figures see *Amarillo City Directory, 1990,* xxii.

26. M. Cox, *Historic Amarillo,* 81; *Amarillo City Directory, 1991,* xviii.

27. M. Cox, *Historic Amarillo,* 81; Eric W. Miller, Amarillo Chamber of

Commerce, interview with Paul H. Carlson, May 12, 2005 (notes in possession of author).

28. "Centennial Events Calendar," 31–32.

29. "Blaze Guts AISD Headquarters" and "We're a Staff without a Home," *Amarillo Globe-Times,* December 10, 1987.

30. "Power People," 46–47, 49.

31. Amarillo Independent School District, *AISD Information Guide,* 1–2, 4–5, 16.

32. "Amarilloans Who Made It to the Big Time," 53.

33. Greene, *50+ Best Books on Texas,* 13–14; W. U. McCoy, introduction to *The Bone Pickers,* by Al Dewlen, ix–xii; L. O'Brien Thompson, interview with Paul H. Carlson and Monte L. Monroe, March 11, 2005.

Bibliography

Manuscript Collections, Theses, and Dissertations

Amarillo Independent School District. Historical Records. Media and Public Relations Office, Administrative Office Building, Amarillo Independent School District.

Amarillo (Texas) Photograph Collection. Southwest Collection, Texas Tech University.

Boaz, Sallie Ruth. "A History of Amarillo, Texas." Master's thesis, University of Texas at Austin, 1950.

Bush, William H. Collection. Amarillo Public Library, Amarillo, Texas.

Flynn, Sean J. "Living History: John L. McCarty and the Texas Panhandle." Ph.D. Dissertation, Texas Tech University, 1999.

Harrington, Sybil and Don File, Southwest Collection, Texas Tech University.

Historic Photograph Collection. Amarillo Public Library, Amarillo, Texas.

Ku Klux Klan (Amarillo, Texas). Records, 1921–25. Southwest Collection, Texas Tech University.

Loving, David Alan. "H. B. Sanborn and the Early Development of the Texas Panhandle." Master's thesis, Texas Tech University, 1998.

McCarty, John L. Collection, Amarillo Public Library, Amarillo, Texas.

Phillips, Francis. "The Development of Agriculture in the Panhandle-Plains Region of Texas to 1920." Master's thesis, West Texas State Teachers College, Canyon, 1946.

Sanborn, Henry B. Collection. Archives. Panhandle-Plains Historical Museum, Canyon, Texas.

Shearer, Ernest C. "The History of Potter County, Texas." Master's thesis, University of Colorado, Boulder, 1933.

Sparks, Mrs. T. C. "A History of the Amarillo Public Schools, 1889–1949." Master's thesis, West Texas State College, Canyon, 1949.

Steele, June M. "Phebe Warner: Community Building in the Texas Panhandle, 1898–1935." Master's thesis, Texas Tech University, 2000.

Toney, Sharon Morris. "The Texas State Parks System: An Administrative History, 1923-1984." Ph.D. dissertation, Texas Tech University, 1995.

Interviews

Bivins, Mrs. Albert, and Cora Green. Interview with Mrs. L. E. Moyer, accompanied by C. Boone McClure. January 20, 1958. Transcript in Wendy Bush O'Brien Marsh and Stanley Marsh 3, Records, Toad Hall, Amarillo.

Currie, Daisey, "The Story of Her Life as Told to Me by Her: The Life Story of Mrs. W. W. Wetsel, I," Transcript in interview files, Archives. Panhandle-Plains Historical Museum, Canyon, Texas.

Lively, Lamar. Telephone interview with Paul H. Carlson. May 18, 2005. Notes in possession of author.

McCartt, Debra. Interview with Paul H. Carlson. May 27, 2005. Notes in possession of author.

Miller, Eric W. Interview with Paul H. Carlson. May 13, 2005. Notes in possession of author.

Thompson, L. O'Brien. Interview with Monte L. Monroe and Paul H. Carlson. March 11, 2005. Tape in Southwest Collection, Texas Tech University.

Ware, Tol. Interview with Monte L. Monroe and Paul H. Carlson. May 27, 2005. Tape in Southwest Collection, Texas Tech University.

Newspapers

Amarillo Daily News, 1909–2005.

Amarillo Evening News, 1895.

Amarillo Globe, 1924–40.

Amarillo Globe-Times, 1987.

Amarillo Livestock Champion, 1888–89, 1900.

The Amarillo Star, 1903.

Amarillo Sunday News and Globe, 1927–2005.

Amarillo Weekly News, 1898–1901.

The Daily Panhandle (Amarillo), 1907, 1909.

Dallas Morning News, 1892–93, 1925.

The Evening News (Amarillo), 1899–1901.

Lubbock Avalanche-Journal, 2004–5.

San Antonio Express-News, 1975.

Tascosa Pioneer, 1887–88.

The West Texas Catholic (Amarillo Diocese), 1980–82.

Articles, Books, and Government Documents

Alexander, Charles C. *Crusade for Conformity: The Ku Klux Klan in Texas, 1920–1930.* Houston: Texas Gulf Coast Historical Association, 1962.

———. *The Ku Klux Klan in the Southwest.* Lexington: University of Kentucky Press, 1965.

Allen, Frederick Lewis. *Only Yesterday: An Informal History of the 1920s.* New York: Harper & Row, 1931, 1964.

Bibliography

Allen, R. G., H. W. Price, and E. V. Reinbold. "The History, Use, and Manufacture of Carbon Black." *Panhandle-Plains Historical Review* 12 (1929): 64–77.

"Amarilloans Who Made It to the Big Time." *Accent West* 16 (May 1987): 53.

Amarillo City Directory, 1981. Dallas: R. L. Polk, 1981

Amarillo City Directory, 1983. Dallas: R. L. Polk, 1983.

Amarillo City Directory, 1990. Dallas: R. L. Polk, 1990.

Amarillo City Directory, 1991. Dallas: R. L. Polk, 1991.

"Amarillo College." In Hammond, *Amarillo,* 186–88.

Amarillo Historic Building Survey and Preservation Program Recommendations. Charles Hall Page & Associates, Inc. Amarillo: City of Amarillo, 1981.

"Amarillo Housing." *Accent West* 4 (March 1975): 9.

Amarillo Independent School District. *AISD Information Guide.* Amarillo: AISD, 2004.

"Amarillo International." *Accent West* 4 (June 1975): 17–19.

Anderson, C. C. "Helium from a Scientific Curiosity to Large Scale Production." *Panhandle-Plains Historical Review* 12 (1939): 24–47.

Archambeau, Ernest R. "The First Federal Census in the Panhandle, 1880." *Panhandle-Plains Historical Review* 23 (1950): 89–101.

———. "The Fort Smith–Santa Fe Trail along the Canadian River in Texas." *Panhandle-Plains Historical Review* 27 (1954): 1–26.

———. "Old Tascosa: Selected News Items from the *Tascosa Pioneer,* 1886–1888." *Panhandle-Plains Historical Review* 39 (1966): 1–183, 198–208.

Ashworth, Robert. "Amarillo Public Schools." In Hammond, *Amarillo,* 190.

Baker, T. Lindsey, and Billy R. Harrison. *Adobe Walls: The History and Archeology of the 1874 Trading Post.* College Station: Texas A&M University Press, 1986.

Bartlett, N. D. "Discovery of the Panhandle Oil and Gas Fields." *Panhandle-Plains Historical Review* 12 (1939): 48–54.

Bergman, Lee. "Caution: Pantex." *Accent West* 11 (February 1982): 36–38, 40–41, 43.

Betty, Gerald. *Comanche Society before the Reservation.* College Station: Texas A&M University Press, 2002.

Blodgett, Jan. *Land of Bright Promise: Advertising the Texas Panhandle and the South Plains.* Austin: University of Texas Press, 1988.

Bonnifield, Paul. *The Dust Bowl: Men, Dirt, and Depression.* Albuquerque: University of New Mexico Press, 1979.

Brooks, Robert L. "From Stone Slab Architecture to Abandonment: A Revisionist View of the Antelope Creek Phase." In *The Prehistory of Texas,* ed. Timothy K. Perttula, 331–44. College Station: Texas A&M University Press, 2004.

Buhite, Russell D., and David W. Levy, eds. *FDR's Fireside Chats.* Norman: University of Oklahoma Press, 1992.

Burt, Daniel S. *The Novel 100: A Ranking of the Greatest Novels of All Time.* New York: Checkmark Books, 2004.

Cantrell, Don. "What Makes Jerry Run?" *Accent West* 34 (April 2005): 48–51, 63.

Carlson, Paul H. "Black Sunday—The South Plains Dust Blizzard of April 14, 1935." *West Texas Historical Association Year Book* 67 (1991): 5–17.

———. "The Campbell Ranch and the Changing Face of Cattle Raising in the Texas Panhandle." *Panhandle-Plains Historical Review* 75 (2002): 27–34.

———. *Empire Builder in the Texas Panhandle: William Henry Bush.* College Station: Texas A&M University Press, 1996.

———. "Panhandle Pastores: Early Sheepherding in the Texas Panhandle." *Panhandle-Plains Historical Review* 53 (1980): 1–15.

Casey, Patrick. "Prescription Politics." *Accent West* 10 (April 1981): 31–36, 54–55.

Cashion, Ty. *Pigskin Pulpit: A Social History of Texas High School Football Coaches.* Austin: Texas State Historical Association, 1998.

"Centennial Events Calendar." *Accent West* 16 (April 1987): 31–32.

Chalmers, David M. *Hooded Americanism: The History of the Ku Klux Klan.* 2nd ed. New York: New Viewpoints, 1981.

Clark, James A. *Three Stars for the Colonel: The Biography of Ernest O. Thompson.* New York: Random House, 1954.

Connor, Seymour V. "Early Ranching Operations in the Panhandle: A Report on the Agricultural Schedules of the 1880 Census." *Panhandle-Plains Historical Review* 27 (1954): 45–69.

Cox, James. *Historical and Biographical Record of the Cattle Industry and the Cattlemen of Texas and Adjacent Territory.* St. Louis, MO: Woodward and Tiernan Printing, 1895.

Cox, Mike. *Historic Amarillo: An Illustrated History.* San Antonio, TX: Historical Publishing Network, 2004.

Crimm, Ana Carolina Castillo. "Mathew 'Bones' Hooks: A Pioneer of Honor." In *Black Cowboys of Texas.* Ed. Sara R. Massey, 219–40. College Station: Texas A&M University Press, 2000.

Crudgington, John W. "Old Town Amarillo." *Panhandle-Plains Historical Review* 30 (1957): 79–113.

DeLeon, Arnoldo. *Tejano Epic: Essays in Honor of Felix D. Almaraz Jr.* Austin: Texas State Historical Association, 2005.

Dethloff, Henry C., and Irvin M. May Jr., eds. *Southwestern Agriculture: Pre-Columbian to Modern.* College Station: Texas A&M University Press, 1982.

Dewlen, Al. *The Bone Pickers.* Lubbock: Texas Tech University Press, 2002.

Dixon, Olive K. *Life of "Billy" Dixon.* Dallas: Southwest Press, 1927.

Dougherty, Russell E., and Mark O. Hatfield. "Should the United States Build the MX Missile?" *AEI: Foreign Policy and Defense Review* 3, no. 2 (1980): 2–23.

"Downtown Revisited." *Accent West* 4 (June 1975): 20–21.

Dunn, Roy Sylvan. "Drouth in West Texas, 1890–1984." *West Texas Historical Association Year Book* 37 (1961): 121–36.

Early, Allen, et al. *Our One Hundred Years Walk with the Lord: A Collection of Reminiscences and Observations by Members of First Presbyterian Church, Amarillo, Texas.* Ed. Mary Kate Trip. Amarillo: First Presbyterian Church, 1990.

Fagan, Brian M. *Ancient North America: The Archaeology of a Continent,* 3rd ed. New York: Thames & Hudson, 2004.

Finch, O. H. "Judge O. H. Nelson." *Panhandle-Plains Historical Review* 19 (1946): 18–23.

Finger, George W. "Sanford Dam and Reservoir." In Hammond, *Amarillo*, 99–107.

Foreman, Jim M. "The Birth of English Field." *Accent West* 5 (March 1976): 16–17.

Franks, Ray, and Jay Ketelle, comps. *Amarillo, Texas, the First Hundred Years, 1887–1987: A Picture Postcard History.* Amarillo: Ray Franks Publishing Ranch, 1986.

———, comps. *Amarillo, Texas, the First Hundred Years II: A Picture Postcard History.* Amarillo: Ray Franks Publishing Ranch, 1987.

Freeth, Nick. *Traveling Route 66.* Norman: University of Oklahoma Press, 2001.

Gammel, Hans Peter Nielsen, comp. *Laws of Texas, 1822–1897.* 10 Vols. Austin: Gammel, 1898.

General Laws of the State of Texas Passed at the Regular Session Twenty-fourth Legislature, 1895. Austin: State Printer, 1895.

Glass, Matthew. *Citizens against the MX: Public Languages in the Nuclear Age.* Urbana: University of Illinois Press, 1993.

Gober, James R., and B. Byron Price, eds. *Cowboy Justice: Tale of a Texas Lawman, Jim Gober.* Lubbock: Texas Tech University Press, 1997.

Goodrich, Lloyd, and Doris Bry. *Georgia O'Keeffe.* New York: Whitney Museum of American Art, 1970.

Gracy, Alice Duggan. "Willis Day Twichell, Civil Engineer." *Panhandle-Plains Historical Review* 18 (1945): 79–90.

Graves, Lawrence, ed. *Lubbock: From Town to City.* Lubbock: West Texas Museum Assocaition, 1986.

The Grand March: A Pictorial History of the First Baptist Church, Amarillo, Texas, 1889–1989. Amarillo: First Baptist Church, 1989.

Green, Donald E. *Land of the Underground Rain: Irrigation on the Texas High Plains, 1910–1970.* Austin: University of Texas Press, 1973.

Greene, A. C. *The 50+ Best Books on Texas.* Denton: University of North Texas Press, 1998.

Guy, Duane F., ed. *The Story of Palo Duro Canyon.* Lubbock: Texas Tech University Press, 2001.

Haley, J. Evetts. *Charles Goodnight: Cowman and Plainsman.* Boston: Houghton Mifflin, 1936.

———. "The Comanchero Trade." *Southwestern Historical Quarterly* 38 (January 1935): 157–76.

———. "Grass Lease Fight and Attempted Impeachment of the First Panhandle Judge." *Southwestern Historical Quarterly* 38 (July 1934): 1–27.

———. *The XIT Ranch of Texas and the Early Days of the Llano Estacado.* Norman: University of Oklahoma Press, 1967.

Haley, J. Evetts, and William Curry Holden. *The Flamboyant Judge, James D. Hamlin: A Biography.* Canyon, TX: Palo Duro Press, 1972.

Hammond, Clara T., comp. *Amarillo.* Amarillo: George Autry, 1971.

Hamner, Laura V. *Short Grass and Longhorns.* Norman: University of Oklahoma Press, 1965.

———, ed. *Light 'n Hitch: A Collection of Historical Writing Depicting Life on the High Plains.* Dallas: American Guild Press, 1958.

Harrison, Lowell H. "Union Veterans in the Texas Panhandle." *Panhandle-Plains Historical Review* 37 (1964): 37–62.

Harrison, Morton. "Gentlemen from Indiana." In Mowry, *The Twenties,* 145–54.

Hawkins, Rusty. "The Canadian River Municipal Water Authority." *West Texas Historical Association Year Book* 81 (2005): 19–31.

Hogrefe, Jeffrey. *O'Keeffe: The Life of an American Legend.* New York: Bantam Books, 1992.

Holden, William Curry. *The Espuela Land and Cattle Company: A Study of a Foreign-owned Ranch in Texas.* Austin: Texas State Historical Association, 1970.

———. *The Spur Ranch: A Study of the Inclosed Ranch Phase of the Cattle Industry in Texas.* Boston: Christopher Publishing House, 1934.

Holliday, Vance T. *Paleoindian Geoarchaeology of the Southern High Plains.* Austin: University of Texas Press, 1997.

Horsley, David. *Into the Wind.* Houston: Winedale Publications, 1999.

Howard, Orville. "Billion Dollar Question." *Accent West* 16 (July 1987): 70–73.

Huebner, J. A. "Late Prehistoric Bison Populations in Central and Southern Texas." *Plains Anthropologist* 36 (1991): 343–58.

Hughes, Jack T. "Lake Creek: A Woodland Site in the Texas Panhandle." *Bulletin of the Texas Archeological Society* 32 [for 1961] (1962): 65–84.

———. "Prehistoric Cultural Development on the Texas High Plains." *Bulletin of the Texas Archeological Society* (1989): 1–55.

Hurt, R. Douglas. *The Dust Bowl: An Agricultural and Social History.* Chicago: Nelson-Hall, 1981.

Jackson, Jack. *Los Mestenos: Spanish Ranching in Texas, 1721–1821.* College Station: Texas A&M University Press, 1986.

Jackson v. State (No. 8482). Court of Criminal Appeals, January 27, 1926. 280 *Southwestern Reporter,* 202–8.

Jennings, Al. *Through the Shadows with O. Henry.* Lubbock: Texas Tech University Press, 2000.

Kavanagh, Thomas W. *Comanche Political History: An Ethnohistorical Perspective.* Lincoln: University of Nebraska Press, 1996.

Kelly, Susan Croce. *Route 66.* Norman: University of Oklahoma Press, 1990.

Kelso, Patrick R. "Census Shows Area Losses and Gains." *Accent West* 9 (November 1980): 51–52.

Key, Della Tyler. *In the Cattle Country: History of Potter County.* Wichita Falls, TX: Nortex, 1966.

Kreidler, Tai. "To Anchor the Wind." *Journal of the West* 29 (October 1990): 46–52.

Krieger, Alex D. *Culture Complexes and Chronology in Northern Texas with Extension of Puebloan Datings to the Mississippi Valley.* University of Texas Publication no. 4640. Austin: University of Texas Press, 1946.

Lambert, Roger. "Drought Relief for Cattlemen: The Emergency Purchase Program of 1934–35." *Panhandle-Plains Historical Review* 45 (1972): 21–37.

Lavender, David. *Bent's Fort.* Garden City, NJ: Doubleday, 1954.

La Vere, David. *The Texas Indians.* College Station: Texas A&M University Press, 2004.

Leuchtenburg, William E. *The Perils of Prosperity, 1914–1932.* Chicago: University of Chicago Press, 1958.

Levi, Barbara G., et al., eds. *The Future of Land-Based Strategic Missiles.* New York: American Institute of Physics, 1989.

Loy, Shawn, ed. *The Invisible Empire in the West: Toward a New Historical Appraisal of the Ku Klux Klan of the 1920s.* Urbana: University of Illinois Press, 2004.

Mabry, W. S. "Early West Texas and Panhandle Surveys." *Panhandle-Plains Historical Review* 2 (1929): 22–42.

———. "Some Memories of W. S. Mabry." *Panhandle-Plains Historical Review* 11 (1938): 31–51.

Malone, Michael P. , and Richard W. Etulain. *The American West: A Twentieth-Century History.* Lincoln: University of Nebraska Press, 1989.

"The Man behind the Big Beef," *Accent West* 15 (January 1986): 57.

Marcy, Randolph B. *Exploration of the Red River of Louisiana, in the Year 1852.* Washington, DC: Beverley Tucker, Senate Printer, 1854.

Marsh, Stanley, 3. "The Bush Memorial Collection." In Hammond, *Amarillo,* 299–300.

"Marsh's Manifest Mesa," *Accent West* 9 (December 1980): 31.

Mason, Richard. "The Cotton Kingdom and the City of Lubbock: South Plains Agriculture in the Postwar Era." In Graves, *Lubbock.*

Masterson, Ben. "The JY Cattle Brand." *Panhandle-Plains Historical Review* 16 (1943): 50–58.

Matthiesen, Leroy T. *Wise and Otherwise: The Life and Times of a Cottonpicking Texas Bishop.* Amarillo: n.p., n.d.

McCarty, John L. "Kenneth Wyatt: Cowboys and Quarter Horses." *Southwestern Art* 3 (1971): 2–6.

———. *Maverick Town: The Story of Old Tascosa.* Enlarged ed. Norman: University of Oklahoma Press, 1968.

McClure, C. B., ed. "The Battle of Adobe Walls, 1864." *Panhandle-Plains Historical Review* 21 (1948): 18–65.

Meadows, William C. *Kiowa, Apache, and Comanche Military Societies: Enduring Veterans, 1800 to the Present.* Austin: University of Texas Press, 1999.

Meinig, D. W. *Imperial Texas: An Interpretive Essay in Cultural Geography.* Austin: University of Texas Press, 1969.

Messinger, Lisa Mintz. *Georgia O'Keeffe.* New York: Thames and Hudson, 1988.

Mojtabai, A. G. *Blessed Assurance: At Home with the Bomb in Amarillo, Texas.* Boston: Houghton Mifflin, 1986.

Morris, John Miller. *El Llano Estacado: Exploration and Imagination on the High Plains of Texas and New Mexico, 1536–1860.* Austin: Texas State Historical Association, 1997.

———, ed. *A Private in the Texas Rangers: A. T. Miller of Company B, Frontier Battalion.* College Station: Texas A&M University Press, 2001.

Mowry, George E., ed. *The Twenties: Fords, Flappers, and Fanatics.* Englewood Cliffs, NJ: Prentice-Hall, 1963.

Murrah, David J. *C. C. Slaughter: Rancher, Banker, Baptist.* Austin: University of Texas Press, 1981.

Nail, David L. *One Short Sleep Past: A Profile of Amarillo in the Thirties.* Canyon, TX: Staked Plains Press, 1973.

Nall, Garry L. "The Cattle Feeding Industry on the Texas High Plains." In Dethloff and May, *Southwestern Agriculture,* 105–15.

———. "Dust Bowl Days: Panhandle Farming in the 1930s." *Panhandle-Plains Historical Review* 48 (1975): 42–63.

———. "Farming on the High Plains: Innovation and Adaptation on Arid Lands in Texas." *Journal of the West* 29 (October 1990): 22–29.

———. "Panhandle Farming in the 'Golden Era' of American Agriculture." *Panhandle-Plains Historical Review* 46 (1973): 68–93.

———. "Specialization and Expansion: Panhandle Farming in the 1920s." *Panhandle-Plains Historical Review* 47 (1974): 46–67.

Neugebauer, Janet M., ed. *Plains Farmer: The Diary of William G. DeLoach, 1914–1964.* College Station: Texas A&M University Press, 1991.

"A New School for Amarillo." *Accent West* 5 (June 1976): 20–22.

Overton, Richard C. *Gulf to Rockies: The Heritage of the Fort Worth and Denver—Colorado and Southern Railways, 1861–1898.* Austin: University of Texas Press, 1953.

Paddock, B. B., ed. *A Twentieth-Century History and a Biographical Record of North and West Texas.* 2 vols. New York: Leois, 1906.

"Panhandle Lakes Program Stimulates Business." *Southwest Business Magazine.* September 1939, 15–17.

Parfit, Michael. "The Dust Bowl." *Smithsonian* 20 (June 1989): 44–57.

Parker, G. A. F. "Incipient Trade and Religion in Amarillo in the Late Eighties." *Panhandle-Plains Historical Review* 2 (1929): 137–44.

Pate, J'Nell L. *Livestock Legacy: The Fort Worth Stockyards, 1887–1987.* College Station: Texas A&M University Press, 1988.

Petersen, Peter L. "A Park for the Panhandle: The Acquisition and Development of Palo Duro Canyon State Park." In Guy, *Story of Palo Duro Canyon,* 145–78.

Plagens, Peter. "Georgia on Our Minds." *Newsweek* 144, no. 8 (August 23, 2004): 64–65.

Price, B. Byron, and Frederick W. Rathjen. *The Golden Spread: An Illustrated History of Amarillo and the Texas Panhandle.* Northridge, CA: Windsor, 1986.

"Power People." *Accent West* 16 (March 1987): 46–47, 49.

Quinby, J. Roy. "Hybrid Sorghum: A Triumph of Research." In Dethloff and May, *Southwestern Agriculture*, 93–105.

Ramsey, Buck. "Should the Panhandle Secede? Heck Yeh!" *Accent West* 9 (July 1980): 36–38, 66–70.

Rathjen, Frederick W. "New Introduction." In Guy, *Story of Palo Duro Canyon*, vi–xi.

———. *The Texas Panhandle Frontier.* Revised ed. Lubbock: Texas Tech University Press, 1998.

Ratliff, Harold. *Autumn's Mightiest Legions: History of Texas Schoolboy Football.* Waco: Texian Press, 1963.

Roddy, Roy. "Texas Helium for War or Peace." *Texas Digest.* June 28, 1941, 12–13.

"Sam Davis, ALT's Down to Earth Angel." *Accent West* 3 (October 1974): 15–17.

Saunder, Guy. "The Empty Saddle." In Hammond, *Amarillo*, 139–42.

Sculle, Keith A. "Traveling in Style: The Park Plaza Motel Chain." *Journal of the West* 41, no. 4 (2002): 63–70.

Seibel, C. W. "The Development of Helium Production as Now Carried on at Amarillo, Texas, by the U.S. Bureau of the Mines, Department of the Interior." *Panhandle-Plains Historical Review* 9 (1936): 43–51.

Shannon, David A., ed. *The Great Depression.* Englewood Cliffs, NJ: Prentice-Hall, 1960.

Sheffy, L. F. "The Experimental Stage of Settlement in the Panhandle of Texas." *Panhandle-Plains Historical Review* 3 (1930): 78–103.

Sinise, Jerry. *Black Gold and Red Lights.* Austin: Eakin Press, 1982.

Snyder, Tom. *Route 66 Traveler's Guide and Roadside Companion: Collector's Edition.* New York: St. Martin's Griffin, 2000.

Speer, Jack. "Amarillo: Cowtown or Slick City?" *Accent West* 12 (January 1983): 23–24, 30–31, 35.

"Spradlin Speaks Out: Were the Critics on Target?" *Accent West* 10 (February 1981): 26–27, 34.

Stanford v. State (No. 8457). Court of Criminal Appeals of Texas, January 21, 1925. 268 *Southwestern Reporter*, 161–62.

State v. Goodnight. Supreme Court of Texas, July 1, 1888. 11 *Southwestern Reporter*, 119–21.

Studer, Floyd V. "Archeology of the Texas Panhandle." *Panhandle-Plains Historical Review* 27 (1955): 87–95.

Stumpf, David K. *Titan II: A History of a Cold War Missile Program.* Fayetteville: University of Arkansas Press, 2000.

Texas Almanac, 1980–1981. Dallas: Dallas Morning News, 1979.

Texas Almanac, 1982–1983. Dallas: Dallas Morning News, 1983.

Texas Almanac, 1984–1985. Dallas: Dallas Morning News, 1985.

Texas Almanac, 2004–2005. Dallas: Dallas Morning News, 2004.

Texas Almanac and State Industrial Guide, 1941–1942. Dallas: Dallas Morning News, 1941.

"Texas State Technical Institute Mid-Continent Campus, Amarillo." In Hammond, *Amarillo,* 188–89.

Thompson, Thomas. *North of Palo Duro: Turnstile Speaks Again.* Canyon: Staked Plains Press, 1984.

———. *The Ware Boys: The Story of a Texas Family Bank.* Canyon: Staked Plains Press, 1978.

Timmons, Paul, et al. *The Centennial Book of Polk Street Methodist Church, Amarillo.* Ed. Garry L. Nall. Canyon: Staked Plains Press, 1989.

Tindall, George Brown, and David E. Shi. *America: A Narrative History.* 4th ed. New York: W. W. Norton, 1996.

Todd, Bruce G. *Bones Hooks: Pioneer Negro Cowboy.* Gretna, LA: Pelican, 2005.

U.S. Air Force Ballistic Missile Office. "Alternative Potential Deployment Areas: Texas/New Mexico." M-X ETR-3 (D301.92: M 69/draft/etr 3). Norton Air Force Base, San Bernardino, California, December 22, 1980.

———. "Socioeconomic Impact Estimates For Texas/New Mexico Deployment Region." M-X ETR-3-A (D301.92: M 69/draft/etr 3A). Norton Air Force Base, San Bernardino, California, December 22, 1980.

U.S. Bureau of Labor Statistics. *National Compensation, Wages, and Salaries.* Washington, DC: Bureau of Labor Statistics, 1997.

U.S. Comptroller General. Report to Congress. "The MX Weapon System: Issues and Challenges." General Accounting Office, MASAD-81-1, February 17, 1981.

U.S. Department of the Interior, Bureau of Mines. "Helium Capital of the World—Amarillo." In Hammond, *Amarillo,* 157–59.

Wallace, Ernest, and E. Adamson Hoebel. *The Comanches: Lords of the South Plains.* Norman: University of Oklahoma Press, 1952.

Wallis, Michael. *Route 66: The Mother Road.* New York: St. Martin's Grifin, 2001.

Warren, Harris Gaylord. *Herbert Hoover and the Great Depression.* New York: W. W. Norton, 1967.

Weaver, Bobby, ed. *Harvest of Memories: The St. Francis Story.* Amarillo: Southwestern Publications, 1983.

Wellman, Paul I. *A Dynasty of Western Outlaws.* New York: Pyramid Books, 1964.

Wheeler, Kenneth W. *The Palo Duro Club: A Centennial History, 1905–2005.* New York: n. p., 2005.

Whisenhunt, Donald W. *The Depression in Texas: The Hoover Years.* New York: Garland, 1983.

———. "The Texas Attitude toward Relief, 1929–1937." *Panhandle-Plains Historical Review* 46 (1973): 94–112.

White, Gene. "We're Bullish on Downtown." *Accent West* 10 (November 1981): 30–31, 33, 35.

Wilson, Carroll. "The M-X Shell Game: Any Takers?" *Accent West* 10 (February 1981): 30–31, 38–39, 41, 46–47.

———. "The Mysterious Case of the Vanishing Elm." *Accent West* 9 (May 1980): 38, 57–59, 62–64.

———. "Peeking over the Hedge." *Accent West* 4 (August 1975): 17–19.

———. "The Wermund Report." *Accent West* 14 (April 1985): 45–47.

———. "Where Is Amarillo GWA-ing?" *Accent West* 5 (March 1976): 20–21, 25.

Witzel, Michael Karl. *Route 66 Remembered.* Osceola, WI: Motorbooks International, 1996.

The World Almanac and Book of Facts, 1987. New York: World Almanac, 1986.

Worster, Donald. *Dust Bowl: The Southern Plains in the 1930s.* New York: Oxford University Press, 1979.

———. *Under Western Skies: Nature and History in the American West.* New York: Oxford University Press, 1991.

Yeilding, Kenneth D., and Paul H. Carlson, comps. *Ah That Voice: The Fireside Chats of Franklin Delano Roosevelt.* Odessa: The John Ben Shepperd Jr. Library of the Presidents, the Presidential Museum, 1974.

Index

Index

www.ingramcontent.com/pod-product-compliance
Lightning Source LLC
LaVergne TN
LVHW041112080826
845145LV00007B/1780

* 9 7 8 1 6 8 2 8 3 3 1 1 7 *